THE DAYS WE CELEBRATE
Celebrations for Special Occasions

OUR AMERICAN HOLIDAYS

Edited by
ROBERT HAVEN SCHAUFFLER
AND OTHERS

A SERIES of anthologies for the use of students and teachers in schools and colleges; consisting of the best verse, plays, stories, addresses, special articles, orations, etc. Applicable to the holidays listed as follows:

CHRISTMAS . . . . *December 25th*
DEMOCRACY DAYS . . . .
EASTER . . . . *March or April*
GOOD WILL DAYS . . . .
HALLOWE'EN . . . . *October 31st*
INDEPENDENCE DAY . . . . . . *July 4th*
LINCOLN'S BIRTHDAY . . . *February 12th*
THE MAGIC OF BOOKS . . . *Book Week*
THE MAGIC OF MUSIC . . . *Music Week*
MEMORIAL DAY . . . . . . *May 30th*
MOTHER'S DAY . . . *Second Sunday in May*
PAN-AMERICAN DAY . . . . . *April 14th*
PEACE DAYS . . . .
ROOSEVELT DAY . . . . . *October 27th*
THANKSGIVING *Last Thursday in November*
WASHINGTON'S BIRTHDAY . *February 22nd*

THE DAYS
WE CELEBRATE

☆ ☆ ☆ ☆

CELEBRATIONS FOR SPECIAL OCCASIONS

MOTHERS' DAY - MUSIC WEEK
GRADUATION DAY - FATHERS' DAY
HALLOWE'EN - BOOK WEEK

Compiled and Edited by
ROBERT HAVEN SCHAUFFLER

EDITOR OF
OUR AMERICAN HOLIDAYS

DODD, MEAD & COMPANY
NEW YORK   1966

394.2
Sch 1
c.1
G

Copyright, 1940
By ROBERT HAVEN SCHAUFFLER

PRINTED IN THE UNITED STATES OF AMERICA
BY THE VAIL-BALLOU PRESS, INC., BINGHAMTON, N. Y.

ACKNOWLEDGMENTS

For their kind help in providing facilities and material for this compilation, special thanks are due to these New York librarians: Miss Thelma Edic, Librarian of the Magazine Reserve; Mr. Franklin F. Hopper, Chief of Circulation; Miss C. H. Meade, Librarian St. Agnes Branch, and her obliging and efficient staff; Miss Amelia Munson, Librarian Teachers' Reference Room, 58th Street Branch; and to the many other branches that kindly loaned books and magazines. Also to Miss Helen Mildred Owen, editor of *The Instructor* for her generosity in allowing so many extracts from a magazine preeminent for the quality of its holiday literature; and to these members of the Dodd, Mead staff: Miss Ruby N. Carr, Miss Madeline C. Duffy, and especially Miss Mary A. Brennan, for their invaluable co-operation in the business end of this undertaking.

For permission to use copyrighted material acknowledgment is made to:

D. Appleton-Century Company, Inc.: "The Topsyturvy Concert," by George Bradford Bartlett, from "The St. Nicholas Book of Plays and Operettas."

Walter H. Baker Company, the copyright holders: "Mothers on Strike," by Carl Webster Pierce.

Anne Madison Beeman: "Book Frolic"; with a Note on Its Production.

William Rose Benét: "Paternity."

The Bobbs-Merrill Company: "Like His Mother Used to Make," from "Afterwhiles," by James Whitcomb Riley. Copyright 1887, 1915. Used by special permission of the publishers, The Bobbs-Merrill Company.

Mrs. George S. Burgess, literary executor of Katharine Lee Bates: "The Ideal," by Katharine Lee Bates.

Elizabeth J. Coatsworth: "On a Night of Snow."

Mary Carolyn Davies: "The Peak."

Dodd, Mead and Company: "The Givers of Life," and "In a Copy of Browning," by Bliss Carman; and "The Quitter," by Robert W. Service.

Doubleday, Doran and Company, Inc.: "Mother O' Mine," from

ACKNOWLEDGMENTS

"The Light That Failed"; and "If," from "Rewards and Fairies," by Rudyard Kipling. From "Rudyard Kipling's Verse," Inclusive Edition, 1885–1932. Copyright, 1891, 1934. Reprinted by permission of Mrs. Rudyard Kipling and the publishers.

Katherine Edelman: "Mother."

The Extension Magazine and the Author: "Mother's Diary," by Elsie Duncan Sanders.

Mildred Focht: "Child's Play," from "Four Trees and Other Poems."

Funk and Wagnalls Company: "Microcosm," from "Broad-Cast," by Ernest Crosby.

Fannie Stearns Davis Gifford: "Evening Song."

Mrs. J. H. Gower: "Saint Cecilia Meets King Jazz," and "Grandma Berry's Sheet-and-Pillow-Case Party."

Harper's Magazine: "Music," by Lionel Wiggam.

Enid Hayward: "Mother of the World."

Theresa Helburn: "Mother."

Marion Holbrook: "Orchids to Father."

Houghton Mifflin Company: "Her Stories," from "Songs for My Mother," by Anna Hempstead Branch; "Music," and "Mother's Birthday," by Frances Gill.

Alfred A. Knopf, Inc.: "Reflection While She Sleeps," from series, "Remembering Mother," by Leonora Speyer, in "Slow Wall." Reprinted by special arrangement with the authorized publishers, Alfred A. Knopf, Inc.

Mary Sinton Leitch: "To My Mother," "The Bankrupt," and "Advice to Would-Be Poets."

Carrie Ward Lyon: "To My Mother," and "You Sing the Air."

Elbridge S. Lyon: "To Pass or Not to Pass," and "The Missing Bookend."

The Macmillan Company: "To His Mother, C. L. M.," by John Masefield, from "Collected Poems of John Masefield."

The late Edwin Markham: "Preparedness," and "Duty."

Virginia Scott Miner: "Faith," and "Gentle Presence."

Bertha Nathan: "Bre'r Rabbit and the Ghosts."

The F. A. Owen Publishing Company, publishers of The Instructor: for "Activities for Mother's Day," by Nella Harvey; "A Mother's Day Activity," by Nora McCarthy; "Originality in Music," by Laura Beth Torrance; "A Test for Music Week," by Ernestine Bennett Briggs; "Autumn and Hallowe'en Fun," and "Hallowe'en Games," by Alice Crowell Hoffman; "A First-Grade Hallowe'en Party," by Helen Emily Snyder; "A Pumpkin Game for Hallowe'en," by Elizabeth Sharp; "Hallowe'en Masks," by Zeda A. Wahl; "Hallowe'en Masks Made of Paper Bags," by Mary B.

ACKNOWLEDGMENTS

Grubb; "The Little Book People," by Goldie Grant Thiel; "Poems in Pantomime," by Kathleen Carmichael Dietz; "A Test for Book Week," by Juanita Cunningham; "Suggestions for Book Week," by Fanora Voight; "A Poetry Booklet," by Gladyce Englerth; "A Book Pageant," by Katharine Nickel; "A Book-Week Dramatization," by Mae Foster Jay; "Teaching Poems," by Jennie E. Roper; "A Book Recital," by Helen Reed; "Teaching Poetry," by Sara Mae Spearing; "Memorizing Poetry," by Margaretta McCoy; "Illustrating Poetry," by Laura A. Holderness; "A Book Week Activity," by Eleanor Haack; and "Magic Ring—A Game of Poetry Appreciation," by Edna Flexer Stuart.

Parents' Magazine and the Authors: "Fatherless," by Marjorie Knapp; "Mothers," by Anne Trumbull; "Laughing Mama," by Anne Herendeen; "Busy Mother," by Mary Louise Tredinnick; "Growth," by Helen Welshimer; "Fathers as Pals," by James Peter Warbasse; "For Fathers Only," by Benjamin H. Carroll; "Leisure and Libraries," by Beatrice Sawyer Rossell; and "For Fathers Only," by Ethel Kawin.

Margaret Parsons: "Mystery at Hallowe'en."

G. P. Putnam's Sons: "Night and Morning," from "Everything and Anything," by Dorothy Aldis.

Delle Oglesbee Ross: "Afternoon with Schumann" and "The Shop Window."

Grace Dorcas Ruthenburg: "Oh, Susannah!," and "Abraham and Isaac."

Jessie B. Rittenhouse, literary executor of Clinton Scollard: "Old Books," by Clinton Scollard.

Scott, Foresman and Company: "The Three Joys of Reading," Anonymous, from "The Elson Readers, Book VII."

Charles Scribner's Sons: "Father's Letter," by Eugene Field.

Mary Stewart Sheldon: "Who Calls Me?," and "Flames of Hallowe'en."

Ruth Reno Smith: "Mother's Hope Chest."

Mirjane Strong: "The Clay Gnome," and "Characters' Cabaret."

The Talbot Press, Ltd., Dublin, Eire: "Wishes for My Son," from "The Complete Poetical Works of Thomas MacDonagh."

Dorothy Brown Thompson: "Memorandum for an Infant Son," "Villanelle," and "On Hallowe'en."

Leonard Charles van Noppen: "Poetry."

May Williams Ward: "Counsel," by George Sterling.

Dixie Willson and Child Life: "Smiling," by Dixie Willson.

The John C. Winston Company: "The Sandman," by Margaret Thomson Janvier, from "The Fireside Encyclopaedia of Poetry."

The Woman's Home Companion: "Father's Day."

INTRODUCTION

Realizing that some readers consider any introduction an impertinent superfluity, I will try to be telegraphically brief.

The present series has been planned to complete and bring down to date the twenty-one volumes of OUR AMERICAN HOLIDAYS, and PLAYS FOR OUR AMERICAN HOLIDAYS. Except for occasions not covered by the first series, most of the plays, poems, stories, essays, articles, games, projects, exercises, activities, etc., which are provided here for each celebration, are of more recent date than the corresponding volume of the standard set. In THE DAYS WE CELEBRATE will be found some of the best work of such authors as Eleanor Farjeon, Rose Fyleman, A. E. Housman, Vachel Lindsay, Alfred Noyes, Walter De la Mare, John Masefield, Leonora Speyer, and Sara Teasdale—all written too recently for inclusion in the parent series.

There is a large proportion of easily staged-and-acted plays, pageants, masques, dances, and tableaux. These have nearly all been planned with an eye to economical production. Most of them have been written specially for these volumes. Much material has been provided for the use of teachers, and of children of all ages.

Together with its two parent series, I trust that THE DAYS WE CELEBRATE will provide a practical and down-to-the-minute library of holiday literature for everybody.

R. H. S.

CONTENTS

CELEBRATIONS FOR MOTHERS' DAY

PLAYS

		PAGE
MOTHER'S HOPE CHEST	Ruth Reno Smith	3
MOTHERS ON STRIKE	Carl Webster Pierce	12

POEMS

TO HIS MOTHER, C. L. M.	John Masefield	29
HER STORIES	Anna Hempstead Branch	30
FROM REMEMBERING MOTHER	Leonora Speyer	31
LIKE HIS MOTHER USED TO MAKE	James Whitcomb Riley	32
MOTHER'S DIARY	Elsie Duncan Sanders	33
MOTHER	Theresa Helburn	33
FAITH	Virginia Scott Miner	34
TO MY MOTHER	Mary Sinton Leitch	34
MOTHER OF THE WORLD	Enid Hayward	35
MOTHER O' MINE	Rudyard Kipling	36
MOTHER	Katherine Edelman	37
MEMORANDUM FOR AN INFANT SON	Dorothy Brown Thompson	38
TO MY LITTLE SON	Julia Johnson Davis	39
TO MY MOTHER	Carrie Ward Lyon	39
THE GIVERS OF LIFE	Bliss Carman	40
FATHERLESS	Marjorie Knapp	44
GENTLE PRESENCE	Virginia Scott Miner	44
MOTHERS	Anne Trumbull	45
EVENING SONG	Fannie Stearns Davis Gifford	45
NIGHT AND MORNING	Dorothy Aldis	46
MOTHER'S BIRTHDAY	Frances Gill	46
LAUGHING MAMA	Anne Herendeen	47
THE SANDMAN	Margaret Thomson Janvier	48
HUSHING SONG	Fiona Macleod	50

ACTIVITIES

ACTIVITIES FOR MOTHER'S DAY	Nella Harvey	51
A MOTHER'S DAY ACTIVITY	Nora McCarthy	52

CONTENTS

CELEBRATIONS FOR MUSIC WEEK

PLAYS

		PAGE
AFTERNOON WITH SCHUMANN	Delle Oglesbee Ross	61
SAINT CECILIA MEETS KING JAZZ	Jean Milne Gower	76
OH, SUSANNAH!	Grace Dorcas Ruthenburg	88

POEMS

AFTER MUSIC	Josephine Johnson	101
MUSIC	Lionel Wiggam	101
YOU SING THE AIR	Carrie Ward Lyon	102
BUSY MOTHER	Mary Louise Tredinnick	102
TO A YOUNG MUSICIAN	Josephine Johnson	103
MUSIC	Frances Gill	104

ACTIVITIES AND A TEST

A TOPSYTURVY CONCERT	George Bradford Bartlett	105
ORIGINALITY IN MUSIC	Laura Beth Torrance	106
A TEST FOR MUSIC WEEK	Ernestine Bennett Briggs	106

CELEBRATIONS FOR GRADUATION DAY

PLAYS

THE SHOP WINDOW	Delle Oglesbee Ross	111
WHO CALLS ME?	Mary Stewart Sheldon	121
TO PASS OR NOT TO PASS	Elbridge S. Lyon	138

POEMS

IF	Rudyard Kipling	145
COURAGE	Josephine Johnson	146
THE IDEAL	Katharine Lee Bates	146
THE BANKRUPT	Mary Sinton Leitch	148
THE DAY OF A THOUSAND DEATHS	Robert Haven Schauffler	148
MICROCOSM	Ernest Crosby	149
EVENING PRAYER	Josephine Johnson	150
DUTY	Edwin Markham	151
PREPAREDNESS	Edwin Markham	151
BUT, HEART, REMEMBER!	Julia Johnson Davis	151
THE QUITTER	Robert W. Service	152

CONTENTS

		PAGE
THE LEVEL WAY	Josephine Johnson	153
THE PEAK	Mary Carolyn Davies	154

CELEBRATIONS FOR FATHERS' DAY

PLAYS

ORCHIDS TO FATHER	Marion Holbrook	157
ABRAHAM AND ISAAC	Grace Dorcas Ruthenburg	171

POEMS

PATERNITY	William Rose Benét	195
FATHER'S LETTER	Eugene Field	196
THE TOYS	Coventry Patmore	198
MAGIC FIRE	Robert Haven Schauffler	200
From IN MEMORIAM	Alfred, Lord Tennyson	201
From TINTERN ABBEY	William Wordsworth	201
CHILD'S PLAY	Mildred Focht	202
From THE FIRESIDE	Nathaniel Cotton	202
From TO DR. BLACKLOCK	Robert Burns	203
From CHRISTABEL	Samuel Taylor Coleridge	203
WISHES FOR MY SON	Thomas MacDonagh	203
GROWTH	Helen Welshimer	205

ESSAYS

FATHERS AS PALS	James Peter Warbasse	207
FOR FATHERS ONLY	Benjamin H. Carroll	210
FATHER'S DAY	Editorial in *Woman's Home Companion*	213
FOR FATHERS ONLY	Ethel Kawin	214

CELEBRATIONS FOR HALLOWE'EN

PLAYS

MYSTERY AT HALLOWE'EN	Margaret Parsons	221
GRANDMA BERRY'S SHEET-AND-PILLOW-CASE PARTY	Jean Milne Gower	240
FLAMES OF HALLOWE'EN	Mary Stewart Sheldon	255
THE CLAY GNOME	Mirjane Strong	265
BRE'R RABBIT AND THE GHOSTS	Bertha Nathan	275

CONTENTS

POEMS

		PAGE
ON A NIGHT OF SNOW	*Elizabeth J. Coatsworth*	285
VILLANELLE	*Dorothy Brown Thompson*	285
SMILING	*Dixie Willson*	286
IMAGINATION	*John Davidson*	287
ON HALLOWE'EN	*Dorothy Brown Thompson*	287

GAMES

AUTUMN AND HALLOWE'EN FUN	*Alice Crowell Hoffman*	289
HALLOWE'EN GAMES	*Alice Crowell Hoffman*	290

A PARTY

A FIRST-GRADE HALLOWE'EN PARTY	*Helen Emily Snyder*	293

ACTIVITIES

A PUMPKIN GAME FOR HALLOWE'EN	*Elizabeth Shark*	299
HALLOWE'EN MASKS	*Zeda A. Wahl*	299
HALLOWE'EN MASKS MADE OF PAPER BAGS	*Mary B. Grubb*	300

CELEBRATIONS FOR BOOK WEEK

PLAYS

CHARACTERS' CABARET	*Mirjane Strong*	305
THE MISSING BOOKEND	*Elbridge S. Lyon*	318
BOOK FROLIC	*Anne Madison Beeman*	328

POEMS

MY BOOKS	*Julia Johnson Davis*	341
IN A COPY OF BROWNING	*Bliss Carman*	342
OLD BOOKS	*Clinton Scollard*	346
POETRY	*Leonard Charles van Noppen*	347
COUNTRY OF BOOKS	*Anonymous*	347
"STONE WALLS—"	*Robert Haven Schauffler*	348
ADVICE TO WOULD-BE POETS	*Mary Sinton Leitch*	349
ENVOY	*Francis Thompson*	349
COUNSEL	*George Sterling*	350

CONTENTS

A PRIMARY STORY

The Little Book People . . . . . *Goldie Grant Thiel* 353

THOUGHTS ON READING

The Three Joys of Reading . . . . . . *Anonymous* 357
Leisure and Libraries . . . . *Beatrice Sawyer Rossell* 361

POEMS IN PANTOMIME

Poems in Pantomime . . . . *Kathleen Carmichael Dietz* 365

A GAME

Magic Ring—A Game of Poetry Appreciation
Edna Flexer Stuart 369

TESTS AND SUGGESTIONS

A Test for Book Week . . . . . *Juanita Cunningham* 373
Suggestions for Book Week . . . . . *Fanora Voight* 377

ACTIVITIES

A Poetry Booklet . . . . *Gladyce Englerth* 383
A Book Pageant . . . . *Katharine Nickel* 383
A Book-Week Dramatization . . . . *Mae Foster Jay* 384
Teaching Poems . . . . *Jennie E. Roper* 384
A Book Recital . . . . *Helen Reed* 385
Teaching Poetry . . . . . . *Sara Mae Spearing* 386
Memorizing Poetry . . . . . . *Margaretta McCoy* 386
Illustrating Poetry . . . . . *Laura A. Holderness* 387
A Book Week Activity . . . . . . *Eleanor Haack* 388

Celebrations for Mothers' Day

PLAYS

MOTHER'S HOPE CHEST *

By Ruth Reno Smith

CHARACTERS

Beth, *a young girl*
Hal, *her brother*
Indian Jim
Wacha, *his little son*
Rain-on-Hair, *an Indian chief*
Omancha, *his son*
Other Indians

Setting: *A frontier home, 1880. Sitting room, simply furnished in keeping with period. Heating stove, table with checked cloth, chairs with "tidies," old-fashioned chest of drawers. Entrance, door at left of rear center. (Arrangement for wind.)*

COSTUMES

Beth: Tight-fitting basque of red, long sleeves and high collar with ruchings; full skirt, white apron. Hair tied with ribbon bow at back.

Hal: Long trousers and coat, shirt light-colored material, bow tie, boots. Cap, overcoat and long wool muffler upon peg behind door.

Indian Jim: Khaki trousers, fringed, belt of beadwork, blanket, fillet of red with feather on head, necklace of beads.

* For permission to produce, apply to the author, Fort Myers, Florida.

WACHA: Breech cloth, moccasins, ear-rings.
RAIN-ON-HAIR: Full Chief's costume.
OMANCHA: Long trousers of khaki, beaded belt, red kerchief, red fillet about head, bead ornaments.
OTHER INDIANS: Similar to Rain-on-Hair, but less elaborate.

SCENE I

Early morning, November, 1880.
(Curtain rises.)

BETH. (*Sorting clothes from chest.*) Mother calls this her Hope Chest, because she says she always *hopes* to find a need for what she keeps in it; but I've often wondered when she'll ever need some of the things here.

HAL. (*At table, absently fingering a book.*) Yes.

BETH. (*Laughing.*) For instance, here are her wedding slippers and our own baby clothes. (*Shakes garments out and looks at them.*)

HAL. To be sure.

(*Low moan of wind.*)

BETH. And here are my old red mittens and toboggan cap. (*Displays.*) To think I ever wore these.

HAL (*Absently.*) Of course.

BETH. (*Looking at him for a moment, then springing up suddenly, moves toward him.*) Hal, what's the matter? You're worried. You haven't been yourself for a week. I thought it was because of Mr. Carter. He isn't worse?

HAL. No, oh, no.

BETH. Then what is it? Something is wrong. You may as well tell me.

HAL. It isn't anything— It isn't anything much.

BETH. Oh, it is— I know it now— We're partners, aren't we, while Father and Mother are away.

HAL. Of course—but—

BETH. Tell me—tell me (*Anxiously.*) is it Rain-on-Hair? (*Boy hangs head.*) I thought so. (*Sits down opposite him.*) Now you tell me all about it this very minute! Tell me every word.

HAL. Oh, it's nothing much—or I hope it isn't much.

BETH. (*Sternly.*) Tell me this minute.

HAL. I—I don't want to worry you—

BETH. We're partners, aren't we? What is Rain-on-Hair up to? I have a right to know.

HAL. I know you have, and yet— Oh, if only I knew what to do. If I knew what Father would do! When he started east everything was all right!

BETH. Of course, but after Mr. Carter took sick—

HAL. Then things fell on my shoulders—

BETH. (*Interrupting.*) Then Rain-on-Hair began to take advantage. Of course I know that, but what is it worries you to-day,—has worried you these past few days? If you don't tell me, I shall go straight to the Indians myself. Tell me!

HAL. Well, they're threatening to leave the reservation!

BETH. (*Dismayed.*) Leave the reservation!

HAL. Yes.

BETH. Oh, that is bad. But maybe, (*Hopefully.*) maybe you are mistaken.

HAL. No, it's all too true!

BETH. But why?

HAL. No reason, except that Rain-on-Hair keeps them stirred up, dissatisfied. If Rain-on-Hair would keep still, the others would quiet down; but with Carter flat on his back and Father away, there's no telling what may happen—and within the next day or two.

BETH. And they really threaten, and seriously, to leave the reservation?

HAL. (*Dejected.*) Yes, they do.

(*Wind moans and sighs.*)

BETH. Even though the Government has forbidden it? Even though the troops could be called?

HAL. Called? Yes, but a hundred miles away and more; besides Father has never had to call the troops here. He has always managed to keep the Indians satisfied, contented. Oh, if only I knew what he would do. If only I could consult Carter.

BETH. But surely they will make no move to go now, just at the beginning of winter, November. (*Wind howls.*) Oh, hear that wind. It's getting colder. Don't worry, Hal, they won't go in such weather. Of course they will not!

HAL. I know they would not, except for Rain-on-Hair.

BETH. Lock him up, until Father returns.

HAL. Which may not be for six weeks if this weather gets worse; besides, his people would rebel in earnest if he were handled that way.

BETH. But have you talked to him, reasoned with him—commanded him?

HAL. I have done all I know to do with him. He thinks I'm only a youngster and have no authority.—Oh, he's a great man among them and they do whatever he says.

BETH. Well, perhaps things are not as bad as you think. They're really like children, as I've often heard Father say—naughty at times, but on the whole easily handled!

HAL. (*Wistfully.*) If Father were only here!

BETH. (*Briskly.*) Ride over to Mr. Carter's and see how he is, and quit worrying. Remember Mother always says, "There's a rightful thing to do in solving any problem." It's right these Indians stay here, so there is a rightful way to keep them here. (*Rises and moves toward chest.*) Perhaps Rain-on-Hair hasn't as much influence as you think.

HAL. (*Moving toward door and taking coat and cap from peg.*) I wish I could believe that.

BETH. (*At chest.*) Quit worrying. We'll find a way. (*Glances

in and draws out a little overcoat.) Oh, look, Hal! Remember this? (*Holds up coat.*)
HAL. (*Brightening.*) It's my little overcoat Father brought from Washington years ago. How proud I was of it. I thought myself quite a man then.
BETH. (*Laughing.*) Yes, quite as big as Father. You said you and Father were twins. (*Draws out other gray coat.*) See, here is Father's.
HAL. (*Looking at coats.*) Brass buttons and all—just like mine! Why do you suppose Mother kept them all these years?
BETH. Because she *hoped* perhaps to find some use for them— Now run along to Mr. Carter's, but don't tell him a word about Rain-on-Hair. Hurry back—and quit worrying!
(*Wind moans.*)
HAL. (*Pausing at door.*) I'll try. Maybe you're right. Surely the Indians won't go in such weather.
(*Exits and wind howls.*)
BETH. (*Puttering about the things in the chest. The mittens, toboggan, and two coats she folds and places on top.*) I'm sure Rain-on-Hair won't lead his people off the reservation now in such weather and the winter coming on. Queer he is, and arrogant, but he loves that little son of his, and is just as proud of him as Father is of Hal.
(*A heavy gust of wind as* JIM *and* WACHA *enter.* WACHA *is hunched over, showing every sign of being thoroughly chilled. Wind moans.*)
BETH. (*Coming forward.*) Oh, Jim—it's cold. (*Draws* WACHA *toward the stove.*) You poor child—you must be nearly frozen. (*Rubs his hands, etc. Severely to* JIM.) Jim, you should never let Wacha go about this way. The child will freeze.
JIM. (*Carelessly.*) Him—no—freeze. (BETH *starts to throw a shawl about* WACHA.) Him—no—cold—him no squaw— Him—all Face! (*Suddenly.*) Where—little white chief?
BETH. He has gone over to Mr. Carter's. Do you want him?

(JIM *nods.*)

JIM. Rain-on-Hair—him—all move.

BETH. (*Greatly dismayed.*) You mean—

JIM. (*Grimly.*) Squaws—take down—teepees—meat—all pack— Sun up—all go! All—Injuns—go.

BETH. (*Aghast.*) To leave the reservation?

JIM. Big Chief Rain-on-Hair—him say—go—all go.

BETH. (*In despair.*) Oh, Jim! (*Suddenly.*) Jim, Jim, run, run on to Mr. Carter's. Tell Hal! Tell him at once. (*Wrings hands.*) Oh, what shall we do? Whatever shall we do? (JIM *turns toward door.* WACHA *follows slowly. The shawl has long since been discarded. Wind howls dismally.*) Oh, leave the boy here! It is too cold!—No, no, take him with you. Take him to his mother. The child will freeze. (*Snatches little gray coat from chest.*) Here, take this! (*Hurriedly bundles* WACHA *into coat and buttons it.*) It belonged to Hal, to Little White Chief! Stop and leave the child with his mother; but tell Hal! Send him here at once!

(JIM *surveys* WACHA *with satisfaction.* WACHA *much pleased. Exeunt. Wind.*)

BETH. (*Wringing hands.*) Oh, it must be true. Jim would know! Oh, whatever shall we do? To get word to the troops now is impossible! To appeal to the Indians, to Rain-on-Hair —Hal has done that!—To try to hold these people by force— with half a dozen half-breeds and that many guns— That would be madness!—Oh, if Father were only here!—Oh, there must be a way! It is rightful! They must not— THEY MUST NOT LEAVE.

(*Door opens slowly. Enter* RAIN-ON-HAIR *followed by* OMANCHA. BETH *is startled.*)

BETH. Oh, Rain-on-Hair!

RAIN. (*Pointing to* OMANCHA.) Him—little Chief—coat—him cold—freeze!

BETH. (*Hurriedly.*) Oh, Rain-on-Hair, you are not taking

your people away! You are not leaving the reservation? Oh, you must not. You cannot!

RAIN. (*Pointing to* OMANCHA.) Him—cold—him freeze—like lit'l Jim!

BETH. Oh, Rain-on-Hair, what would the Great White Father at Washington say? What would White Chief Parsons say?

RAIN. Big Jim—no—give—lit'l white chief—coat. (*Motions toward* OMANCHA.) Him—big chief boy—him want—white chief coat.

BETH. (*Suddenly understanding.*) You mean—

RAIN. Lit'l chief—freeze—bad— (*Pretends to shiver.* OMANCHA *does likewise.*)

BETH. You mean—you mean you want a coat—a coat for him?

(OMANCHA *nods.*)

RAIN. Him—freeze—bad.

BETH. (*Helplessly.*) Oh, I have no coat! (*Starts. Runs to chest and snatches father's coat. Moves toward* RAIN-ON-HAIR *and straightening shoulders, raises hand.*) See, Big Chief Rain-on-Hair, tomorrow at sunup your people would move off the reservation. Rain-on-Hair, if you convince them they should stay—that they must stay here, Little White Chief Parsons will give to Omancha a coat like Wacha's! A coat like Wacha's— Do you understand? (RAIN-ON-HAIR *and* OMANCHA *regard her fixedly.*) If you will make them stay, you shall have a coat—quite as fine as Wachas— See—with pockets—and buttons—brass buttons (*Points to buttons.*) and you shall have these (*Brings from chest the cap and mittens.*) besides! See! (*Displays them.*)—Ah, you are a great man, Rain-on-Hair, a very great man and a prophet. You can make your people stay.

OMANCHA. (*To father.*) Lit'l Red Chief want—white chief coat—want him—bad—Lit'l Jim—no give—

BETH. (*To* RAIN-ON-HAIR.) You shall have the coat for Omancha, tonight—at sunset—and these mittens and cap—Rain-on-Hair, if you will keep your people here—on the reservation—and in peace, until twelve moons or more have passed. Oh, will you promise? (RAIN-ON-HAIR *stands motionless, arms folded.* OMANCHA *turns to him appealingly.*) Will you promise, Rain-on-Hair?
(*Tableau as curtain falls.*)

SCENE II

Evening, same day.
Same scene, except the lamps are lighted. As curtain rises BETH *is hastily sewing brass buttons on a little coat.* HAL *clumsily removes basting threads.*

HAL. If only it will work. He can do anything with his people—and if he wants the coat badly enough—
BETH. Omancha wants the coat, Hal, and Rain-on-Hair loves Omancha as any father loves an only son. He will do anything for him! You'll see.
HAL. Yet perhaps he will not keep his promise even when he has the coat.
BETH. (*Firmly.*) He will keep his promise. He has honor—though he is only an Indian. We can trust him. We MUST trust him.
HAL. He should be coming.
BETH. He will come!—There, that is done. (*Holds up the little coat.*) At first I thought we never could make Father's great coat over in so short a time—but it seemed the rightful thing to do—as Mother would have said. Wasn't it lucky she had it in her Hope Chest?
(*Enter* RAIN-ON-HAIR, OMANCHA, OTHER INDIANS *and* JIM.)

BETH. Oh, Rain-on-Hair, you have come, just as you said at sunset! (*Holds up coat.*) See, it is finished—even the pockets and brass buttons. See. (RAIN-ON-HAIR *grunts and turns to* OTHER INDIANS *who survey coat stoically.* BETH *puts coat on* OMANCHA *and buttons it. Runs to chest and taking up cap and mittens, places them on* OMANCHA.) See, Rain-on-Hair! Aren't they beautiful? Omancha cannot be chilly now. (OMANCHA *appears much pleased.* RAIN-ON-HAIR *regards him, then nods slowly to* OTHER INDIANS *who nod in return.*) And now you will keep your promise, Rain-on-Hair! See, Little White Chief Parsons awaits your answer. (*Stands back a step.*)

HAL. (*Stepping forward.*) Yes, Big Chief Rain-on-Hair—your promise. You have persuaded your people to stay?

RAIN. (*Turning to* INDIANS. *They nod.*) Big Chief—people —stay—twelve moons and more—stay now— Lit'l Red Chief— (*Pointing to* OMANCHA.) Him—no cold—now—him—white chief—now.

BETH. (*Relieved.*) Thank God!

HAL. (*Extending hand.*) Thank you, Rain-on-Hair. Twelve moons or more, your people stay. Red Men, White Men, Friends.

(*They shake hands solemnly.* INDIANS *slowly file out.* OMANCHA *is last, evidently much pleased with his finery.* JIM *remains in background until last.*)

JIM. (*Coming forward.*) Rain-on-Hair— Him say—stay— All stay— Lit'l White Chief—no worry more— Injun stay— twelve moons—more— Lit'l Red Chief—Omancha—him no more freeze.

HAL. Thank you, Jim. (*Exit* JIM. *Thoughtfully.*) And to think Mother's Hope Chest solved the problem!

BETH. (*Joyously.*) Just as she hoped! Oh, Hal.

(*They catch hands and spin around gayly as curtain falls.*)

MOTHERS ON STRIKE *

By Carl Webster Pierce

CHARACTERS

Mrs. Stanton ⎱ striking members of "Mothers' Lo-
Mrs. Warren ⎰ cal, No. 1."
Bob Stanton, Jr., *a freshman in high school*
Ruth Stanton, *a senior in high school*
Robert Stanton, Sr., *a business man*
John Warren, *another business man; friend to* Robert

Time: *Late in a November afternoon.*

Scene: *Living-room in the* Stanton *home. Entrances upper center and right. Through center entrance is seen hat-tree and table in hall. Window down left, near which is an armchair, and beside chair an end table, on which lies some knitting. Fireplace left; near it an antique footstool. Easy chair and library table right center. On table several magazines and some school-books in a strap.*

Curtain discovers Mrs. Stanton *on her knees before table, with dust-pan and brush.*

Mrs. Stanton. Oh, dear! Will there never be an end to it? It's one thing after another, just as fast as I can fly. (*Gets up and starts to leave room; sees school-books on table, then goes to door upper center and calls.*) Bob! Bob, come here!
Bob. (*Offstage.*) In a minute.
Mrs. Stanton. No. This minute.
(*Enter* Bob, *upper center.*)
Bob. (*Carelessly.*) What d'ye want?

---

* For permission to produce this play, apply to **Walter H. Baker Company**, 178 Tremont St., Boston, Mass.

Mrs. Stanton. What did I tell you about leaving your school things scattered all over the house? Please take those books to your own room. What do you think your father bought your desk for?

Bob. All right. I was in a hurry and forgot.

Mrs. Stanton. And you must remember to use the door mat. I spent a long time cleaning this room this morning, and you've tracked in great chunks of mud.

Bob. Oh, gee! I always forget that mat. I'm generally in a hurry when I come in.

Mrs. Stanton. And in a hurry to get out again. Please run down cellar and get some wood for the fireplace. A blaze will be cheerful this evening.

Bob. Oh, I'll get the wood after dinner. I have to go down to the garage for some of their "free air" now. My bike has a flat tire. I won't forget your wood.

(*Exit, upper center.*)

Mrs. Stanton. (*With a discouraged sigh as she looks at the table.*) Well, if he didn't forget the books! (*Glances at clock on mantel.*) Oh, I didn't know it was so late. (*Goes to window and looks out.*) No one in sight yet. (*Paces back and forth.*) I wish they'd hurry so that it will be over with, and at the same time I hope they don't. I wonder how Ethel is looking forward to this evening's performance. (*Takes embroidery scissors from end table, nervously manicures a finger, throws them down again.*) I hope that her courage is holding up better than mine.

(*Enter* Mrs. Warren, *upper center; she has a newspaper in her hand.*)

Mrs. Warren. Here I am for one last word.

Mrs. Stanton. I was just on the verge of calling you.

Mrs. Warren. I must hurry right back. John will be home any time now, and everything must go off on schedule.

Mrs. Stanton. Oh, Ethel, how will it all turn out? I'm half

afraid to do it.

Mrs. Warren. It's going to be hard for us. I can't help wondering what effect it will have on John.

Mrs. Stanton. And I've spent a solid hour trying to figure out how my husband will take it.

Mrs. Warren. We shall soon find out.

Mrs. Stanton. I only hope that we are doing the right thing. When I think it over I'm not at all sure of myself.

Mrs. Warren. (*Taking* Mrs. Stanton *by the shoulders.*) See here, Margaret, I feel the same way but we must prod our courage when those moments of failure come. It will all be ended one way or the other—success or failure—within a few hours. Really, this uneasiness is merely an undeserved jab by a conscience which has been so ground down by absolute servitude that it is afraid to do justice to itself now. (*Laughs.*) There! That harangue has acted as an extra prop to my own confidence. (*Crosses and looks out window.*)

Mrs. Stanton. Of course, we must carry out our plans to their full extent—both of us. How awkward if one or the other were to relent; what an embarrassing situation for the unrelenting one. (*Laughs nervously.*)

Mrs. Warren. Concerted action is absolutely necessary. Unions always win their demands by hanging together.

Mrs. Stanton. (*Dolefully.*) When they *do* win them.

Mrs. Warren. There you go. Careful!

Mrs. Stanton. Perhaps the steps we're taking are too drastic.

Mrs. Warren. No, no. We're in the right. When demands are reasonable and fair they're always granted, and goodness knows that we're asking nothing unreasonable.

Mrs. Stanton. It was your suggestion that started us, and I do hope it turns out as well as you predict.

Mrs. Warren. Oh, I brought the paper down to show you where I got the idea. (*Reads.*) "Country-wide Rail Strike Imminent." And from this item: (*Reads.*) "The Governor has ordered a survey of the foodstuffs now in the state, and in the event of the actual occurrence of a strike, the state may be put upon war-time rations." That gave me the germ of an idea for us to use in awakening our families to the fact that we are human beings and not housekeeping machines. It will only take a jolt or two to make them realize how careless and selfish they are.

Mrs. Stanton. I hope so. You should have heard Bob a few minutes ago. Oh, if it will only work, how happy we all will be!

Mrs. Warren. Don't you worry about it not working. Pugilists always aim to give their opponents a blow in the stomach, judging by what I gather from my better informed son, and I guess that's the portion of the anatomy which our dinner strike will hit.

Mrs. Stanton. I hope that one blow will be sufficient for a —a knockout.

Mrs. Warren. Yes, let's hope that our walkout will be a knockout! (*Crosses to window.*)

Mrs. Stanton. My! Doesn't that sound ferocious and slangy?

Mrs. Warren. And American. Oh, here come Ruth and Robert; they've just turned the corner.

Mrs. Stanton. I guess the die is cast.

Mrs. Warren. I must go upstairs. We don't want it known yet that we are working together. Don't forget the details. (*Hurries* Mrs. Stanton *into chair near window.*) And speak up firmly. Here are your properties for the first act of the domestic drama. (*Gets magazine from table and places it in* Mrs. Stanton's *lap, and spreads knitting conspicuously over end table.*) There, the stage is all set; play your part well.

Mrs. Stanton. Good-bye, dear. I'll see you again soon.

Mrs. Warren. Keep your nerve and we'll win out.

(*Exit* Mrs. Warren, *upper center.* Mrs. Stanton *nerv-*

ously flutters leaves of magazine; wistfully glances out of window, then determinedly opens magazine and for a moment seems absorbed in it, then again closes it.)

MRS. STANTON. Will it straighten things out or only make them worse? (*Rises and wanders aimlessly about room.*) But I can't go back on my agreement with Ethel. I'll see it through; it's now or never. (*Sits and again opens magazine.*) I know that it's nothing intentional, but it makes life so hard and uninteresting and monotonous for us.

(*Door closes in distance; she starts.* MR. STANTON *and* RUTH *appear in door, upper center. He stops to remove coat and hat; she peers into room.*)

RUTH. Hello, Mumsey. I thought you were in the kitchen. (*Runs and kisses her mother, then draws back in astonishment.*) For goodness' sake! Dad, come here. Will you look at this! Mother's actually reading my movie magazine. What do you know about that?

MR. STANTON. (*Crosses to* MRS. STANTON; *carries newspaper.*) Knitting, too. Why, Ma, you haven't touched any knitting for months. What's up?

MRS. STANTON. (*Greatly confused.*) I—I— Well, I thought that I would today.

MR. STANTON. (*Sits right center.*) I'm glad that you're getting interested in things. Haven't I been telling you for weeks that you make altogether too much of a job out of housework?

MRS. STANTON. No, I don't, Robert. You don't realize what a hard day's work it is to run a house.

MR. STANTON. Pshaw! Isn't half the trouble you think it is. If you women folk would only systematize your work as we men do ours, you'd find it nothing at all.

MRS. STANTON. Who's the one who really does your work at the office? Of course you plan it all, but how about your stenographers and office boys and clerks?

MR. STANTON. Oh, that's different.

Mrs. Stanton. What's the difference? You have help, don't you?

Mr. Stanton. Yes.

Mrs. Stanton. A little help counts for a great deal.

Mr. Stanton. (*Face buried in newspaper.*) All right, Ma. I'm sorry that you have to do so much. (*Pause.*) Ho-hum, I'm tired after the day at the office.

Ruth. And I'm tired after a hard day in school. I wish Virgil had been a plumber or a motorman or anything but a poet.

Mr. Stanton. What will it be like next year when you're in college?

Ruth. Worse still. I guess I'll get married and keep house. It's a much easier life than studying one's head off.

Mrs. Stanton. Ruth, some day when you're married, I'll challenge you to make that statement again.

Ruth. Oh, I know it's true. (*Removes coat and hat.*) I guess I'll take my things off, although I haven't hardly got time. I'm going around to Mildred's tonight. I was talking to her over the phone this afternoon, and what do you think! Walter has proposed. I'm just dying to see her diamond. She got it last night.

Mr. Stanton. Is Bob in yet?

Mrs. Stanton. I think I heard him come in just a minute ago.

Mr. Stanton. Ruth, tell him to bring my slippers and jacket, will you, please?

Ruth. All right. (*Exit, upper center.*)

Mr. Stanton. Those crazy kids. They're always too excited over some trivial affair to take time to eat. I feel right now as if I could eat my weight in wildcats. (Mrs. Stanton *jumps nervously;* Mr. Stanton *unlaces his shoes.*) Had a good day at the office. Got old man Conway's signature on that contract I've been after. That means that perhaps we can buy a new car in the spring.

Mrs. Stanton. You've been after that contract quite a while.

Mr. Stanton. And so have many others. I feel pretty good over landing it. (*He turns his attention to the paper.* Mrs. Stanton *is now working at her knitting.* Mr. Stanton, *after a moment, reads.*) "Country-wide Rail Strike Imminent." H'm! Strikes seem to be the favorite pastime of the country. I wonder if they ever do any good.

Mrs. Stanton. (*Emphatically.*) So do I!

Mr. Stanton. I have my doubts.

Mrs. Stanton. (*With a sigh.*) So have I.

Mr. Stanton. Don't sound so mournful over it, Margaret. The rail strike won't concern us.

Mrs. Stanton. No, not the rail strike.

Mr. Stanton. By George, it might, too. Listen to this: (*Reads.*) "The Governor has ordered a survey of the foodstuffs now in the state, and in the event of the actual occurrence of a strike, the state may be put upon wartime rations." (*Laughs.*) It seems to me that would be an unfavorable point for the railroad men. You know the old rule states that the way to a man's heart is through his stomach, and a corollary to that might be "and his good humor depends upon the satisfying thereof." It would be funny if they were to lose public sympathy on that score, wouldn't it? It would be going too far to deprive people of food merely for a labor strike.

Mrs. Stanton. (*Looking helplessly around.*) What shall I—

(*Enter* Bob, *upper center, with slippers and jacket.*)

Bob. Here you are, Dad.

(Mr. Stanton *removes coat and shoes and puts on articles* Bob *has brought.*)

Mr. Stanton. How would a blaze in the fireplace feel this evening? It's rather chilly.

Mrs. Stanton. I asked Bob to get the wood some time ago.

Bob. Oh, that wood! I'll get it after dinner.

(MR. STANTON *settles comfortably in chair and resumes his reading.* BOB, *shoes and coat in hand, starts to exit upper center.*)

MR. STANTON. Bob, the footstool, please. (BOB *gets it from beside fireplace.* MR. STANTON *places his feet on it with a sigh of content, then glances down at stool.*) Say, this old thing doesn't wobble any more. Did you fix it, Bob?

BOB. No. I haven't touched it.

MRS. STANTON. I tinkered it up this morning. It's one of the family antiques, and we should take care of it.

MR. STANTON. That's too bad. I intended to fix it some evening.

BOB. (*Patting his stomach.*) I think that Mammoth Cave is entirely surrounded by me, I feel so hollow. Didn't take much time for lunch this noon, you know.

MRS. STANTON. I know you didn't. (*She hastily drops her knitting, opens magazine and becomes deeply interested in it.*)

BOB. Won't have much time for dinner, either; just time to gulp a bite.

MR. STANTON. What's the hurry?

BOB. Fred's uncle is going to take us for a nice long auto ride tonight, and we've got to get started early.

MR. STANTON. (*Sarcastically.*) Don't spoil an auto ride for a little thing like the good of your gastronomic department, will you? (*Exit* BOB, *upper center.* MR. STANTON, *from depths of newspaper.*) I'm rather hungry myself. Dinner 'most ready?

(MRS. STANTON *catches her breath and waits, but he evidently forgets his question. After a few moments, during which* MRS. STANTON *bestows several furtive glances upon her husband,* RUTH *enters upper center.*)

RUTH. What's the matter, Mother? The kitchen fire's out, and dinner isn't even started.

MRS. STANTON. (*Closes magazine and speaks very nervously.*) Bob didn't have time to get me any coal when he came in from school; he had important football practice and started away in a hurry after swallowing a bite of lunch.

MR. STANTON. What's that? Dinner not ready? Why, Margaret, I wanted to get away early to lodge this evening.

RUTH. (*Impatiently.*) And I told Mildred I'd be around by seven-thirty. It's six-thirty now.

MRS. STANTON. (*With an attempt to be firm, but greatly agitated.*) Call Bob. I've something I wish to say to all of you.

RUTH. (*Goes to door upper center and calls.*) Bob! Bob, Mother wants you.

MR. STANTON. Margaret, what is it? You look as pale as a ghost. Do you feel ill?

MRS. STANTON. No. I'm all right.

RUTH. What's the matter, Mother? I've never seen you look like this.

MRS. STANTON. Wait until you're all here.

RUTH. (*Again goes to door and calls.*) Bob, did you hear me? Come here at once.

BOB. (*Off stage.*) Hold your horses. (*Enters upper center.*) I'm too tired to run. Been playing football ever since school. (*To* MRS. STANTON.) Ma, I'm so hungry I could eat raw meat. How about dinner?

MRS. STANTON. There will be no dinner tonight.

MR. STANTON. What!

RUTH. What do you mean?

BOB. Aw, quit your foolin', Ma. Didn't I tell you that I'm hungry as a wolf, and in a hurry, too?

MRS. STANTON. (*Firmly.*) I tell you there will be no dinner tonight so far as I'm concerned. (*Takes a deep breath.*) *I am on strike!*

MR. STANTON.		On strike!
RUTH.	(*Together.*)	Mother!
BOB.		For the love of Mike!

Mrs. Stanton. (*Defiantly.*) Mothers' Local, Number One, held an indignation meeting this afternoon, and voted unanimously for a walkout. It is the opinion of all members that Bob is capable of carrying coal and of doing errands; that Ruth is not too tired when she gets home to leave the movie magazine until after dinner and help in the dining-room; and that Father can attend to odd jobs and spend an evening at home occasionally—or take his wife out for a good time.

Mr. Stanton. Margaret—

Mrs. Stanton. (*Quietly and tremulously.*) We know that none of you realize the existing conditions. It's just a sort of unconscious selfishness which is gradually becoming worse. Life's been one long monotonous drudgery the last few months, just because of your carelessness, and now you must all be made to see it. Everyone is striking—everyone from gravediggers to policemen. Most of them want more money and shorter hours, but we only want the position of homekeeper differentiated from the job of housekeeper. If you can't in some way meet this demand, you must hire a housekeeper—a strikebreaker.

(*Exit* Mrs. Stanton, *right, bravely trying to keep back her tears. The family is speechless for a moment.*)

Bob. Well, what do you know about that? Just the night I was in a hurry to get out,—and starving, too.

Ruth. (*On the verge of tears.*) Bobby! How can you talk like that? Why didn't you get the coal this noon?

Bob. You needn't say anything. Did you hear what she said about you and your movie magazines?

Mr. Stanton. Children, stop that everlasting squabbling and listen to me. (*Very thoughtfully.*) You're both to blame for what has happened, and I'm sorry to have to confess that I am, too. We ought to be heartily ashamed that such a thing has occurred in our family.

RUTH. (*Soberly.*) I never realized. I suppose that we've left lots of things for Mother to do that we should have looked out for.

BOB. Aw, I didn't intend to be mean this noon, but the fellers were waitin' for me.

MR. STANTON. That's it. None of us has done—or, rather, not done, things intentionally, but in the hurry and rush of life we've not taken time to see beyond our own horizon. (*Pause.*) What do you say if we three make a little agreement to endeavor to see how the other fellow is getting on? I'm sure that we'll not be sorry. If we do our level best to see that those about us are happy, we'll find that happiness comes to us, too.

BOB. I'll do my part. Gee, Dad, I wouldn't have had this happen for the world.

RUTH. And I'll do mine. We've all had a lesson that we deserve. Come on, Bob. We'll start to do things right now. Let's go out in the kitchen and see what we can do about dinner. After this, every evening when we get home our first concern will be to see what we can do to help Mother.

BOB. Ruth, the very next time you hear me say a mean thing to Ma, pull my ears.

(*Exit* RUTH *and* BOB, *upper center.*)

MR. STANTON. (*Pacing back and forth.*) Ye gods! I must have sounded fine telling that poor, overworked, little woman how hard I've been working today, and how little she's had to do.—And she's been doing it for me for nineteen long years! (MR. WARREN *appears in door, upper center, unobserved by* MR. STANTON.) Sometimes we men are just poor, blind fools.

MR. WARREN. You said it, Robert.

MR. STANTON. (*Turning with a start.*) Hello, you old sinner. How did you get in?

MR. WARREN. Bob Junior let me in the back door. Say, old man, what did I hear you say about the male of the species just as I came in?

Mr. Stanton. I was telling myself what an egotistical, selfish, self-satisfied brute I am; and, by George, I'll wager that you're just as bad as I or just a degree or two short of it.

Mr. Warren. Heap it up. Add ten degrees more for me.

Mr. Stanton. (*Bitterly.*) You can't beat me.

Mr. Warren. I can prove that I'm far ahead of you.

Mr. Stanton. Impossible. (*Grimly.*) You don't know what makes me so sure.

Mr. Warren. Look here, I'm not going to lodge this evening. I have some work to do at home. You're a better specimen of a man than I because—because—

Mr. Stanton. Well?

Mr. Warren. Because I've been so inconsiderate of my wife that she's been forced to go on strike to defend her rights. I guess that you can't beat that in your character shredding contest. Robert, you don't know how dirt cheap I feel.

Mr. Stanton. (*Gazes intently at him; speaks quietly.*) Your wife—on strike?

Mr. Warren. That's what I said.

Mr. Stanton. (*Extending hand.*) Good. Shake on it, John.

Mr. Warren. I'm not kidding you, and I didn't come down here to joke about it.

Mr. Stanton. I should hope not. Shake, we're both one hundred per cent jackasses.

Mr. Warren. I don't understand you.

Mr. Stanton. You say that your wife is on strike?

Mr. Warren. Yes, on strike. S-T-R-I-K-E, strike! No dinner tonight. She says that I was too busy reading the paper over my coffee this morning to offer any suggestions for tonight's dinner; and that that son of mine tore off to a football game with that angelic child of yours without getting her any coal, and that—

Mr. Stanton. Say, did she happen to mention a union,— Mothers' Local, Number One?

Mr. Warren. What do you know about it?

Mr. Stanton. Why, man, my wife's an active member of it; and my kids are junior members of the Loafers' League, along with yours.

Mr. Warren. Huh! If the kids are junior members, do you realize who are the seniors?

Mr. Stanton. I do. That's what I was talking to myself about when you came in.

Mr. Warren. Then from the tenor of what I overheard of your conversation with yourself, I take it that you think as I do—that our wives have just cause for complaint.

Mr. Stanton. I do. And I'll bet you and many another falsely called "head of the house" has been handing expense money over to his wife every week, and then complacently telling himself what a model husband he is. I tell you, John, I've had a jolt that I won't forget for a long while.

Mr. Warren. So have I. But we deserved it; richly deserved it. Isn't it funny how a man will get in a rut? If anyone had told us that there were men who treated their wives as ours have been treated, we'd have been ready to go gunning for them.

Mr. Stanton. John, you and I used to be mighty particular when we were first married, and before—that those two women had no cares or worries that we could prevent, didn't we?

Mr. Warren. Certainly we did.

Mr. Stanton. What do you say if we start a second courtship, and be careful not to take things for granted, and not to slip back into the old ruts?

Mr. Warren. Fine. That sounds good to me.

Mr. Stanton. What do you say if we—

(*He talks to* Mr. Warren *very earnestly for several seconds, so low that the audience cannot distinguish the words, and* Mr. Warren *very enthusiastically seems to agree with him.*)

Mr. Warren. (*Slapping him on the back.*) That's a great idea, old man. We'll both—
(*Again the audience is unable to get the words for a few seconds.*)
Mr. Stanton. Yes. Just like we used to.
Mr. Warren. (*Looks at watch.*) We'll have to hurry. Well, old boy, I guess that we'll know enough to behave ourselves in the future, won't we?
Mr. Stanton. You can bet that I'm going to mind my *p's* and *q's* when I get out of this scrape.
Mr. Warren. We'll swap notes on the way down town in the morning. So long.
Mr. Stanton. Good luck. (*They shake hands sincerely. Exit* Mr. Warren, *upper center.* Mr. Stanton *starts to go off right, hesitates a moment, then starts for door upper center.*) Guess I'll go tell the kids. (*Exits, upper center.*)
(*After a pause* Mrs. Stanton *enters right, and paces distractedly around.*)
Mrs. Stanton. Why didn't I let things go along as they were? Perhaps I've imagined things worse than they really are. (*Sound of coal being shovelled is heard faintly. She listens a moment, then throws her shoulders back defiantly.*) Bob's gotten around to the coal! (*Glances at ceiling.*) I'll keep my word, Ethel. (*Pauses to think.*) When I think it over, I don't know but I did exactly the right thing. Maybe it will make them more considerate. (*As she continues to pace back and forth her doubt returns.*) Probably we expected too much of them. If this should cause any hard feeling in the family I— (*Several hammer blows are heard in the distance; they continue at intervals for the next few seconds. She stands still and listens.*) Sounds as if something were being fixed. H'm! Perhaps we have followed the best course after all.
(*Sits in chair near window. Enter* Mr. Stanton, *upper center.*)

Mr. Stanton. Margaret, dear, I've come to have a little talk with you. I'm truly ashamed that it's been necessary for you to teach us this lesson; but we all deserved it, and it has struck home.

Mrs. Stanton. (*Breaking down at the last moment.*) Why did I do it? I had no right to upset everyone's plans. I'm so sorry. (*Rises.*) I'll go and get you a bite so that you can go to your meeting.

Mr. Stanton. (*Gently pushing her back into chair.*) Well, if that isn't just like a woman! Here you've won your point, given us all a lesson that we sorely needed, and now you want to spoil it all.

Mrs. Stanton. (*Between sobs.*) It was a mean thing for me to do.

Mr. Stanton. It was the best thing that you could have done. John thinks so, too. We've talked it over together. Too bad you women folk didn't think of it sooner. Will you give us another chance? We are going to do our level best to meet the demands of Mothers' Local, and we'll try to show from now on that we belong in it. Ruth has dinner under way; Bob has already fixed the catch on the refrigerator; and tomorrow night I'm going to put on my overalls and tackle the odd jobs which have been piling up around the house.

Mrs. Stanton. I'm so glad. Will you try to forget the disagreeable scene which took place here tonight?

Mr. Stanton. No, ma'am! We'll keep it in mind as a well-deserved lesson, and one which has been of priceless value to us. (*Softly.*) Margaret, remember the good old courting days when I used to call on you at least twice a week, and we used to run out somewhere for a good time every once in a while?

Mrs. Stanton. I'll never forget them. You see, Robert, every woman treasures them in her memory and lives them over again, when they've long been dead in a man's life.

Mr. Stanton. (*Sits on end table and takes his wife's hand.*)

Never mind the memories. Sweetheart, after dinner, while Ruth and Bob are doing the dishes, let's run down town to the movies.

Mrs. Stanton. Mothers' Local, Number One, will unanimously vote to accept the terms offered.

(*She leans over and kisses* Mr. Stanton.)

CURTAIN

POEMS

TO HIS MOTHER, C. L. M.

By John Masefield

In the dark womb where I began
My mother's life made me a man.
Through all the months of human birth
Her beauty fed my common earth.
I cannot see, nor breathe, nor stir
But through the death of some of her.

Down in the darkness of the grave
She cannot see the life she gave.
For all her love, she cannot tell
Whether I use it ill or well,
Nor knock at dusty doors to find
Her beauty dusty in the mind.

If the grave's gates would be undone,
She would not know her little son,
I am so grown. If we should meet,
She would pass by me in the street,
Unless my soul's face let her see
My sense of what she did for me.

What have I done to keep in mind
My debt to her and womankind?
What woman's happier life repays

Her for those months of wretched days?
For all my mouthless body leech'd
Ere Birth's releasing hell was reach'd?

What have I done, or tried, or said
In thanks to that dear woman dead?
Men triumph over women still,
Men trample women's rights at will,
And men's lust roves the world untamed,
. . . .
O grave, keep shut lest I be shamed!

HER STORIES

From *Songs for My Mother*

By Anna Hempstead Branch

I always liked to go to bed—
   It looked so dear and white.
Besides, my mother used to tell
   A story every night.

When other children cried to go
   I did not mind at all,
She made such faery pageants grow
   Upon the bedroom wall.

The room was full of slumber lights,
   Of seas and ships and wings,
Of Holy Grails and swords and knights
   And beautiful, kind kings.

And so she wove and wove and wove
   Her singing thoughts through mine.

I heard them murmuring through my sleep,
  Sweet, audible, and fine.

Beneath my pillow all night long
  I heard her stories sing,
So spun through the enchanted sheet
  Was their soft shadowing.

Dear custom, stronger than the years—
  Then let me not grow dull!
Still every night my bed appears
  Friendly and beautiful!

Even now, when I lie down to sleep,
  It comes like a caress,
And still somehow my childish heart
  Expects a pleasantness.

I find in the remembering sheets
  Old stories, told by her,
And they are sweet as rosemary
  And dim as lavender.

FROM REMEMBERING MOTHER

By Leonora Speyer

(Reflection while she sleeps)

I do not ask my children's tears
(A grave's a green, contented spot),
May they go laughing down the years—
(My little loves, grieve not!)

But lest a shrouded mother hears
(Too faintly) that familiar mirth,

Good father Death, seal well these ears,
This mother's heart, with earth.

LIKE HIS MOTHER USED TO MAKE

By James Whitcomb Riley

"I was born in Indiany," says a stranger, lank and slim,
As us fellows in the restaurant was kind of guyin' him,
And Uncle Jake was slidin' him another punkin pie
And an extra cup of coffee, with a twinkle in his eye—

"I was born in Indiany—more'n forty years ago—
And I hain't been back in twenty—and I'm workin' back'ards slow.
And I've et in every restaurant 'twixt here and Santa Fe,
And I want to state this coffee tastes like gettin' home to me!

"Pour us out another, Daddy," says the feller, warmin' up,
A-speakin' 'crost a saucerful, as Uncle tuck his cup.
"When I seed your sign out yonder," he went on to Uncle Jake—
"Come in and git some coffee like your mother used to make—

"I thought of my old mother and Posey county farm;
And me a little kid ag'in, a-hangin' on her arm,
As she set the pot a-bilin'—broke the eggs an' poured 'em in—"
And the feller kind o' halted, with a trimble in his chin.

And Uncle Jake he fetched the feller's coffee back and stood
As solemn for a moment as an undertaker would;
Then he sort o' turned and tiptoed to'rd the kitchen door, and next—
Here comes his old wife out with him a-rubbin' off her specs—

And she rushes for the stranger, and she hollers out, "It's him!
'Thank God, we've met him comin'! Don't you know your
    mother, Jim?"
And the feller, as he grabbed her, says, "You bet I hain't for-
    got—"
But wipin' of his eyes, says he, "Your coffee's mighty hot!"

MOTHER'S DIARY

By Elsie Duncan Sanders

I found a little record of her days
At the old lonely home. A few short lines
Each day were all she wrote. My mother's ways
Were simple. When she planted columbines
She put it down; the day she set a hen;
The little calf she weaned from mother-cow;
Her daily household tasks, and often when
She visited the sick . . . But O, somehow
One line apart from others seems to stand:
"I went to the postoffice," she would say . . .
I look upon it—here in her own hand—
That one short line she wrote from day to day.

Dear God, on high, can Mother see tonight
These tears for letters that I failed to write?

MOTHER

By Theresa Helburn

I have praised many loved ones in my song,
        And yet I stand
Before her shrine, to whom all things belong,
        With empty hand.

Perhaps the ripening future holds a time
For things unsaid;
Not now; men do not celebrate in rhyme
Their daily bread.

FAITH

By Virginia Scott Miner

We children turned to Mother
For her approving nod—
As sure of understanding
As when mother turned to God!

TO MY MOTHER

By Mary Sinton Leitch

Your form is dim: your hands, your brow, your face,
Are lost, and only some elusive grace
Remains of you for memory to prize:—
A fluttering bit of lace,
A ribbon—oh, the past is pitiless
And will not yield you to my searching eyes.
Is this forgetfulness?

Mother, not so, for your escape is of
The body, not the spirit, and my love
Holds you, forgotten, intimately sweet,
And precious far above
The need of flesh to keep remembrance true.
Forgotten?—Ah, my very pulses beat
In memory of you!

MOTHER OF THE WORLD

By Enid Hayward

I stopped in Oklahoma
Where a shack to a red hill clung,
And where nothing would grow except children,
Flaxen-haired, squat, brown babies!
Ten I counted, ragged and dirty—
The mother stood in the doorway.
Her hair hung cleated, sunburned to her head;
Her skin was rich and blistered like a man's
Hot from the ploughing; her body
Was ugly and strong, but her face
Lifted like a sunflower to the sun.
Shading her eyes with work-widened hands
She leaned against the doorway of the shack
Gazing not at me but through me,
Seeing not me—but the brown babes in the dirt.
Mother of the world she was
With dreams of making a new world in her eyes.

Visioned her children grown to youth
Beautiful and bold; saw her daughters
Graceful as maples silver-leafed, wind-blown,
With throats curved softly as catalpa blossoms
Flushed faintly with the tint of sunset gold.
Brides of strong men and bearing children,
Walking with their own brown babes at breast.
She saw her sons, stronger than their sire,
A new race to themselves, new men—
Slim saplings deepened into giant oaks!

Visioned the great muscled arms of her children
Ploughing, planting, making of common labor

Work divine; she pictured them
Templing the continents with their architecture,
Spanning the starry rivers with their bridges,
Rearing their coral columns to the sun!
All things perfect, planned by mortals,
Should know the imprint of her children's hands—
And, where they set their feet, new cities spring,
And where they stopped to plough, a new world grow!
Within the sun-glazed shack she stood,
Mother of the world, dreamer of dreams,
Beautiful to look upon, for in her eyes
Lay a dream of her brown children.

MOTHER O' MINE

By Rudyard Kipling

If I were hanged on the highest hill,
    Mother o' mine!
    Oh, mother o' mine!
I know whose love would follow me still,
    Mother o' mine!
    Oh, mother o' mine!

If I were drowned in the deepest sea,
    Mother o' mine!
    Oh, mother o' mine!
I know whose tears would flow down to me,
    Mother o' mine!
    Oh, mother o' mine!

If I were damned o' body and soul,
    Mother o' mine!
    Oh, mother o' mine!

I know whose prayers would make me whole,
   Mother o' mine!
   Oh, mother o' mine!

MOTHER

By Katherine Edelman

Of all the love that has been known
   Since time and earth began,
Of all the faith that has been shown
   Since God created man,
Of all the noble, stirring deeds
   That grace the written page,
A mother's boundless love and faith
   Stand out through every age.

Her deeds have moved the sternest hearts
   To wonder and to tears,
Her love has kindled faith and trust
   Through all the changing years;
Her sacrifice, unselfishness,
   Her trust through praise or blame
Have shrined her in the hearts of all
   And glorified her name.

For though the world may frown or sneer,
   Though failure may be ours,
Her love still folds, encircles us,
   A rosary of flowers;
A comforting, sustaining force,
   A star that brightly gleams,
That softens every care and hurt,
   And shares our hopes and dreams.

MEMORANDUM FOR AN INFANT SON

By Dorothy Brown Thompson

You may not find it easy, son, on Mother's-Days-to-be,
To think of anything for which you should be thanking me,
And so I list some reasons in a handy memorandum
Before you even reach an age of wit to understand 'em,
And you may take them out each year as Mother's Day recurs,
And say, "At least, she did this much, and therefore praise be hers."

I may have failed on many counts of duties mothers do,
Yet I have never tried to make a prodigy of you;
You have not posed for Hollywood, nor sung for Major Bowes,
Nor gone Terpsichorean on a toddler's tapping toes;
You can't speak Esperanto, nor beat champions at chess—
And yet I hope your intellect will flourish none the less.

I do not tremble for your health nor analyze your brain
(I hope you're nearly normal and approximately sane),
I do not try experiments with fads in education
Nor study cults of Attitude and Complex and Fixation;
I leave you pleasantly alone, entirely reconciled
To thinking you are just a boy, and not a Problem Child.

You never have been entered in a beauty contest yet;
I do not ape your baby talk with honeyed epithet;
I do not make you kiss your aunts nor sit on strangers' laps;
I've put you into rompers and your bonnets now are caps;
I do not make you play with girls, nor buy you dolls for toys,
But give you stern equipment such as appertains to boys.

If I should keep a baby book of "cunning things" you say,
I shall not leave it where your friends may find it some sad day;

And when you come to college years, I shall not show your dates
Your baby shoes electroplated into paperweights;
And no artistic pleasure in your infant pulchritude
Can make me have you photographed in curls, or in the nude.

Son—keep this list for Mother's Days, and may you never dread one,
But pin a flower on your coat, a large one—and a *red* one!

TO MY LITTLE SON

By Julia Johnson Davis

In your face I sometimes see
Shadowings of the man to be,
And eager, dream of what my son
Will be in twenty years and one.

But when you are to manhood grown,
And all your manhood ways are known,
Then shall I, wistful, try to trace
The child you once were in your face?

TO MY MOTHER

By Carrie Ward Lyon

I dreamed your beauty floated near me still,
   Lighting the common pathway I must tread.
   My heart stirred strangely, though the years have sped
Since you were laid to rest upon the hill;
For real, more real than waking, was the thrill
   That caught my spirit to your smile and said:

"The heart speaks truly that by love is led,
And drifted years are swept away at will."

You wave farewell from your high peak of dream,
   And still new color floods the earth and sky,—
   Part of the vanished splendor you and I
Visioned together in the evening's beam?
      How strange, how sweet, if the grim gates of death
      Should lift as lightly as a zephyr's breath!

THE GIVERS OF LIFE

By Bliss Carman

I

Who called us forth out of darkness and gave us the gift of life,
Who set our hands to the toiling, our feet in the field of strife?

Darkly they mused, predestined to knowledge of viewless things,
Sowing the seed of wisdom, guarding the living springs.

Little they reckoned privation, hunger or hardship or cold,
If only the life might prosper, and the joy that grows not old.

With sorceries subtler than music, with knowledge older than speech,
Gentle as wind in the wheat-field, strong as the tide on the beach,

Out of their beauty and longing, out of their raptures and tears,
In patience and pride they bore us, to war with the warring years.

II

Who looked on the world before them, and summoned and chose our sires,
Subduing the wayward impulse to the will of their deep desires?

Sovereigns of ultimate issues under the greater laws,
Theirs was the mystic mission of the eternal cause;

Confident, tender, courageous, leaving the low for the higher,
Lifting the feet of the nations out of the dust and the mire;

Luring civilization on to the fair and new,
Given God's bidding to follow, having God's business to do.

III

Who strengthened our souls with courage, and taught us the ways of Earth?
Who gave us our patterns of beauty, our standards of flawless worth?

Mothers, unmilitant, lovely, moulding our manhood then,
Walked in their woman's glory, swaying the might of men.

They schooled us to service and honor, modest and clean and fair,—
The code of their worth of living, taught with the sanction of prayer.

They were our sharers of sorrow, they were our makers of joy,
Lighting the lamp of manhood in the heart of the lonely boy.

Haloed with love and with wonder, in sheltered ways they trod,
Seers of sublime divination, keeping the truce of God.

IV

Who called us from youth and dreaming, and set ambition alight,
And made us fit for the contest,—men, by their tender rite?

Sweethearts above our merit, charming our strength and skill
To be the pride of their loving, to be the means of their will.

If we be the builders of beauty, if we be the masters of art,
Theirs were the gleaming ideals, theirs the uplift of the heart.

Truly they measure the lightness of trappings and ease and fame,
For the teeming desire of their yearning is ever and ever the same:

To crown their lovers with gladness, to clothe their sons with delight,
And see the men of their making lords in the best man's right.

Lavish of joy and labor, broken only by wrong,
These are the guardians of being, spirited, sentient and strong.

Theirs is the starry vision, theirs the inspiring hope,
Since Night, the brooding enchantress, promised that day should ope.

V

Lo, we have built and invented, reasoned, discovered and planned,
To rear us a palace of splendor, and make us a heaven by hand.

We are shaken with dark misgiving, as kingdoms rise and fall;
But the women who went to found them are never counted at all.

Versed in the soul's traditions, skilled in humanity's lore,
They wait for their crown of rapture, and weep for the sins of war.

And behold they turn from our triumphs, as it was in the first of days,
For a little heaven of ardor and a little heartening of praise.

These are the rulers of kingdoms beyond the domains of state,
Martyrs of all men's folly, over-rulers of fate.

These we will love and honor, these we will serve and defend,
Fulfilling the pride of nature, till nature shall have an end.

VI

This is the code unwritten, this is the creed we hold,
Guarding the little and lonely, gladdening the helpless and old,—

Apart from the brunt of the battle our wondrous women shall bide,
For the sake of a tranquil wisdom and the need of a spirit's guide.

Come they into assembly, or keep they another door,
Our makers of life, shall lighten the days as the years of yore.

The lure of their laughter shall lead us, the lilt of their words shall sway.
Though life and death should defeat us, their solace shall be our stay.

Veiled in mysterious beauty, vested in magical grace,
They have walked with angels at twilight and looked upon glory's face.

Life we will give for their safety, care for their fruitful ease,
Though we break at the toiling benches or go down in the smoky seas.

This is the gospel appointed to govern a world of men,
Till love has died, and the echoes have whispered the last Amen.

FATHERLESS

By Marjorie Knapp

I, who was once too indolent to do
The childhood tasks that were assigned to me
Without slow, bitter tears, now smile to see,
Though I am weary when the day is through,
How each new morning vigor comes anew.
Where love is, how a mother's task may be
An easy thing! O little brood of three,
With what supreme content, I work for you!

I watch you sleeping in the quiet night,
My loneliness forgotten for your sake,
And wonder—does your father, long away
In the far spaces, dim beyond our sight,
Listen to hear your laughter when you wake,
Or my voice singing at the close of day?

GENTLE PRESENCE

By Virginia Scott Miner

As one is suddenly aware
  Of what he scarcely sees,
I turn—and lo, the rocking chair
  Is moving in the breeze.

I saw no figure, saw no face—
I knew it was the air—
Yet felt for one brief moment's space
My mother's presence there!

MOTHERS

By Anne Trumbull

The world is a marvelous
  Spinning top
Of great affairs
  That never stop.
Broad as the nations
  It narrows down
To the little streets
  Of a friendly town;
Uncles and aunts
  And sisters and brothers,
To the tempered point
  That it spins on—
    Mothers!

EVENING SONG

By Fannie Stearns Davis Gifford

Little Child, Good Child, go to sleep.
The tree-toads purr and the peepers peep;
Under the apple-trees grass grows deep;
  Little Child, Good Child, go to sleep!

Big star out in the orange west;
Orioles swung in their gypsy nest;

Soft wind singing what you love best;
  Rest till the sun-rise; rest, Child, rest!

Swift dreams swarm in a silver flight.
Hand in hand with the sleepy Night
Lie down soft with your eyelids tight.
    Hush, Child, little Child! Hush.—Good-night—

NIGHT AND MORNING

By Dorothy Aldis

The morning sits outside afraid
Until my mother draws the shade;

Then it bursts in like a ball,
Splashing sun all up the wall;

And the evening is not night
Until she's tucked me in just right,
And kissed me and turned out the light.

Oh, if mother went away
Who would start the night and day?

MOTHER'S BIRTHDAY

By Frances Gill

Daddy says today is Mother's birthday.
Mother isn't living here,
God took her to His house, where she'd be well.
But, Oh! if we had her near,
I could sew her something for a present;

I could pick her lots of flowers,
And make her room so sweet;
And see her smile her rainy smile—
No mother smiles like ours.

Today is Mother's birthday, Daddy says.
I think God lets the Angels know;
They'll make a party for her; she'll love that.
And I—I think that I'll tell Daddy so.

LAUGHING MAMA

By Anne Herendeen

(For A. B. C.)

You were never a Great Big Mother:
You were always folding yourself up
To just my size.

When I crawled on one elbow and one knee
You sat on the floor too.
You were my sailor's snug harbor.

We were going on seven
When, as "Mrs. Smith" and "Miss Jones,"
We gossiped of the terrible trials of large families.

When we graduated to "Casino,"
With the piano bench for our table,
No one would ever have believed you had a cupboard full of
    whist prizes.

We were fully thirteen, I should think,
When we went chestnutting with Trilby horse
(Wading upstream for minnows).

Maker of plans, surprises, parties;
Impregnable bulwark against all bullies.

A dancing Mama, a singing Mama, a reading Mama,
A keen Mama who was never fooled on a horse,
An exquisite Mama, distilling their perfume from rose leaves.

A Mama in overalls among the strawberries,
A Mama in white shoulders and opal ball gown.

Always behind steadying,
Always ahead vitalizing,
Always beside me laughing.

A laughing Mama
Surrounded by laughing servants
And laughing rooms,
Laughing food and laughing gardens.

O, laughing Mama,
If ever you make a will——
Leave me your clean shining laughter!

THE SANDMAN

By Margaret Thomson Janvier

The rosy clouds float overhead,
   The sun is going down;
And now the sandman's gentle tread
   Comes stealing through the town.
"White sand, white sand," he softly cries,
   And as he shakes his hand,
Straightway there lies on babies' eyes

His gift of shining sand.
Blue eyes, gray eyes, black eyes, and brown,
   As shuts the rose, they softly close,
When he goes through the town.

From sunny beaches far away—
   Yes, in another land—
He gathers up at break of day
   His store of shining sand.
No tempests beat that shore remote,
   No ships may sail that way;
His little boat alone may float
   Within that lovely bay.
Blue eyes, gray eyes, black eyes, and brown,
   As shuts the rose, they softly close,
When he goes through the town.

He smiles to see the eyelids close
   Above the happy eyes;
And every child right well he knows,—
   Oh, he is very wise!
But if, as he goes through the land,
   A naughty baby cries,
His other hand takes dull gray sand
   To close the wakeful eyes.
Blue eyes, gray eyes, black eyes, and brown,
   As shuts the rose, they softly close,
When he goes through the town.

So when you hear the sandman's song
   Sound through the twilight sweet,
Be sure you do not keep him long
   A-waiting in the street.
Lie softly down, dear little head,

Rest quiet, busy hands,
Till, by your bed his good-night said,
　He strews the shining sands.
Blue eyes, gray eyes, black eyes, and brown,
　As shuts the rose, they softly close,
When he goes through the town.

HUSHING SONG

By Fiona Macleod

Eily, Eily,
　My bonnie wee lass:
The winds blow,
　And the hours pass.

But never a wind
　Can do thee wrong,
Brown Birdeen, singing
　Thy bird-heart song.

And never an hour
　But has for thee
Blue of the heaven
　And green of the sea:

Blue for the hope of thee,
　Eily, Eily;
Green for the joy of thee,
　Eily, Eily.

Swing in thy nest, then,
　Here on my heart,
Birdeen, Birdeen,
　Here on my heart,
　Here on my heart!

ACTIVITIES

ACTIVITIES FOR MOTHER'S DAY

By Nella Harvey

1. Plan a program and invite the mothers.
2. Learn appropriate poems. Practice them in order to recite them well.
3. Collect appropriate stories. Two or three of the best may be chosen and read for the program.
4. Dramatize stories.
5. Learn appropriate songs.
6. Make a program booklet, so that the numbers on the program need not be announced.
7. Make a welcome arch.
8. Make favors for mothers, such as white flags, with the word "Mother" in red letters on each one.
9. Plant flower seeds; later reset the plants and give them to the mothers on Mother's Day.
10. Make booklets about mothers of famous men.
11. Make baskets for messages of remembrance, one for each day in the week.
12. Make greeting cards for the mothers.
13. Write invitations to the mothers asking them to attend the program.
14. Arrange and decorate the room for Mother's Day.
15. From magazines collect pictures of mothers or of family life. Mount them on brown wrapping paper and paste them on the blackboard. Print appropriate titles or

sentences below them.
16. Plan refreshments for a party.
17. Prepare the food in the classroom the day before.
18. Make napkins of paper towels; measure, cut in fancy shapes, and decorate with colored paper.
19. Use paraffined cups for the flowerpots, and decorate them.
20. Arrange and decorate the room.

A MOTHER'S DAY ACTIVITY

(*For Primary Grades*)

By Nora McCarthy

This activity is an example of how one of our national days may be capitalized for training in citizenship, character, health, and safety.

I. How the activity was initiated.

We were learning the names of the great days of the year. The important days of each month were being spelled. Mother's Day was named as the greatest day in May. One child asked, "Are we going to make something for our mothers this year?" We discussed many gifts that we might make. The idea of making a booklet was suggested. The children decided to call the booklet "Home." The experiences of home life were discussed and dramatized, and supplied firsthand subject matter. The making of the booklet was an activity that brought every child into a spirit of hearty co-operation, and stimulated worth-while interests.

II. Aims.
    A. Children's.
        1. To have fun making a book about their families.
        2. To keep the making of the book a secret.

3. To please their mothers with the booklets on Mother's Day.
B. Teacher's.
1. To develop habits of good citizenship.
2. To develop a knowledge and greater appreciation of the relationships, duties, and responsibilities of the members of the home, school, and community.
3. To teach the children to work together to accomplish a definite task.
4. To teach children to respect the rights of others.

III. Progress of the activity.

Questions concerning home life were freely discussed, and the children talked over how to treat others, how to guard their health, and how to protect themselves against the dangers of street, home, and school. The following codes in regard to citizenship, health, and safety were originated after the discussion.

A. Citizenship.
1. In school.
   a) I will keep the schoolroom neat and attractive.
   b) I will walk in the halls.
   c) I will obey the rules of the school.
   d) I will do better work in school each day.
   e) I will not disturb my neighbor while he is doing his work.
   f) I will play fair.
   g) I will be a good loser.
   h) I will be a modest winner.
2. At home.
   a) I will be polite.
   b) I will be helpful.
   c) I will be obedient.
   d) I will be neat.
   e) I will do acts of courtesy.

f) I will run errands.
g) I will not quarrel with my sisters or brothers.
h) I will always be kind to all of our guests.
B. Health.
1. I will walk, stand, and sit correctly.
2. I will take good care of my eyes and ears.
3. I will wear the proper clothing.
4. I will play out-of-doors each day.
5. I will sleep and rest enough.
6. I will keep my body clean.
7. I will think kind, healthful thoughts.
8. I will be cheerful and try to make others happy.
C. Safety.
1. I will look in both directions before I cross the street.
2. I will not touch live wires.
3. I will not catch on cars.
4. I will watch where I am going.
5. I will obey the policeman.
6. I will help old people.
7. I will help little children.
8. I will think "Safety First."

IV. Activities.
A. After forming the citizenship, health, and safety codes, we carried on the following activities.
1. A code was assigned as a single topic. The children began to think consistently and to give oral compositions.
2. Stories were retold, in which the children practised correct language form through imitation of the author.
3. Stories partially told were completed, in order to develop the child's imagination and to form a motive for oral work.
4. Pictures relating to our codes were cut from maga-

zines and papers and brought to school.

5. Poems and quotations relating to the codes were collected.

B. After much oral work, the children began their written compositions. They made the following rules for self-criticism.

1. Is the title in the middle of the page?
2. Do all the important words in the title start with capital letters?
3. Did I skip a line between the title and the story?
4. Did I indent the first line of the paragraph?
5. Does each sentence begin with a capital letter?
6. Is there a question mark or period at the end of each sentence?

C. After much discussion, the following titles were chosen for our written compositions.

Our Family, My Mother, Our Home, How to Act, My Father, How to Cross a Street, How to Get Ready for School, Our Evenings at Home, How to Keep Healthy, and Two Poems.

D. After a composition was written for the booklet, a crayon drawing was made to illustrate it.

1. The title was written under each illustration.
2. Pattern letters, H, O, M, and E, were drawn on ¼" squared paper, and made 2" high and 1¼" wide.
3. The letters and a cut-paper design were cut from construction paper, and were mounted on a sheet of contrasting color, 8" x 9".
4. The covers and sheets of the booklet were fastened with brass paper fasteners.

V. Outcomes.

A. This project linked home and school more closely together.

B. The teacher gained valuable information concerning

the children's home life, in a way that parents did not resent.

C. The children composed a playlet for Mother's Day.

D. The children learned to appreciate the duty they owe to society in return for the rights enjoyed.

E. The children learned to express themselves more easily and correctly in oral and written English.

F. Every parent became interested, and showed keen enjoyment when the books were presented.

VI. Interesting incidents.

One day the superintendent paid our grade a visit. One boy, who was always very attentive, was called upon twice. He had no idea as to what question had been asked. After our visitor left I asked him the reason. He replied, "Well, I wrote about him in my composition, 'How to Act,' yesterday. I was taking a good look at him so that I could draw his picture today."

One of the little girls drew a picture of her mother on the blackboard. The illustration was that of a very slender woman. One boy exclaimed, "Mary's mother is fat, and she should make her look fatter." Whereupon Mary replied, "Oh, I want her to look thin because my mother is trying to reduce."

BIBLIOGRAPHY

Citizenship

Ringer, Edith H., and Downie, L. C.: "Citizenship Readers," Primer, *Home;* Book 1, *City and Country;* and Book 3, *The Good Citizens Club* (Lippincott).

Health

Andress, J. M.: *Boys and Girls of Wake-up Town* (Ginn).
Andress, J. M., and Andress, A. L.: *A Journey to Health Land* (Ginn).

Lawson, Edith W.: *Better Health for Little Americans* (Beckley-Cardy).

Newmayer, S. W., and Broome, E. C.: *Health Habits* (American Book Co.).

Whitcomb, C. T., Beveridge, J. H., and Townsend, E. E.: *My Health Habits,* Book 3 (Rand McNally).

Safety

Loper, Leila: *Safety First Stories and Pictures* (Hall & McCreary).

Peardon, Celeste, and Comegys, Zelina De M.: *Adventures in a Big City* (Macmillan).

Ringer, Edith H., and Downie, L. C.: *School Days,* "Citizenship Readers," Book 2 (Lippincott).

Roberts, M. M.: *Safety Town Stories* (Lyons & Carnahan).

Celebrations for Music Week

PLAYS

AFTERNOON WITH SCHUMANN *

A Play for Music Week
To Be Used with School Orchestra

By Delle Oglesbee Ross

PERSONS IN THE PLAY

Robert Schumann, *a young musician, about 23*
Clara Wieck, *a gifted young pianist, about 14*
Frau Schumann, *Robert's mother, very large and masterful*
Gottlieb Rudel, *Robert's guardian*
Friedrich Wieck, *Clara's father, with whom Robert is studying*
Baroness Ernestine von Fricken, *about 17, with whom Robert is having a secret affair*
Gisbert Rosen, *Robert's intimate friend, a young student*
Members of the Orchestra, *all young students*

Time: *The year 1833.*

Place: *Leipzig.*

Scene: *A room in the home of* Friedrich Wieck.

Notes: All are dressed in the fashion of the early 1830's. Robert Schumann is sentimental, melancholy and given to hys-

---

* This play may be produced without royalty where no admission is charged. Otherwise, a fee of $3.00 must be paid to the author, 317 North Marion St., Oak Park, Ill.

teria. Clara Wieck, though young, is mature and already in love with Schumann. Ernestine von Fricken is a fashionable, simpering, young lady.

The selections mentioned for the orchestra are merely suggestions and may be changed to others if desired. However, they should be contemporaneous with the period of Schumann, and the second selection should be one of Schumann's compositions.

Ballet Music from Rosamunde . . . . *Franz Schubert*
Traumerei . . . . *Robert Schumann*
Scherzo from Midsummer Night's Dream . *Felix Mendelssohn*

Chronological order has not been adhered to in this play; for events happening before and after have been crowded into this one afternoon; but the circumstances are authentic.

A music room in the house of FRIEDRICH WIECK. *The furnishings should suggest the ornate decorations of the period. The window has heavy draperies; the table holds elaborate vases and ornaments, as well as piles of music. If possible, there should be one or two heavy oil paintings on the wall. At center back are French doors leading to a terrace. The orchestra is placed diagonally across left back, the chairs arranged informally. Across the corner, right back, is a grand piano. Right center is the door opening into the hall. A divan is placed at one side, front, of the door, on the other side a chair. At left front is a table, with large chair and small ottoman at right; another chair at left of table.*

As the scene opens the musicians are entering and taking their places. ROBERT SCHUMANN, *who is to direct, stands by the music desk, which is placed to command both orchestra and pianist. He motions to the members of the orchestra regarding their places.* CLARA WIECK *is seated at the piano watching the rest.* SCHUMANN *taps with his baton.*

SCHUMANN. Attention! Shall we commence with something of the divine Schubert's?
CLARA. The Ballet Music from Rosamunde, Robert?
SCHUMANN. Yes—yes—that will be a good beginning.
VIOLINIST. I am a little weak in that second phrase—
SCHUMANN. Then we will practise—yes—that one passage—
(*The* VIOLINIST *plays first, then the orchestra with him, for a few moments.*)
SCHUMANN. Now! We are ready? So!
(*He taps his music desk, lifts his baton. The orchestra plays.*)
SCHUMANN. Ah, that is good! Ah, the wonderful—the marvelous Schubert!
CLARA. Cut down in the flower of his youth—
SCHUMANN. (*Shaking his head sadly.*) To die so young, with all the glory of his future before him. Sad—sad!
CLARA. Let us play another, Robert.
SCHUMANN. But your father, Clara—
CLARA. Pooh! Father can wait—
SCHUMANN. He will be angry—
CLARA. But this is the same as practising—this playing with the orchestra—besides it is fun!
SCHUMANN. Well, well, dear child—
CLARA. Don't call me a child, Robert. In some ways I am much older than you!
(*The boys in the orchestra laugh.* ROBERT *taps his music stand, and turns over some music sheets.*)
SCHUMANN. Now then! Now then! No nonsense! Are we not here for serious work? What shall it be next?
(*He continues turning the music. The musicians tune their instruments.* CLARA *plays softly.* GOTTLIEB RUDEL *opens the door, then stands aside to allow* FRAU SCHUMANN *to enter the room, which she does with great majesty and*

dignity. *She is very large and is dressed in a rich and severe manner.*)

SCHUMANN. Mother!

FRAU SCHUMANN. Ah, my dear son, you did not expect me!

RUDEL. It is a pleasant surprise, I trust—

SCHUMANN. (*Petulantly.*) You know I dislike surprises. It upsets my poor nerves!

FRAU SCHUMANN. (*Embracing him.*) Don't be childish, Robert.

SCHUMANN. You have no conception of my sufferings—

CLARA. His nerves are so sensitive.

(GOTTLIEB RUDEL *places the large chair by the table, and* FRAU SCHUMANN *is seated, spreading her skirts.* RUDEL *stands back of her chair.*)

RUDEL. (*Pompously.*) Now, my young friend, we have come from Zwickau to see how the law studies are progressing—

SCHUMANN. The law!

(*The boys in the orchestra wink at each other, and laugh softly.* CLARA, *having risen when the guests enter, now turns again to the piano, running her fingers lightly over the keys.*)

RUDEL. Indeed yes—the law! One would think you had never heard of it—

SCHUMANN. (*Tragically.*) Oh, yes, sir, I have heard of it!

RUDEL. It has been some months, now, since you came to Leipzig, and we have had no reports—

SCHUMANN. Reports!

FRAU SCHUMANN. Yes, reports! Do you think we will wait forever to hear how your career is shaping?

SCHUMANN. But, my dear Mother—

FRAU SCHUMANN. But, my dear Son—we do not have patience with dilatoriness—

RUDEL. Your brothers are industrious and diligent—can you claim that you are the same?

SCHUMANN. Wait—

FRAU SCHUMANN. We have waited too long. Already your brothers have made places for themselves in the world—

SCHUMANN. (*In a loud voice.*) Listen to me! I have given up the law!

RUDEL. Given up the law!

FRAU SCHUMANN. What is this I hear? If my ears are not proving false to me!

SCHUMANN. Music is my life! My life is music!

FRAU SCHUMANN. Music!

SCHUMANN. How can I spend my life with dry-as-dust law?

RUDEL. Bah!

SCHUMANN. When there is music! Music to fill my soul with ecstasy! Music to bring joy and solace to a weary world!

RUDEL. Bah!

FRAU SCHUMANN. Nonsense! I will not allow it! To make music your life-work—what a thing for a grown man to do!

SCHUMANN. You do not understand—

FRAU SCHUMANN. When you might have a profession that is honorable—lucrative—

SCHUMANN. (*Wrings his hands.*) But I will, mama—I *will!* Do you not see—

CLARA. (*Rises and approaches* FRAU SCHUMANN.) Oh, Frau Schumann, are you saying the profession of music is not honorable?

FRAU SCHUMANN. Perhaps not dishonorable, but a poverty-stricken one, you must admit—

CLARA. Not always is that true—

SCHUMANN. What does all that matter—when one's soul yearns to express beauty in the form of perfect harmony?

CLARA. Ah, Robert is right!

FRAU SCHUMANN. I judge in your eyes Robert is always right—*nicht wahr?*

(*She is slightly sentimental,* CLARA *is somewhat confused.*)

SCHUMANN. Now and then I discover that I have imagination and perhaps a turn for creating things myself—
CLARA. If you could but hear what he creates, Frau Schumann. Robert, let us play the *Traumerei* for them—
SCHUMANN. Their souls are doubtless too filled with material yearnings to understand it—but we will do our poor best—
 (*He turns to the orchestra, taps with his baton. They tune their instruments and arrange the music on their stands.* CLARA *sits again at the piano.*)
SCHUMANN. Come lads, do your best with my poor effort.
 (*They play Traumerei.*)
CLARA. (*Stands and enthusiastically addresses* FRAU SCHUMANN *and* RUDEL.) There! Do you not see? He is a musician—not a lawyer!
FRAU SCHUMANN. Very pretty—
SCHUMANN. Very pretty, indeed! Very pretty! Do you see nothing more than mere prettiness in that?
FRAU SCHUMANN. Do not become so agitated, my son—
SCHUMANN. Ah, that I should go through this agony! Misunderstood—ill— My nerves tearing me to pieces—
CLARA. Ah—poor Robert—
FRAU SCHUMANN. You are sympathetic, *liebes Fräulein*—
CLARA. Oh—
SCHUMANN. I will not give up the music! I will not study the law! Never— Never!
 (*He stamps and tears his hair. The musicians in the orchestra, one by one, slip through the French window, showing by pantomime that they are bored with the argument, but sympathize with* SCHUMANN.)
RUDEL. (*Staring at* SCHUMANN.) Histrionics! I know what will bring this young man to his senses—
FRAU SCHUMANN. If you do, for Heaven's sake, tell me!
RUDEL. We will stop his allowance—

SCHUMANN. (*Stopping short in his tantrum.*) Stop my allowance! You would not dare!

RUDEL. Why not?

FRAU SCHUMANN. It is a thought, indeed.

SCHUMANN. (*Almost screaming.*) Stop my allowance! It is not enough now— I am in debt—you know that! I must borrow here—and beg there—to get along—

RUDEL. Your allowance is quite adequate for a student. It is because you squander it that you are always out of money.

SCHUMANN. Can you sit there, Mama, and hear your son so libeled?

CLARA. Cruel—

FRAU SCHUMANN. I fear it is only too true—

RUDEL. We will see how you manage without an allowance—if you insist upon the music—

SCHUMANN. Then I will destroy myself! Yes—I will destroy myself like my poor sister who found life too hideous to endure!

CLARA. Oh, *lieber Gott*—Robert! Robert! (*She weeps.*)

FRAU SCHUMANN. (*Screams.*) No—do not say that! To have one child take her life! Oh, not another! That you should threaten such a thing!

SCHUMANN. But I will! I swear it! I will not live without music—

FRAU SCHUMANN. We must not insist perhaps, Rudel. He is serious—

RUDEL. Do you think so?

SCHUMANN. Stop my allowance—demand that I continue with the law—you will see!

FRAU SCHUMANN. We must be lenient, Rudel. Perhaps we should allow a trial of the music—I think he will see his mistake—

RUDEL. It is you who will make the mistake—

CLARA. Ah, Frau Schumann, you are a true mother—

FRAU SCHUMANN. He is my youngest one—my last child—the thought melts my better judgment.

(SCHUMANN *is wiping his face with trembling hands. He sinks down upon the piano chair. A voice is heard calling* CLARA. FRIEDRICH WIECK *enters.*)

WIECK. Clara, what do you mean, wasting your time in this way?

CLARA. I have been practising with the orchestra, Papa.

WIECK. (*Sarcastically.*) Where then is this orchestra? Trifling, that's what you are doing—

SCHUMANN. She has been working with us—we have only just stopped.

CLARA. Here is Frau Schumann and Herr Rudel, Papa—

WIECK. (*Rather gruffly.*) I greet you.

(*He bows to each, they return the greeting.*)

FRAU SCHUMANN. You will pardon our intrusion into your home, Herr Wieck.

RUDEL. We asked for you upon our arrival, but the servant informed us you were out.

WIECK. I have but this moment returned. Had I been home, my daughter would have been busy with her preparations instead of trifling here—

CLARA. Oh—Papa!

FRAU SCHUMANN. We felt it was necessary to visit this son of mine—who seems also to be trifling with his time—

WIECK. Schumann? I should say that he has been most industrious—

RUDEL. (*Ironically.*) With music?

WIECK. But what is more important?

RUDEL. Bah—these musicians!

CLARA. Frau Schumann has graciously consented to Robert continuing seriously with the music, Papa—

WIECK. Good! The fellow undoubtedly has ability—

FRAU SCHUMANN. You anticipate, *Fräulein.* I have not actually decided—

WIECK. (*Paying no attention.*) His great fault is his extravagance. He knows not the value of money—and he reads too much of Jean Paul Richter. Too sentimental—too morbid—

RUDEL. If he does not know the value of money, then he must learn—

WIECK. Perhaps life will teach him. Yes, yes, he is too extravagant—too sentimental—too maudlin—too fond of the fair sex—but otherwise he is a good musician—

CLARA. Papa, you know how the ladies run after Robert—

WIECK. And I do not think Robert makes much haste in running away, my child—

CLARA. They are always making excuses—

WIECK. For romantic excursions—secret engagements—

FRAU SCHUMANN. You are not so foolish, Robert?

SCHUMANN. I could hardly engage myself upon my present income, do you think—

WIECK. But there is this Baroness—

SCHUMANN. (*Hastily.*) I must be attentive to the friend of my friend Gisbert—

WIECK. Ah so! Come, Clara, you must pack—you must practise your concerto—you—

FRAU SCHUMANN. Your daughter shows great talent, Herr Wieck—

WIECK. She is a genius! A prodigy! Even now she is preparing for the grand concert tour—

FRAU SCHUMANN. And you encourage her?

WIECK. Encourage her! Of course I encourage her!

(CLARA *is leaning over* SCHUMANN; *they are whispering together.*)

FRAU SCHUMANN. But will not this life of public appearances prevent her from fulfilling a woman's destiny? To marry and manage her children and household?

WIECK. That is my hope, Frau Schumann. She is too precious

to waste upon a life of domesticity—

FRAU SCHUMANN. Life may teach you something, too, Herr Wieck, as to that—

(WIECK *glares at her, then claps his hands.*)

WIECK. Come—come—Clara. Time is passing—there is much to be done—

CLARA. I'll try to come down again, Robert—

SCHUMANN. Do so, Clara, your Fridolin needs you. He leans upon your sympathetic understanding—

WIECK. Come—I say! I am not at all satisfied with the cadenza in the second movement. It still needs hours of work—

(CLARA *curtsies to* FRAU SCHUMANN *and* RUDEL, *kisses the tips of her fingers to* SCHUMANN, *she and her father go out door right.*)

FRAU SCHUMANN. A dear child!

SCHUMANN. A very dear child! Her tender thoughtfulness consoles me and inspires me—

RUDEL. Why should you be consoled?

SCHUMANN. Ah, my dear Rudel, you have no idea of my sufferings. My nerves so easily unstrung. My financial worries—

RUDEL. I repeat—they are of your own making—

SCHUMANN. And now this cruel threat—to take away my music or my allowance.

FRAU SCHUMANN. Perhaps we should discuss this further—

RUDEL. (*Interrupting.*) As a man of business—

SCHUMANN. Business! Business! I am sick of business!

FRAU SCHUMANN. Take heed, my son, business is the very foundation of our lives—

SCHUMANN. I am an artist—that is—I want to be an artist. No. I *am* an artist! And I am not concerned with business!

FRAU SCHUMANN. Foolish boy—

SCHUMANN. My father left money for my education. He would have encouraged me in my musical ambitions.

FRAU SCHUMANN. Alas, I fear he would. He was ever shortsighted where you were concerned—

SCHUMANN. Then music was his plan for me—you admit it, Mama?

FRAU SCHUMANN. His—not mine—

RUDEL. But you are no longer a boy to spend your life in schools—you are a man—

FRAU SCHUMANN. And you have accomplished nothing!

(SCHUMANN *strides back and forth.*)

SCHUMANN. That is because I have wasted too many years trying to do something that is obnoxious to me. Law! Pah!

RUDEL. You are ruining your life with your stubbornness.

SCHUMANN. (*Loudly.*) Why do you worry me?

(GISBERT ROSEN *and* ERNESTINE VON FRICKEN *enter.* GISBERT *leads her in, supporting the tips of her fingers.* ROBERT *is quite confused when he sees her. He looks quickly at his mother, then shakes his head at* ERNESTINE; *but she does not notice.*)

ERNESTINE. Such shouting, dear Robert, you are as red as a turkey cock!

(SCHUMANN *greets her, kisses her hand, then claps* GISBERT *on the shoulder.*)

SCHUMANN. Ah, my dear Ernestine, how good of you to bring my old Gisbert. I have missed you both.

ERNESTINE. (*Very coy.*) Missed us! La—'tis only yesterday.

SCHUMANN. (*Hastily.*) Oh, yes, it seemed much longer.

(GISBERT *looks quite astonished.*)

ERNESTINE. (*Making eyes at* SCHUMANN.) A pretty speech! Flatterer! I fear you are as naughty as ever.

FRAU SCHUMANN. Who are your friends, Robert?

SCHUMANN. A thousand pardons, Mama. The Baroness Ernestine von Fricken, my mother, Frau Schumann. My guardian, Herr Rudel. (ERNESTINE *curtsies prettily.* FRAU SCHUMANN *inclines her head.* HERR RUDEL *bows very low.*) My dear friend, Gisbert Rosen, you already know through my letters.

(GISBERT *bows deeply to* FRAU SCHUMANN, *then exchanges bows with* RUDEL.)

FRAU SCHUMANN. Indeed it seems we are not strangers, Herr Rosen, for my son's letters have been filled with Gisbert—Gisbert.

ERNESTINE. And not with Ernestine? Fie—Robert!

SCHUMANN. I would not risk that temper of Gisbert's—

ERNESTINE. Of Gisbert?

GISBERT. Of me?

(SCHUMANN *stands behind his mother and makes signs to* GISBERT *and* ERNESTINE *not to betray to his mother that the affair is between* ERNESTINE *and himself, instead of* GISBERT. GISBERT *is inclined to be irritated.* ERNESTINE *does not understand and continues to cast loving glances at* ROBERT.)

FRAU SCHUMANN. Of course, my dear, young men do not discuss young ladies in their letters.

ERNESTINE. (*Looking at* SCHUMANN.) Oh, of—of—course not.

SCHUMANN. Baroness, do be seated on this divan. (*He goes to her quickly and leads her to the divan near the door.* GISBERT *seats himself in the nearby chair.* HERR RUDEL *sits in the chair left of the table, while* SCHUMANN *leans gracefully against the back of the divan.*) I am sure our dear Gisbert will not challenge me if I remain near you.

GISBERT. Schumann, you are—

SCHUMANN. I know what you would say—

GISBERT. We came hoping for some music—

ERNESTINE. Ah, your heavenly music, Robert!

FRAU SCHUMANN. Is it this kind of flattery that has stolen your poor wits, my son?

RUDEL. (*Shaking his head.*) To give up the law!

GISBERT. What is this?

SCHUMANN. (*Darting angry glances at his mother and*

RUDEL.) They came with demands that I sacrifice my music to law! Imagine it!

ERNESTINE. But you are not serious?

FRAU SCHUMANN. Serious? And why not, pray?

ERNESTINE. (*Very coyly.*) Oh, but he is so gifted—a genius! I am in Heaven when I listen to his music—or when I sing to his accompaniment.

FRAU SCHUMANN. You seem to take this matter to heart, dear Baroness.

ERNESTINE. Oh—yes—yes—we—

SCHUMANN. She knows how dear my happiness is to Gisbert. Is it not so, Gisbert?

GISBERT. What— Oh, of course—of course— (*He sees what* SCHUMANN *is trying to do, and becomes amused.*) My dear Ernestine and I could never be happy if our friend is not happy also—

SCHUMANN. Good old Gisbert!

GISBERT. Yes, indeed!

(*They exchange glances.*)

ERNESTINE. And he would be so tragic without his music. To myself I call him "the Master."

RUDEL. (*Consulting his watch.*) If we return to Zwickau with the afternoon coach, my dear Frau Schumann—

FRAU SCHUMANN. (*Standing and gathering gloves, purse, etc.*) Yes, my good Rudel, we must not miss the coach.

SCHUMANN. You have decided, Mama, and you, Herr Rudel?

RUDEL. It is, of course, your mother's decision. But I—

FRAU SCHUMANN. Yes, it is, in the end, my decision.

SCHUMANN. Ah, dear Mama, I tremble to know—

FRAU SCHUMANN. (*Slowly.*) We will allow the music to continue—for a time—at least—

SCHUMANN. (*Seizes her hands. She embraces him.*) Ah, Mama! (CLARA *enters, right.*) Ah, Clara, do you hear?

CLARA. What is it, Robert? I returned as soon as I could.

SCHUMANN. The music! She has decided! I am not to be stricken dumb, but can continue to pour out my soul in music!

CLARA. (*Bows before* FRAU SCHUMANN, *and kisses her hands.*) You are truly a mother! I knew you would not be harsh.

FRAU SCHUMANN. Now, now, my dear, you are all so excitable.

RUDEL. We really must be off.

FRAU SCHUMANN. Embrace me, my son. Farewell! (*She kisses him on the brow, then turns to* CLARA.) I think yours are the capable hands in which to leave him, though you are so young—

CLARA. Thank you—

ERNESTINE. But I—I am—

GISBERT. Of course you are devoted to any friend of mine.

FRAU SCHUMANN. (*In a satisfied voice.*) That is as it should be. I wish every happiness to such loyal friends of my son. (ERNESTINE *looks quite amazed and angry. She rises.*) Farewell, young ladies. Farewell, Gisbert Rosen—and Robert—

(*The girls curtsey, the young men bow.* FRAU SCHUMANN *and* RUDEL *depart, right.*)

SCHUMANN. (*Pacing up and down.*) Now I must work—work! I must devote every moment to it. I will finish the device to hold my fourth finger steady—I will—

CLARA. You must finish the *Papillons*.

SCHUMANN. Ah, yes, so much to do—so much—

ERNESTINE. (*Putting her hand on his arm.*) You have scarcely noticed me, Robert, nor told me that I look well—or—have you no time for poor little me?

SCHUMANN. (*Absently.*) Don't bother me!

CLARA. Oh, Robert, don't be rude to Gisbert's friend—

ERNESTINE. (*Horrified.*) Gisbert's—friend? (CLARA *and* SCHUMANN *are at the music desk, examining some manuscript, and do not hear her.*) Robert, do all our pledges mean nothing?

GISBERT. Come, Baroness, we had better go and leave these immortals to their dreams.

SCHUMANN. (*Absently.*) Oh, do not go. We will have some music presently.

CLARA. I will call the boys in— (*She goes to the French window.*) They are in the garden—

ERNESTINE. (*Stamps her foot.*) We are leaving—at once!

CLARA. (*As she steps through the window.*) Adieu, Baroness, adieu, Gisbert. No doubt you are sufficient unto yourselves—

(GISBERT *bursts into a laugh, claps* SCHUMANN *on the shoulder, holds out his hand to* ERNESTINE, *and leads her from the room.* SCHUMANN *pretends indifference, but is evidently ashamed. He bows deeply as they leave.*)

SCHUMANN. Fare thee well then, Ernestine—

ERNESTINE. (*Gives him a languishing look, then puts her handkerchief to her eyes.*) Ah, Robert—it is then—farewell!

(SCHUMANN *puts his hands to his eyes, and staggers to the large chair, and by pantomime indicates that he is suffering agonies of exhaustion. He then raises his head and gets up from the chair as* CLARA *precedes the members of the orchestra through the French window. They take their places, softly tune their instruments, turn music, etc.* CLARA *runs down front, catches* SCHUMANN'S *hands and pulls him to the music desk.*)

CLARA. We must not loiter, Robert. Papa will be coming after me—but I want some more glorious music—

SCHUMANN. Then you will be off to your concerts and the applause of the entranced throngs.

CLARA. But I do not want to go until I have seen peace return to Schumann's brow.

SCHUMANN. Dear Clara! You are so young—so unspoiled—and yet you have the wise and tender heart of a woman.

CLARA. That is because I am an artist. Years have nothing to do with it—

SCHUMANN. Well, thank goodness you are not like these silly young ladies of fashion!

CLARA. (*Seats herself at the piano, then turns and looks at* SCHUMANN.) Robert, my first concert is here in Leipzig, you know—

SCHUMANN. Yes, I know. I am looking forward to it with joyful anticipation—

CLARA. On my program I shall play your F ♯ minor sonata—

SCHUMANN. How good of you, Clara—

CLARA. I shall play it because it is my only chance to tell you —tell you—well I cannot tell you privately how I feel in my heart—we are so seldom alone—so I will tell you publicly—

SCHUMANN. (*Surprised and delighted.*) Clara—Clara—

CLARA. (*Raises her hand as he starts to her.*) What shall we play? our friends are waiting—

SCHUMANN. Ah, yes we must play— Shall it be the *Scherzo* from Mendelssohn's *Midsummer Night's Dream?*

CLARA. Delightful!

SCHUMANN. Careful with the first violins. So! Ready— (*He raises his baton. The orchestra plays.*)

CURTAIN

SAINT CECILIA MEETS KING JAZZ *

A Musical Pageant

By JEAN MILNE GOWER

PLACE: *A garden or auditorium.*
TIME: *Present—Music Week.*

---

* For permission to produce, $5.00 must be sent to Mrs. J. H. Gower, 56 West 70th Street, New York City, N.Y. Special terms will be granted to small groups.

PERSONS

(In order of their appearance.)

THE AUDIENCE
SAINT CECILIA'S HEAVENLY HERALDS
SAINT CECILIA
SAINT CECILIA'S MESSENGERS *and* ATTENDANTS
EARTHLY HERALDS OF KING JAZZ
KING JAZZ
COURT ATTENDANTS TO KING JAZZ *and* PAGES
ST. CECILIA'S MUSICIANS, *folk-song and classic*
KING JAZZ'S SWING-TIME ORCHESTRA, CROONERS, BLUES SINGERS, ETC.

NOTE: *The quantity and quality of music used is left to the discretion of the Director. If the Pageant be used by several neighborhood groups of Girl- and Boy-scouts or Y.W.C.A. and Y.M.C.A. branches meeting in some central place, the individual groups may be coached separately and come together only for the dress rehearsal. Settings and costumes may be simple or elaborate as desired.*

SCENE: (If in a garden.) *A flower-decked pavilion stands slightly to left of centre. Shrubbery and trees edge the expanse of lawn and rustic seats are placed conveniently.* (If in an auditorium.) *An ornamental chair may be used on a dais banked with palms and flowers, while vases of bright blossoms give the needed color. An organ (off) plays stately music, Bach, Handel, Beethoven, or any well known classical excerpt.*

Enter four HERALDS. *They wear pale gold tunics and carry long slender trumpets through which they announce the coming of their mistress.*

HERALDS. (*In unison.*)
        Hail, Saint Cecilia! Hail! Hail! Hail!

(*They turn and make obeisance.*)
(*Enter, from left,* SAINT CECILIA *and* ATTENDANTS. SAINT CECILIA *wears flowing white draperies and carries a silver lute. Her four* ATTENDANTS *wear similar robes in pale blue, rose, primrose and lavender. The four small* MESSENGERS *are in simple white smocks. They precede the retinue and stand at attention on either side of the pavilion each holding aloft a lily as* ST. CECILIA *mounts to her seat on the dais. The organ still plays softly its classic measures as the* ATTENDANTS *group themselves about their patron saint.*)
FIRST HERALD. (*With three calls on his trumpet.*)
 Hear ye! Hear ye! Hear ye!
(*Then, to appropriate music off stage, he chants to the* AUDIENCE.)
 Once more Cecilia, martyred maid of Rome,
 Our Patron Saint of Music, has come home
 From higher spheres. Again she visits Earth,
 The planet Fate predestined for her birth.
(*The* ATTENDANTS *bow low and the small* MESSENGER-PAGES *swing the lilies as though they were censers before* ST. CECILIA.)
SECOND HERALD. (*Also calling attention with his trumpet.*)
 Hear ye! Hear ye! Hear ye!
(*Music, off, continues as he chants.*)
 Across wide spaces, as she sped along,
 Our Saint has heard strange conflict in Earth's song
(*Derisive saxophone laughter off, at right.*)
 Moaning and wailing like some beast in pain,
(*Illustration, off.*)
 Unseemly crooning sodden with things profane.
(*A crooner, off, becomes emotional.*)
(ST. CECILIA'S ATTENDANTS *cast anxious glances toward the right but she herself appears to be serene.*)
THIRD HERALD. (*Blowing a more emphatic call for attention.*)

Hear ye! Hear ye! Hear ye!
Affrighted lest Earth's harmony be lost,
Our Saint has sped through sound waves tempest-tossed,
To bid all music-lovers to draw nigh
And call again old melodies from on high.
(*Laughter from right.*)

FOURTH HERALD. (*Sending out his challenge.*)
Hear ye! Hear ye! Hear ye!
Come hither all, who for the best aspire,
Sing songs your forebears sang to lute and lyre.
Greet ye our Patron Saint, the Heavenly Muse,
With strains that must all baser themes confuse.

SAINT CECILIA. (*Rising and holding out her hands to* AUDIENCE.)
Dear ones of Earth, I greet you with great joy
And thank you for your greeting to me here.
May ours be happiness without alloy
Throughout this week of melody and cheer.

AUDIENCE. (*If it does its duty and fulfills its part.*) Hear! Hear! (*Applause.*)

(*Enter, from right,* KING JAZZ, *his* HERALDS, GENTLEMEN-IN-WAITING, *and* PAGES. KING JAZZ *is in full evening dress with a silk hat, huge diamond stud and spectacular rings. His four* HERALDS *wear gaudy raiment and head-gear ranging from a Panama to a topper. They carry bright colored megaphones through which they chant as they cakewalk in, followed by four small black* PAGES *in striped pajamas—all chewing gum.*)

FIRST JAZZ HERALD. (*Swaggering and speaking in a falsetto voice through megaphone accompanied by jungle drums off.*)

HEEEEEAR YE! *Hear Ye! Heeeeeear Ye!*
What ho, Saint Ciss! Lo, Jazz, our mighty king,
(*Latest popular tune.*)

And his retainers now their welcome bring!
And, though your ideas are a bit passé,
We'll teach you nifty tricks to take away.
   (St. Cecilia *glances round at her* Attendants *who are obviously aghast. She then bows gravely in acknowledgment of the address.*)
   Second Jazz Herald. (*Turning a handspring before using his megaphone.*)
Hear ye-he-he-he-he! Hear Ye-he-he-he! Hear Ye-he-he-he-he!
Just watch your step! We'll teach you how to rumba
   (*Late hit tune off.*)
And sing each up-to-date exotic number.
We'll teach you how to swing a funeral dirge
And give it quite a bacchanalian urge.
   (*A strain or two of Chopin's Funeral March with impertinent variations.*)
   (*During the chanting of this, two of* St. Cecilia's Attendants *have found themselves moving to the new rhythm in spite of themselves. The others looked dazed and disgusted. Two of them cover their ears and* St. Cecilia *appears disturbed.*)
   Third Jazz Herald. (*Approaches solemnly with his megaphone under his arm and his hands in prayerful pose. Then he speaks through his megaphone in a patient, pedagogic voice. Hymn-like music with twists to suit words.*)
Cheer Ye! Cheer Ye! Cheer Ye!
Our good King Jazz will teach you, too, to croon,
To sing torch-songs and swing each solemn tune.
He'll teach you to sob sentimental Blues
That will make angels tremble in their shoes.
   First Celestial Attendant. (*Horrified.*)
      Sacrilege!
   Second Celestial Attendant.
      Obscene!

THIRD CELESTIAL ATTENDANT.
         A pagan Cult!
FOURTH CELESTIAL ATTENDANT. (*To* ST. CECILIA.)
    Dear Mistress, let us flee from such insult.
SAINT CECILIA. (*Thoughtfully*.)
    Nay, sisters, we must strive to understand
    What dire disease has fallen on this land.
FOURTH JAZZ HERALD. (*Applauding and megaphoning triumphantly*.)
    Hear ye! Cheer ye! Cheer Ye!
    Hi! 'At-a-girl, Saint Ciss! No quitter you!
    But you'll find we're a pretty husky crew.
    We've no *disease,* but lots of *devotees*
    Who think we're tops—and so we strive to please.
KING JAZZ. (*Swaggering forward and doffing his topper as he bows before her*.)
    That's O.K., Sister. We've got what it takes
    To make the old world buzz. Why, Holy Snakes!
    If we'd gone on with your old chestnut stuff
    We'd be in the dark ages sure enough.
SAINT CECILIA. (*With dignity and judicially*.)
    Pray tell me, is it possible that you
    Believe this senseless clatter to be *new?*
    Why, such discordant themes and sounds were rife
    In chaos before Earth bore human life.
KING JAZZ. (*Pretending to feel doubtful and scratching his head*.)
Ouch, Lady! One on me! *I* wouldn't know
What sort of shows they staged *that* long ago;
But this is what I'd like to put to test
Whether these folks (*Indicating* AUDIENCE.) like your or my
    stuff best.
    (*Derisive saxophone, off, mingles with strains of Handel's largo*.)

SAINT CECILIA. (*Smiling.*)
>That's fair enough. Let this great concourse here
>Show forth its preference as my groups appear
>With classic themes, folk-song and madrigal
>And yours in their eccentric carnival.

KING JAZZ. (*Laughing confidently and seating himself on a flamboyant very tall gilt chair which his* PAGES *have just dragged in and placed beside the pavilion and, as the* PAGES *adjust the purple canopy bearing the royal arms, he speaks.*) Poor Ciss, I weep for you! (*To* PAGES.) Scram, pages! Bring
All of our peppiest guys that play or sing.
Find us some gals, too, for I've got a hunch
I'll need both sexes in my modern bunch.

>(*Exeunt to right black* PAGES *in disorder.*)

SAINT CECILIA. (*Calmly to her* CELESTIAL MESSENGERS.)
Go, Spirit Messengers, from far and near
Bring those to whom old songs and themes are dear.
Tradition, classic standards are at bay
Against crass tonal dissonance of today.

>(*Exeunt* MESSENGERS *to left.*)

KING JAZZ. (*Reprovingly to* ST. CECILIA.)
"Them is harsh words"—as some wise guy opined
But, Sister Ciss, you've got us wrong you'll find.

SAINT CECILIA. (*Smiling.*)
>I am content to stand by the decree
>Of these wise judges in all amity.

KING JAZZ.
That's mighty white of you. Now let's be friends
No matter how this cuckoo contest ends.

ST. CECILIA.
>Yes, let us lend that aid to harmony
>And greet the verdict with tranquility.

(*During this long conversation,* ST. CECILIA'S ATTENDANTS *and* KING JAZZ'S GENTLEMEN-IN-WAITING *have also* been trying to understand each other. *As their superiors are now conversing quietly a few remarks of the* ATTENDANTS *are audible before the* MESSENGERS *and first group of contestants appear.*)

FIRST GENTLEMAN-IN-WAITING. (*Admiringly.*)

Say, you're *some* gals! Them glad-rags look like sky—

FIRST CELESTIAL ATTENDANT. (*Puzzled.*)

Rags? These are heavenly garments from on high—

SECOND CELESTIAL ATTENDANT.

Woven on looms of purest melody.

SECOND GENTLEMAN-IN-WAITING. (*Teasingly.*)

Oh, yeah? They're ripping, Lady! (*Pretending shock.*) Excuse me!

THIRD CELESTIAL ATTENDANT.

How strangely you all speak—such quaint, queer words—

THIRD GENTLEMAN-IN-WAITING.

Us? Why we thought *you* were the queer birds!

FOURTH GENTLEMAN-IN-WAITING.

    What say we teach you gals to talk our lingo,
    To sing our songs and dance our steps, by jingo.

(*He pairs them off and their feet seem to be testing the rhythm.*)

FOURTH CELESTIAL ATTENDANT. (*Drawing back.*)

    No, really we must stop—it is not seemly—
    Although (*Aside.*) I think I might like it *extremely.*

(*Faint sound of old-fashioned music from left.*)

FIRST HERALD OF SAINT CECILIA. (*Facing left and sounding his bugle.*)

    Behold, the fair competitors appear!

FIRST HERALD OF KING JAZZ. (*Facing right and using his megaphone as jazz is heard.*)

    Sit tight! Our crew of crooners draweth near!

NOTE: *The* ST. CECILIA *groups should wear colorful costumes native to the country they represent. Classical or other musical selections should represent the well-known composers of each country, chosen by the Director with reference to the occasion and capacity of the performers.*

The KING JAZZ groups must be spectacular in dress and behavior. They preface each offering with a short jazzed parody of some classic which has just been rendered by one of their rivals "swinging" it into modern rhythm. They then proceed with their program of current "hit" dance tunes and songs—the more absurd and emotional, the better.

(*The following grouping of performers of adjacent countries may be followed if time precludes separate assignments. The groups may be introduced by* HERALDS *using the following couplets, or simple announcements may be made. The members of the contesting parties should be stage-managed by the* MESSENGERS *and darkey* PAGES.)

FIRST HERALD OF ST. CECILIA. (*Glancing to left as organ peals.*)

Behold, our fair competitors appear!

FIRST HERALD OF KING JAZZ. (*Shielding his eyes with his hand as he peers toward the right.*)

And, lo, our crew of crooners too draws near!

SAINT CECILIA. (*Politely.*)

I think, sir, we should not anticipate.

KING JAZZ. (*Blandly.*)

Sure. We'll know soon enough who gets the gate.

(*Enter left, ushered by* MESSENGERS *the* ST. CECILIA *Groups, English—Scotch—Welsh—Irish. Music: excerpts from Purcell, Elgar, Coleridge-Taylor. Folk-songs, Shakespearean ballads, "Drink to me only with thine eyes," "Under the Greenwood Tree" etc. Scotch, Welsh and Irish ballads.*)

SECOND HERALD OF ST. CECILIA.

These lads and lassies bring from olden days
Their English, Scottish, Welsh and Irish lays.

(ENSEMBLE *sing program as arranged by Director, then*

retire to positions near pavilion, ushered by the CELESTIAL MESSENGERS. AUDIENCE *registering reaction to performance.*)

SECOND HERALD OF KING JAZZ. (*Acting the part of a Cockney as he beckons in the motley group from right—led by capering* PAGES *to some jazzed English tune.*)

    The British h'Isles, sez you? Well, listen 'ere,
    We'll pep 'em h'up a bit with Yankee cheer!

(ENSEMBLE *go through program arranged making sport of their rivals.* AUDIENCE *applauds or hisses as various members respond to the antics.*)

THIRD HERALD OF ST. CECILIA. (*As second group is ushered from left by the* CELESTIAL MESSENGERS.)

    Now Germany, Austria, Hungary are bringing
    Music that sets our very hearts a-singing.

(ENSEMBLE *play or sing excerpts from Wagner's operas, Mozart, Dvořák, Liszt, Schubert, Brahms, German folk-songs.* AUDIENCE *applauds as they join the others near pavilion.*)

THIRD HERALD OF KING JAZZ. (*Greeting the group which the goose-stepping darkey* PAGES *usher in to the tune of "Ach, du lieber Augustine."*)

    We may not "sprechen Deutsch" so good, but say,
    Just hear us translate it to U.S.A.

(ENSEMBLE *impersonating a German band gone mad and showing how they think German folk-songs ought to sound.* AUDIENCE *showing what they think about it, as the performers group themselves with others on right.*)

FOURTH HERALD OF ST. CECILIA. (*Greeting the third group being brought on by the* MESSENGERS.)

    France, Spain and Italy from Southlands bring
    Sweet music that must down the ages ring.

(ENSEMBLE, *such composers as Massenet, Saint-Saëns, Debussy, Gounod, Scarlatti, Verdi and Rossini furnish va-*

riety for this group, who enter to the gentle strains of "Clair de Lune," or the gay "Funiculi, Funicula." AUDIENCE *doing its part as the* CELESTIAL MESSENGERS *assemble the group, left.*)

FOURTH HERALD OF KING JAZZ. (*Welcoming a pair of absurd looking French Apache dancers, a Spanish toreador and senorita, an Italian gondolier and peasant girl.*)

The Latin tongue's too tough for us, it's true,
But hear our saxophone say "Parlez vous"!
(*Illustrates.*)
(ENSEMBLE *Americanizing well-known music into modern rhythm.* AUDIENCE *applauds and what not as this group retires to right.*)

FIRST HERALD OF ST. CECILIA. (*As the Russian, Chinese and Japanese contingents in their native dress are brought forward by the* CELESTIAL MESSENGERS.)

Russia, Japan and China, drawing near,
Bring Eastern music now to charm the ear.
(ENSEMBLE, *Russia has Rubinstein, Tchaikovsky and others to choose from and Sir Arthur Sullivan's "Mikado" music would give the needed flavor for the Japanese.* AUDIENCE *as before, while these join the pavilion group.*)

FIRST HERALD OF KING JAZZ.

The Far East's music drives us nuts, but we
Will mix the darn stuff in a fricassee.
(ENSEMBLE *swing the Volga Boat Song and drum on bowls with chop-sticks.* AUDIENCE *registers its reaction as the party finish their contribution.*)

SECOND HERALD OF ST. CECILIA. (*As the Scandinavian group, in their picturesque costumes, enter.*)

From Denmark, Norway, Sweden come again
Belov-ed strains to gladden hearts of men.
(ENSEMBLE *perform selections from Grieg, Sinding, Sibelius—also folk-songs.* AUDIENCE *as before while the singers*

retire to left.)
SECOND HERALD OF KING JAZZ.
>We bane no Scandinavians; but, you bet,
>We'll make a Greta-Garboish furore yet.

(ENSEMBLE *swing a classic tune and dance as they sing in deep contralto some ultra romantic ditty.* AUDIENCE *as before.*)
THIRD HERALD OF ST. CECILIA.
>United States joins Music's caravan
>Echoing Negro, Indian, and Plainman.

(ENSEMBLE, *music from MacDowell, Goldmark, Steven Foster, etc. Spirituals, "Land of the Sky-blue Water," Cadman, plantation songs.* AUDIENCE *applauds according to their appreciation as group joins others.*)
THIRD HERALD OF KING JAZZ.
>Back home again with cowboys, Indians, darkies!
>So, folks, sit tight—we'll show you what a lark is!

(ENSEMBLE, *medley of cowboys yip-yip-yipping, Indian war-cries, Darkies wailing or crooning.* AUDIENCE *responding as last performers are ushered back by the pickaninny* PAGES.)
SAINT CECILIA. (*Rising and addressing audience.*)
>This strange encounter, friends, has brought to me
>Much wonder as to whether it can be
>That the divinity of Music's inspiration
>Is waning in this earth-mad conflagration.

KING JAZZ.
>Now, folks, get wise; we leave it up to you
>Whether *our* stuff's not got more kick to do
>The worried world the good it's hankering after
>Than classic dope. What you guys need is laughter!

FOURTH HERALD OF ST. CECILIA.
>Pray rise, all ye who deem our cause divine
>And grant to music this your loyal sign.

(*Portion of* AUDIENCE *favoring* ST. CECILIA *rise and ap-*

plaud.)

FOURTH HERALD OF KING JAZZ.
Now, on your feet, you folks who've got good sense!
And, win or lose, we still know we're immense.

ENSEMBLE OF BOTH SIDES, HERALDS, MESSENGERS AND PAGES.
The Saint Cecilias have it!
  or } The Music Contest ends!
The King Jazz faction has it!
Long live all music lovers and let us be good friends.
Let harmony from Music Week go echoing down the year
With inspiration of goodwill for every listening ear.

OH, SUSANNAH! *

A Play for Music Week

BY GRACE DORCAS RUTHENBURG

CHARACTERS

(*In order of their appearance*)

LIVVY
STEPHEN FOSTER
CHILDREN: MIT, MITTY, ANDY, SAM, SELINA
JOE
SUE
MISTER RICE
MEMBERS OF HIS CAST
MRS. FOSTER
MRS. PENTLAND

* All rights reserved. Copyright applied for. No performance of this play may be given without written permission from, and payment of, three dollars royalty to Grace Dorcas Ruthenburg, 471 Park Avenue, New York City.

(*This program is designed to show the sources from which Stephen Foster drew his folk melodies: the spirituals, the popular comic numbers of the early minstrels, the parlor ballads of the day; all of which he absorbed and built upon. There is nothing arbitrary about the selections chosen. The play can be adapted to the skills and numbers you have on hand. Switch it about or substitute as you choose, only remember that comparatively few airs familiar to modern ears were extant in 1835.*)

Before the curtain rises, a chorus appears in the costumes of the early nineteenth century.* They sing a series of Foster melodies: "My Old Kentucky Home," "Uncle Ned," "Old Dog Tray," "Old Black Joe," *and* "Old Folks at Home."

As the final chorus comes to an end, the choristers part and move off into the wings, the music evaporating gradually as the curtain rises on:

The Foster kitchen in what is now part of Pittsburgh, Pa. A simple, cheerful room, comfortably furnished with a stove, a table covered with a red-checked tablecloth, and a sunny window filled with blooming geraniums. The window, and a door to the right of it backstage, look out on the side yard. Another door downstage right leads to the rest of the house.

OLIVIA PISE, *"Livvy," the Fosters' colored servant, is ironing clothes, thumping the iron in rhythm to the air of* "Go Down, Moses!" †

She breaks off at the sound of a drum beaten in the yard

---

* If you don't want to bother about costumes, you can keep this chorus hidden backstage, or if you want to use the audience as chorus, pass out mimeographed copies of the songs and dress the director alone in costume. For the final chorus, it is better to use a rehearsed group, as few people know the air of "Open Thy Lattice, Love," which is used at the final curtain. This last group may appear or not, as you prefer.

† It is impossible to fix the date of the origin of most early spirituals. This one might have been familiar to Livvy, as might "Roll, Jordan," "Trouble's Gwine Ter Weigh Me Down," "Po' Rosy," or "Ride On, King Jesus," most of which are to be found in "Seventy Negro Spirituals," compiled by Fisher, Boston: Oliver Ditson Co., 1926.

outside. As she crosses to the stove to change her irons, she looks out of the window.

LIVVY. La, there's that child at his drummin' again. Never seed such a one fo' music. If tain't a drum, it's a whistle. Tain't a whistle, it's a flute. (STEPHEN FOSTER, *nine years old, bursts into the kitchen. He is almost crying.*) Now whut's the matter, Stevie child?

STEPHEN. Livvy, Livvy, it's going to be their last night.

LIVVY. Las' night o' what?

STEPHEN. The last night Mr. Rice is going to give an entertainment at the ice cream parlor, and he's going to have a new song!

LIVVY. Whut's that to cry about?

STEPHEN. But we can't go! We haven't any of us got ten cents.

LIVVY. Is that all? Why don't yo' have a little gumption? Why don't you all give a show yourselfs and earn the money? Then you can go tonight.

STEPHEN. Earn it how?

LIVVY. You kin sing as good as a lot of them show folks any time. You'n Mitty an' Andy Robinson an' that little friend of yours, that Selina Kelly, she can sing good.

STEPHEN. (*Catching fire.*) That's what! We'll give a show and everybody in the family can come! What'll we sing?

LIVVY. Well, you sing "Auld Lang Syne" awful pretty, an' there's those tunes you learned when I took you to the shoutin' church with me.

STEPHEN. Oh, Livvy, Livvy, you're so smart and so good! I'll go call the others. They're playing right out here in the yard. (*Goes to the rear door and calls.*) Mit! Mitty! Andy! Sam! Selina! Come here! Quick!

(*The* CHILDREN *come in.*)

CHILDREN. What is it? (*Ad libbing*, "What do you want?" etc.)

STEPHEN. Livvy's thought of a way for us to earn some money and go to the entertainment tonight.

CHILDREN. (*Ad libbing.*) How? Tell us! Quick!

STEPHEN. We'll give a performance in the carriage house and charge admission. Mit, you can recite "Lord Ullin's Daughter."

SELINA. Andy and I can sing a duet!

STEPHEN. And we can all sing a spiritual like the ones Livvy knows.

LIVVY. (*Looking out of the window.*) Yo' all got some audience comin' a'ready, I reckon.

(JOE, *a negro, knocks.* LIVVY *opens the door. He is obviously coming to call on* LIVVY.)

STEPHEN. It's Joe!

LIVVY. W'y, come in, Mist' Joe.

STEPHEN. Joe, will you be in our show?

JOE. Law, Mist' Stevie, how'm I goin' look in a show?

STEPHEN. You can do a breakdown! I saw you yesterday on Dr. McDowell's back porch. Try it, Joe!

CHILDREN. (*Ad libbing.*) Come on, let's see you. Please, Joe.

JOE. (*Pleased.*) Gimme time to git my breaf.

(*He pauses, then begins clapping for time. The* CHILDREN *clap for him,* LIVVY *joining in, her eyes ashine. He dances a breakdown or pigeon-wing, ending up with a low bow directed at his audience but chiefly at* LIVVY.)

LIVVY. (*Gratified.*) Git along, how'm I goin' git my ironin' done with you breakdownin' (Or cuttin' pigeonwings.) all ovah my kitchen flo'?

STEPHEN. (*Grinning.*) Come on, all of you, let's go tell people about the show. Ma's in the parlor with Miz Pentland. (*To* LIVVY.) We'll be right back. Then will you teach us one of your church songs, Livvy?

LIVVY. I reckon.

(*The* CHILDREN *go out, ad libbing:* "Maybe Ma'll lend us her sealskin cape." "Etty's got a parasol she'll let us use." "William left his silk hat here." "My, won't you look handsome, though!" *etc.*)

STEPHEN. (*As he goes out.*) Joe, you stay and listen to us!

LIVVY. (*To* JOE, *as soon as the* CHILDREN *are gone.*) They bound an' determined they goin' to earn de money to see Mist' Rice's company at the ice cream pa'lo' tonight.

JOE. Tonight?

LIVVY. This is the lastest night.

JOE. Ain't goin' be any lastest night. This aft'noon's all they is.

LIVVY. Whut you mean it's all they is?

JOE. I sure 'nough hate to disapp'int that passel o' children, but I just come from the ice cream pahlor and they ain't goin' to be no show tonight. Steamboat cap'n say he got to take off fo' Cincinnati six o'clock, and Mist' Rice say they bound to make it. I'm goin' he'p 'em carry their baggage down to the wha'f.

LIVVY. Them po' chillun, an' they countin' on earnin' the money to go. Joe, you run 'splain to Mist' Rice. He powe'ful nice man, got a big heart like all them show folks have. Yo' tell him six chillun's goin' be powe'ful sorry 'f he ketch that six o'clock boat.

JOE. He ain't goin' listen to me. They was fixin' to pack up fo' I left there. They be sta'tin' by now.

LIVVY. Yo' hurry. Tell him six chillun, that makes sixty cents. That ought to keep him in town.

(JOE *goes out. The* CHILDREN *come back in fragments of costume of the period—one has borrowed a vest with brass buttons, another a high silk hat, another gloves and a cane, etc.*)

STEPHEN. Ma and Miz Pentland said they'd come, and Etty and Ann Eliza and Miz McDowell. We'll have enough to take all of us and you, too, Livvy. Are you 'most through ironing?

LIVVY. Just wait till I shove m' irons onto the back of the stove. (SUE *puts the irons away.*) Now then, what you want to learn? "Whut a Tryin' Time?" * "Po' Rosy?"

SELINA. "Roll, Jordan!"

MITTY, ANDY, SAM. "Go Down, Moses!"

LIVVY. How many wants "Go Down, Moses?" (*Four hands fly up, including* STEPHEN'*s.*) Looks like we goin' sing "Go Down, Moses." (SELINA *pouts, but soon is singing the loudest of any.*) Y'll know it about as well as I do.

(LIVVY *sings the spiritual, motioning to the* CHILDREN *to come in on each refrain.*)

CHILDREN. We know it! You sing it with us! You sing better'n we do anyhow!

STEPHEN. Come on, brother Mit, you'd better say "Lord Ullin's Daughter." You haven't recited it since the end of school. Maybe you've forgotten some.

MIT. (*Who likes to recite.*) I don't mind. Lemme think a minute.

(*Striking an elocutionary pose, recites* "Lord Ullin's Daughter." † *Applause.* LIVVY *wipes her eyes. There is a commotion outside.* JOE *comes in.*)

JOE. (*With a solemn face.*) Chillun, I has to announce the disappointin' fact that they ain't goin' be no ice cream show tonight!

CHILDREN. (*Groaning. Ad lib.*) Oh, Joe! No show! Why not? We were going to go!

STEPHEN. (*Desperately.*) But—but we've got the money promised!

---

* Fisher, "Seventy Negro Spirituals."
† To be found in "The Home Book of Verse," edited by B. E. Stevenson (Henry Holt).

JOE. (*Grinning.*) Instead o' which, ladies an' gen'men, Mist' Rice IN PUSSON will give a special gala performance in the Foster kitchen with all his company IMMEGIT! * . . . MIST' RICE!

(MISTER RICE, *originator of the minstrel show, enters with members of his cast:* MRS. SNAVELY, MISS TRUXALL *and* MR. BANES. *They can be followed by a troop of the neighborhood children.*)

MISTER RICE. (*Sweeping off his silk hat with a flourish.*) My dear young friends! (*He pauses dramatically while the children applaud.*) My first, fast, and foremost rule! "Never disappoint the audience!" Can I? No! Will I? No! Am I going to? Again, NO! When I met Joe here flying down the road, what did I do? What could I do? One thing! I did it. I am doing it! I came along in his wake and here I be! Presenting my MATCHLESS entertainment EXCLUSIVELY for your benefit!

STEPHEN. (*Catching his breath.*) Oh, Mr. Rice! You don't mean—you can't mean you're going to give a show right here in the kitchen?

MISTER RICE. (*Thundering.*) ON ONE CONDITION!

MIT. (*Fearfully.*) What's that?

STEPHEN. You mean the—the money? But we can't pay you yet. We have to earn it first.

MISTER RICE. I mean this: As one artist to another, I'll trade song for song.

STEPHEN. Oh, is that all! Why, that'll be fun! (*To the* CHILDREN.) Won't it?

CHILDREN. (*Chorusing.*) Yes!

STEPHEN. Let's tell Ma and Miz Pentland the show's now.

(SELINA *goes to call* MRS. FOSTER *and* MRS. PENTLAND,

---

* If you want to omit the quartet, you can bring Rice in alone, altering the text slightly to indicate that the rest of the company have gone on down to the wharf.

who enter shortly with SELINA. *They stand near the door right.*)

MISTER RICE. (*Bowing to* STEPHEN.) Allow me! You first!

STEPHEN. Me? What would you like?

CHILDREN. (*Ad lib.*) "Zip Coon!" Do "Zip Coon!" With your guitar!

MIT. (*To* MISTER RICE, *proudly.*) He can play the flute, too, you know. And the piano. And the first time he ever tried a flageolet he could play "Hail, Columbia!"

MISTER RICE. (*Genially.*) What have we here? A genius, maybe?

STEPHEN. Oh, no, sir, I just like music is all. Would you like me to sing Zip Coon?

MISTER RICE. I should be honored.

STEPHEN. (*Singing.*)

"Oh, old Zip Coon he is a larned scholar,*
Oh, old Zip Coon he is a larned scholar,
Oh, old Zip Coon he is a larned scholar,
Sings possum up a gum tree and coony in a holler.

Possum up a gum tree, coony on a stump,
Possum up a gum tree, coony on a stump,
Possum up a gum tree, coony on a stump,
Possum up a gum tree, coony on a stump!
Den over dubble trubble Zip Coon will jump,

O Zip a duden, duden, duden, Zip a duden day, etc.

Oh, it's old Suky blue skin, she is in lub wid me,
I went the udder afternoon to take a dish ob tea;

---

* "Zip Coon" was sung in 1835 to the air since better known as "Turkey in the Straw." If you need the music, it can be found in a number of collections, including "Read 'Em and Weep," by Sigmund Spaeth, New York: Doubleday, Doran Co., 1926. If it seems endless, slash it down to what seems reasonable. Stephen can vary it, too, with stamps and other gestures.

What do you tink now Suky hab for supper,
Why chicken foot an' possum heel widout any butter. (*Chorus.*)

Did you eber see the wild goose sailing on de ocean,
O de wild goose motion is a bery pretty notion;
Every time de wild goose beckons to de swaller,
You hear him google google google google gollar. (*Chorus.*)

I went down to Sandy Holler tother arternoon
And the first man I chanced to meet war old Zip Coon.
Old Zip Coon he is a natty scholar
For he plays upon de banjo Coony in de holler! (*Chorus.*)

My old Missus she's mad wid me,
Kase I wouldn't go wid her into Tennessee.
Massa build him barn and put in de fodder.
'Twas dis ting and dat ting, one ting or odder. (*Chorus.*)

I pose you heard of de battle New Orleans,
Whar Old Gineral Jackson gib de British beans;
Dare de Yankee boys do de job so slick,
For dey cotch ole Packenham and rowed him up de creek.

I hab many tings to tork about but don't know which come fust,
So here de toast to Old Zip Coon before he gin to rust.
May he hab de pretty girls, like de King ob ole,
To sing dis song so many times before he turn to mole.

CHILDREN. (*They can join in each chorus if desired.*) Now, you, Mr. Rice!

    MISTER RICE. Let me think, with what shall we oblige?
    STEPHEN. (*Eagerly.*) Will you do "Jim Crow" for us?
    CHILDREN. (*Ad lib.*) "Jim Crow!" Please, do "Jim Crow!"
Oh, goody, goody!

Mister Rice. The very thing! (*Slyly.*) If I haven't forgotten it. . . .
Children. (*Prompting him swiftly.*) "Now listen all you gals and boys—"
Mister Rice. That's right. I'm sure you can all sing it yourselves.
(*They nod eagerly.*)
Mister Rice. (*Flattered, singing the verses and motioning for them to come in on the choruses.**)

"Come, listen, all you gals and boys,
  I'se just from Tuckyhoe;
  I'm goin' to sing a little song.
  My name's Jim Crow."

All. (*As* Mister Rice *beckons to them to join in.*)
"Weel about and turn about an' do jis so,
Ebery time I weel about I jump Jim Crow!"

Mister Rice.
"I went down to de river;
  I didn't mean to stay;
  But dere I see so many gals
  I couldn't get away.   (*Chorus as before.*)

"And arter I been dere awhile
  I t'ought I push my boat,
  But I tumbled in de river
  An' I find myself afloat.   (*Chorus.*)

"I git upon a flatboat.
  I cotch de Uncle Sam;
  Den I went to see de place where
  Dey killed de Packenham.   (*Chorus.*)

---

* The music of this classic is to be found in "Gentlemen, Be Seated," Paskman and Spaeth. New York, Doubleday, Doran, 1928. It, too, can be cut perhaps with profit.

"An' den I go to New Orleans
  An' feel so full of fight
Dey put me in de Calaboose
  An' kept me dere all night. (*Chorus.*)

"When I git out I hit a man;
  His name I now forgot;
But dere was nothing left of him
  'Cept a little grease spot. (*Chorus.*)

"Anudder day I hit a man,
  De man wuz mighty fat.
I hit so hard I knockt him in
  To an old cockt hat. (*Chorus.*)

"I whipt my weight in wildcats,
  I et an alligator.
I drunk de Mississippi up!
  Oh, I'm de very creature. (*Chorus.*)

"I sit upon a hornet's nest;
  I dance upon my head;
I tie a wiper round my neck
  An' den I go to bed. (*Chorus.*)

"I kneel to de buzzard
  An' I bow to de crow;
An' ebery time I weel about
  I jump jis so!" (*Chorus.*)

(*Applause. A steamboat whistles in the distance.*)

MISTER RICE. (*Mopping his brow elegantly.*) That whistle says it's half past five o'clock and I must be stepping on my way. (*With a bow to the ladies present.*) Shall we all have one last chorus together, say of "Auld Lang Syne?"

STEPHEN. (*Shy but eager.*) Mit here can recite "Lord Ullin's Daughter," and Selina and Andy can sing, and Joe was going to do a breakdown for you.

MISTER RICE. (*Gallantly.*) It would be an honor to see and hear them. Joe shall do a breakdown as he shuffles my grips on board. The rest of you I'll hear when I come back next spring!

MRS. FOSTER. Then you're returning! That's splendid! I think the occasion calls for some celebration. Livvy, what's the state of the cookie jar?

LIVVY. (*Grinning.*) It's in right good condition, ma'am!

(*She and* MRS. FOSTER *pass the cookies while the rest sing.*)

ALL. (*Singing.*)

"Should auld acquaintance be forgot
And never brought to mind,
Should auld acquaintance be forgot
In the days of Auld Lang Syne?" etc.

(*The whistle toots again.*)

MISTER RICE. (*Making a sweeping bow to the company, cookie in hand.*) Goodbye, all. (*Holding out his hand to* STEPHEN.) You gave us a fine performance, my lad. I'd have to work hard to beat it. You'll be a musician yourself some day or I miss my guess.

STEPHEN. Oh, I would like to be, sir. I'd be so happy if I could write a song that would be sung by your company.

MISTER RICE. When you write one, let me know. (*The whistle blows impatiently.*) Joseph, our grips!

(*With a final bow around,* MISTER RICE *strides out, munching, and singing the refrain of "Auld Lang Syne." The* CHILDREN *troop after with the exception of* STEPHEN, *who dreamily picks up his guitar.* As the sound of singing fades in the*

---

* If you don't have a guitarist at your disposal, you would be justified in employing a clarinet, flageolet, or even a whistle, at all of which Stephen Foster

distance, he plays the melody with them as long as it is audible. When it can no longer be heard, he begins tentatively a few notes of a simple little air of his own improvisation. He tries it over once or twice, and is repeating the phrase more and more firmly as the curtain falls. The air is picked up by singers backstage, who hum softly, increasing in volume as they emerge to sing the full-fledged air of FOSTER'S *earliest song, "Open Thy Lattice, Love,"* * *and rippling into the closing jollity of "Camptown Races," and "Oh Susannah!"*)

could lend hand or tongue at this period, or at least a little later on. A piano unfortunately seems unlikely in a kitchen.

* For the music, see "Stephen Collins Foster: 25 Songs," Collected, Edited, and Provided with New Accompaniments by John Tasker Howard. J. Fischer & Bro., New York, 1934.

POEMS

AFTER MUSIC

By Josephine Johnson

This is my liberation! Not for me
Do sweet sounds interwoven mark the skill
Wherewith the master wrought them. Well or ill,
I care not, so they take me utterly—
So the tide gather from the dusty shore
High into realms of airy light, where I
Am but a mote in an infinity
Ordered and beautiful. I ask no more.

Nor does the prisoner ask what set him free,
Nor do the famished question whence the bread.
They only know their shackles cease to be
And that miraculously they are fed.
. . . My tears rain down, but for a little space
I dream a God, and think to see his face!

MUSIC

By Lionel Wiggam

Your ears are flooded and your mind is spent
Before this cataract that flutes invent;
The violins are sources for a stream
Whose waters drown your body in their theme.

Before the trumpets' flight of plangent birds,
Imperious death speaks unimportant words;
And even love is speechless and remote
When strings let fly the proud, the arrowy note.

Listen: the bell, the violin, the reed!
The radiant, sovereign sounds proclaim you freed:
Your feet are feathered—let your body soar
Until the aching ear can hold no more.

YOU SING THE AIR

By Carrie Ward Lyon

You sing the Air and I a second part,
   Whose counter strain with your theme shall agree,
   And point by point establish harmony:
You sing the air and practice it by heart.
Thus will the music show the better art,
   If mine is captive that yours may go free,
   Delighting all who hear your melody.
Being attuned to listen let us start.

So we are set; good counterpoint contriving,
   My aching pause and grievous dissonance
   Anticipate your mood of happy chance,
Prepare the potent chord of your arriving.
   And sometimes in your ecstasy I share
   Who have no separate will; you sing the Air!

BUSY MOTHER

By Mary Louise Tredinnick

Lord, in this surfeit of immediateness,
Demands of hunger and the press

Of growing bodies, eager brains,
Let me live so when naught remains
Save what is left in recollection's eye,
This tired inadequateness which is I,
They will forget; but when they hear
Sweet sound of music or the clear
Far shine of stars above the winter's snow,
Or ancient craftsmanship sets eyes aglow,
Then may they say, in instant, quick response,
With warmth which lights a flame in memory's sconce,
"These things are beautiful, I know,
My mother always loved them so."

TO A YOUNG MUSICIAN

By Josephine Johnson

Play me no music, lest I turn and weep!
Play me no music, for they must be strong
Who would have done with sadness and with song,
With everything save will to climb the steep
Stern road unto the end—and music ever
Stripped me alike of armor and of pride,
Leaving defenceless all my naked side,
Taking my lance to blunt, my sword to shiver.

Not now, not now, O beautiful and holy!
Not now, O rain of mercy, tide of love!
Leave me to silence and to courage wholly
Until the end. But when the end shall prove
All my disaster published to the sun,
Drown me with music, and my tears shall run!

MUSIC

By Frances Gill

A lady comes to us, and plays
Upon her violin;
Songs of fairies and of birds.
How does she keep them in
A place so small? They dance, and spring,
And gurgle from that little box. I want to sing,
And laugh,—and sometimes cry.

One day she left it in the room.
I was there, too.
I played it was my own,
And I would do a little song on it. Dear me, you know
It didn't sound the same at all—
It didn't go!
But still—I want to try.

Music is very hard, I think
And we all love it so.

ACTIVITIES AND A TEST

A TOPSYTURVY CONCERT

By George Bradford Bartlett

This is one of the funniest entertainments ever seen, and one of the easiest to prepare.

It needs only a screen or a curtain stretched across any room.

The height of the curtain may be determined by the size of the children who sing in the concert, for they stand in a row behind the screen or curtain.

It is well to have these singers nearly of the same size, as the screen or curtain should conceal all of their bodies except the head and neck.

The only preparation required is that the arms and hands of each should be covered with stockings, and that shoes be worn upon each hand, with the soles of the shoes pointed forward, so that the toes will be turned toward the spectators, who are seated in front of the curtain at a little distance. At the conclusion of each verse the singers stoop down all together and very quickly, and each, lowering the head, elevates the arms above the curtain.

The effect thus produced is that all the singers seem to be standing on their heads.

They keep time with their feet (or rather hands) to the music of the song, and the sudden changes, when done simultaneously, will never fail to amuse.

The idea of this unique performance probably originated in the fertile brain of a Frenchman; but it has been adapted for the use of children, and will prove an enjoyable addition to holiday merrymakings.

ORIGINALITY IN MUSIC

By Laura Beth Torrance

Not having sufficient funds with which to buy instruments for a rhythm band, my first-grade pupils set about to make these instruments themselves. We bent triangles from wire coat hangers. Metal tops for bottles were flattened and strung on wire hoops, for tambourines. A wooden frame made and painted by the children was hung with bottles filled with colored water in graduated quantities, to form an instrument like the xylophone. These bottles and the triangles were struck with large nails. Two kettle lids made effective cymbals. Horseshoes struck with nails, bells, a toy drum, smooth cedar sticks, two wooden blocks covered with sandpaper, together with a few phonograph records, completed our rhythm-band equipment.

A TEST FOR MUSIC WEEK

By Ernestine Bennett Briggs

I. *If the sentence is true, write* T *after it; if false, write* F.

    1. Primitive man made musical instruments of bone.

    2. The ancient peoples knew how to write down their music.

    3. The Greek chorus was a group of singers who took part in a sort of musical play.

    4. Many of the first songs of America were religious in character.

    5. The jig is a slow dance.

    6. Stephen Collins Foster wrote "Old Folks at Home."

7. The violin is larger than the viola.
8. The piccolo is an instrument of percussion.
9. Lowell Mason is famous as a composer of hymns.
10. Johann Sebastian Bach wrote beautiful compositions for the organ.
11. "The Star Spangled Banner" was written by Francis Scott Key.
12. Brahms was a very successful composer of chamber music.
13. "The Ring of the Nibelungs" consists of a number of great operas.
14. Haydn was one of the first composers to write music for string quartets.
15. Edward MacDowell is considered America's greatest composer.

II. *Underline the word or group of words that makes the sentence true.*

1. The favorite instrument of ancient Greece was the (trumpet, lyre, drum).
2. Stephen Collins Foster was born in (Pennsylvania, Kentucky, Missouri).
3. (Sousa, Foster, Damrosch) has been called the "march king."
4. In the modern orchestra there are (two, three, four) groups of instruments.
5. The Puritans permitted only the singing of (ballads, psalms, lyrics).
6. The waltz is written in (4/4, 2/4, 3/4) time.
7. The tarantella is (a Spanish, an Italian, a German) dance.
8. Pavlowa was a famous (violinist, pianist, dancer).
9. The minuet originated in (America, France, England).
10. The "Cremona masters" were a group of (opera singers, violin-makers, dancers).

CELEBRATIONS FOR MUSIC WEEK

11. The opera "Hansel and Gretel" was composed by (Humperdinck, Delibes, Mozart).

12. The correct name for the 'cello is (violincello, 'cello, violoncello).

Key to Tests

I.
1. True
2. False
3. True
4. True
5. False
6. True
7. False
8. False
9. True
10. True
11. True
12. True
13. True
14. True
15. True

II.
1. lyre
2. Pennsylvania
3. Sousa
4. four
5. psalms
6. ¾
7. Italian
8. dancer
9. France
10. violin-makers
11. Humperdinck
12. violoncello

Celebrations for Graduation Day

PLAYS

THE SHOP WINDOW *

*A Play for Junior High School
Graduation Day*

By Delle Oglesbee Ross

PERSONS IN THE PLAY

Lilla, *the class poetess*
Ruth, *the best-loved girl in the class*
Ginny, *a Romantic*
Margie, *who loves clothes*
Tommy, *always in difficulties*
Gerald, *just one of the boys*
Emile, *a student from France*
Peter Arkwright Carter, III, *who has won the American Legion medal*
First Window Dresser ⎫
Second Window Dresser ⎬ *who are actually alive*

Time: *Late afternoon of a June day.*

Place: *The campus in front of Holmes School. A setting in the window of a store.*

Notes: *Being the latest word in shop window dummies, the young people are displaying smart clothes for Junior High*

---

* This play may be produced without royalty where no admission is charged. Otherwise a fee of three dollars must be paid to the author, 317 North Marion St., Oak Park, Ill.

graduates. MARGIE, *alone, is very much overdressed in a formal gown.*

The two WINDOW DRESSERS *are costumed as Greenwich Village artists. They wear berets, smocks, flowing ties, and cloth slippers. They never speak, but express everything in pantomime.*

The window setting is the campus of Holmes School. A white path runs diagonally from left to right across the scene. A gaily painted bench is under a tree, left front; another is similarly placed a little further down right front. Another tree or two at right back, shrubs and bright flowers border the path and campus . . . a heavy frame and a curtain of thin gauze give the effect of the shop window, into which the audience gazes as though they were the passersby.

Two WINDOW DRESSERS *are arranging the window display, and move the characters, which are supposed to be dummies, to get effects. No dummy moves from its place without the help of the artists, who converse in pantomime.*

As the scene opens they are both in the window. One has placed LILLA *on the bench, left. The other stands* GERALD *behind the bench, and is trying different positions. Each time they both suggest changes by gestures. They have left* EMILE *and* GINNY *on the path at back, and have been so careless as to leave them leaning cosily against each other. At right back* MARGIE, RUTH, TOMMY, *and* PETER ARKWRIGHT CARTER, III, *have been left in a group without any particular care.* TOMMY *has toppled over onto the grass at the girls' feet, while* PETER *stands alone, very still, with his back to them. The late afternoon sun shines through the trees shedding a mellow light upon the scene. The* FIRST WINDOW DRESSER *puts a roll of manuscript, tied with rose and blue ribbons, into* LILLA'S *hand.*

LILLA. Oh, here is my manuscript. I wondered what I had done with it.

GERALD. It's the class poem, isn't it?
LILLA. Yes, shall I read it to you?
GERALD. (*Quickly.*) Oh, no! I mean—I want to remember it as you read it this afternoon—
LILLA. Wasn't everything beautiful today?
GERALD. It really was. You know—
LILLA. My granny said we were "standing with reluctant feet where the brook and river meet"—
GERALD. Well, I don't know as *my* feet are reluctant, exactly—in fact I'm rarin' to go—
LILLA. But where, Gerald?
GERALD. Oh—camp this summer—high school, of course—then—college—
LILLA. I hope I can go to college—but I don't know—yet—
GERALD. (*Smugly.*) I'm going to Yale!
LILLA. Oh—*Gerald!*
GERALD. That's what the parents say—if I work hard these next four years—
LILLA. Isn't that where Peter the Great is going?
GERALD. Well, if he is—I'm not!
LILLA. Do you feel that way about him? Where is he?—Still talking to the Colonel—or General—or whatever he is?
GERALD. Can you see him?
LILLA. No, can you?
GERALD. Not the way I'm standing—(*The* FIRST WINDOW DRESSER *motions to the* SECOND WINDOW DRESSER *who turns* GERALD *so that he faces right back.*) Hullo! Now I do—he's standing way over by the tree. Ruth and Margie are there too—and Tommy—taking his ease as usual. Peter Arkwright Carter the third has his back to 'em—
LILLA. His back to them! H'm—
        Contemptuous of their beauty
        He only heeds the call of Duty—
GERALD. Pretty bad, Lilla! Pretty—bad!

LILLA. You are so cruel, Gerald! Where are the others? Ginny —who is she with? They *would* put me so I can't see a thing—
GERALD. Wait a minute—(*The* SECOND WINDOW DRESSER *turns him quickly back to the original position.*) Just caught a glimpse of her—she's up there on the path—she's with—
LILLA. Is it Emile?
GERALD. Yeah—they're doing a spot of necking—
LILLA. Necking! How revolting!
GERALD. Yes—isn't it—
LILLA. I wouldn't have thought it of Emile—
GERALD. Must be his French blood—you know—"The French are fond of light wines and women."
LILLA. Well, anyway, Peter needn't be so stuck-up over that American Legion medal—
GERALD. Oh, he won it fair and square. *He* always wins—everything!
LILLA. And I can't bear for Ruth to lose out and that old Suzanne Denmore go off with the girls' medal—
GERALD. Ruth would have it if I'd had the say-so—
LILLA. Me too!

(*The* WINDOW DRESSERS *are now satisfied with the pose, and go back to the huddled group. They pick up* TOMMY, *and push him down to the bench, right. They put him on the ground, where he leans lazily against the end of the bench, facing* LILLA *and* GERALD.)

TOMMY. Hullo—there!—How'd you like the doings?
GERALD. Good enough!
LILLA. Marvelous—only I think they got the medals mixed—
TOMMY. You mean Ruth?
LILLA. Yes, I do.
TOMMY. Sh! They're coming—

(*The* WINDOW DRESSERS *bring* RUTH *and* MARGIE *and pose them on the bench, right. After much consultation they leave* RUTH *on the bench, and stand* MARGIE *by the tree. The*

First Window Dresser *goes outside and looks through the front of the window to get the effect.*)
Tommy. Yoo hoo—up there on the path—
Ginny. Don't bother us—
Emile. Have you no—no—delicacy?
Gerald. Have you?
(*They all laugh. The* Window Dressers *decide to place* Margie *back on bench.*)
Margie. Cable me from Paris, Ginny, all the latest fashions—
Ginny. Oh, be still!
Tommy. Well, Emile, guess you won't be taking any *medals* back—
Margie. Only Ginny!
Gerald. Well, of course she *is* a prize!
Ginny. Oh, hush up!
Emile. It would have made me proud indeed if I had been given the honor—but a better man won—
Ruth. That's white of you, Emile, to take it like that—
Lilla. Well—a better man didn't win the one you should have had, Ruthie—
Margie. That old Suzanne!
Ruth. Now, look here, kids, I am disappointed, of course, but Suzanne won that medal because she was a better student than I—
Lilla. But other things—
Ruth. We were even on most scores, but she beat me in scholarship—
Lilla. But we wanted you to have it—
Tommy. Well—leave it lay—leave it lay! The other gal won—
Margie. So what!
Ruth. There it is. So what!
(*The* Second Window Dresser, *at the direction of the* First Window Dresser, *brings* Ginny *down to the bench,*

left, to sit by LILLA, *then takes* EMILE *off stage, left back.*)
GINNY. Hey—hey—what are you doing?
EMILE. This is detestable—*mon Dieu!* To be separated!
GINNY. I won't sit here!
TOMMY. Ah, but you are—my duck!
EMILE. (*From outside.*) To be torn apart!
GINNY. Oh—Emile—come back—

(*The* SECOND WINDOW DRESSER *returns, and again at the direction of the* FIRST, *turns* PETER *around. They observe the effect,* PETER *looks rather pathetic, so he pulls* TOMMY *up and places him as though strolling down the path. He brings* PETER *to the bench, right, to lean over the back.* MARGIE *immediately falls off. The* WINDOW DRESSERS *are in desperation.*)

RUTH. Margie, how rude!
(MARGIE *giggles.*)
PETER. Why do you all dislike me so?
GERALD. We—we—
PETER. All through Junior High it has been the same—you all avoid me—
LILLA. We really didn't mean—
RUTH. (*Gravely and sweetly.*) But, Peter, you see—we were afraid of you—
PETER. Afraid!
RUTH. Yes. You were always so superior—
PETER. Oh—
RUTH. You never seemed interested in the silly little everyday things we did—and you were always so well dressed.
MARGIE. And you never used slang—and you always knew all the important people that came to the school—
PETER. But—listen—
GERALD. And you set out to win all the best offices—president of Junior Civics—
LILLA. Class president—valedictorian—

MARGIE. American Legion Medal—the biggest thing of all—
TOMMY. What's more—you always did win!
GERALD. How do you do it?
PETER. I had to!
RUTH. What do you mean?
PETER. You see—it was like this. My grandfather was an important man—my father was, too—
RUTH. But you—
PETER. I have to be just as important. It is expected of me.
GERALD. But you're just a kid—
PETER. I can't remember when I didn't have extra tutoring—summers and holidays—I was never allowed to play with other children—or do childish things—
RUTH. How terrible!
PETER. I simply longed to be in your jolly doings—to let things go and have a good time—
TOMMY. Well, why didn't you?
PETER. I didn't dare! If I came home with anything but the highest marks, Mother wept—
GERALD. Did you ever have low marks?
PETER. Not low, exactly, but sometimes not double A's—
TOMMY. Whew!
PETER. Then I was told over and over what was expected of me. I tell you I didn't dare fail!
MARGIE. I should say not!
PETER. I am an only child, you know. Sometimes it is pretty lonely.
RUTH. If we had only known, Peter.
PETER. I simply could not take time to become acquainted.
TOMMY. Well, I'll bet you're a regular guy, all right, if a fellow knew you—
GERALD. Queer how parents always think they must decide your life for you—
LILLA. My mother said she knew I would be a poet as soon

as I opened my big blue eyes—

TOMMY. Bilge-water!

LILLA. Tommy—you are mean! (TOMMY *and* GERALD *make derisive noises.*) I *am* a poet. I wrote the class poem, didn't I?

TOMMY. Huh! That doesn't make you a poet!

LILLA. Oh, we who from this school now go,
> Some eagerly, some shy and slow—
> Salute you!

GERALD } We've heard it!
TOMMY }

RUTH. Oh, don't tease her! It's a good class poem, Lilla dear.

(*The* SECOND WINDOW DRESSER *decides upon another change. He places* PETER *and* RUTH *on the path,* TOMMY *behind the bench, right, picks* MARGIE *up from the ground and sets her down hard on the bench, right, and carefully arranges her gown.*)

LILLA. Have you noticed the golden light coming through the trees?

TOMMY. (*Absently.*) U-m—

LILLA. The golden light of our future
> Shines on us through the trees.
> The whisper of our destiny
> Is borne on the summer breeze.

(GINNY *falls over on her.* SECOND DRESSER *picks her up and takes her up the path, left back, and off the stage.*)

GINNY. (*As she goes.*) Emile—Emile—

TOMMY. Do you have those spasms often, Lilla?

MARGIE. I think that was lovely.

RUTH. So do I—

PETER. It must be fun to make up poetry—

LILLA. (*Sentimentally.*) Oh not *fun!* It is soul-satisfying—thrilling!

TOMMY. Piffle! How do you get that way!

(*The* SECOND WINDOW DRESSER *now takes* TOMMY *to*

stand near the tree, right back.)

TOMMY. Well, here I go again!

GERALD. You must be restless—

(SECOND WINDOW DRESSER *faces him towards* RUTH *and* PETER, *whom he takes from the path to the grass, where they appear to be approaching* TOMMY.)

PETER. You are such a jolly chap, Tommy—

RUTH. He is, Peter, there's always a lark when Tommy is around—

TOMMY. Oh, I have my serious moments. You wouldn't believe it—but *once* I had my eye on that medal—

RUTH. Why—Tommy!

TOMMY. I took it off pretty quick!

PETER. Why didn't you make a try for it?

TOMMY. With you on the job? Ho! Not a chance!

PETER. I am sorry.

TOMMY. Oh, don't worry—the good times I've had in Junior High make up for it—

RUTH. I'm sorry to leave old Holmes School, aren't you?

TOMMY. I sure am!

PETER. And so am I. Especially now that I'm beginning to know you all. I'm not going to High School, you see—

TOMMY. Not going to High School!

RUTH. Where are you going, Peter?

PETER. To an eastern school to prepare for Yale.

GERALD. Do you have to go east to prepare for Yale?

PETER. Peter Arkwright Carter, I, went there, so did Peter Arkwright Carter, II, so of course Peter Arkwright Carter the third must go also—

GERALD. I see—

PETER. But to tell the truth, I think you will do a swell job of preparing right here in High School—wish I was to stay here—

GERALD. Well, our High has a pretty fine rep for getting a

fellow ready for any college—

TOMMY. Sure—if we can take it—they can dish it out!

PETER. I truly wish I could be here to get my spoon in the dish.

(*The* SECOND WINDOW DRESSER *poses* MARGIE *down front, right, holding her skirt out with her finger tips to show its width. The* WINDOW DRESSERS *consult, and are pleased. The* FIRST DRESSER *leaves the front of the window.*)

MARGIE. I really think this dress is keen—

LILLA. It is lovely—

MARGIE. Did you notice that young girl who stopped and sketched it? Bet she copies it for her commencement—

LILLA. Don't you think it's a little grown-up?

MARGIE. Oh I don't know. I'll need more grown-up things this summer. I'm going to Culver, you know.

LILLA. Culver! No, really!

GERALD. You'll knock the eyes out of all those cadets!

MARGIE. (*Very self-satisfied.*) Oh, you ought to see some of my others, real formals!

LILLA. At your age!

MARGIE. (*Tosses her head.*) I'm fourteen! And there will be just oodles of dances and things—

(*The* SECOND WINDOW DRESSER *brings* GINNY *in, and places her on bench, right. He changes her pose several times. She still calls frantically for* EMILE.)

GINNY. Oh—Emile—don't go away without saying "Good bye"!

RUTH. Ginny, don't be silly—

GINNY. I'm not silly! He'll go back to France—and I'll never see him again— Oh— Oh—

GERALD. Well, I'm afraid you can't help yourself, my young lady—

GINNY. Oh—Emile—Emile—

TOMMY. Can't anyone stop that racket?

(*The* FIRST DRESSER *now pushes* EMILE *down the path to the bench.*)

EMILE. I'm coming—I'm coming, Ginny, my adorable!

GINNY. I knew you would come, Emile—

GERALD. Then you know more about what we can do than we ourselves do.

EMILE. Wait—wait for me—

GINNY. That's all I *can* do! Oh—Emile!

(*The* FIRST WINDOW DRESSER *places him on the bench by* GINNY. *Both* DRESSERS *step back to view the scene.* GINNY *and* EMILE *promptly fall against each other, her head on his shoulder. The* WINDOW DRESSERS *dance and stamp and tear their hair in temperamental rage.*)

THE CURTAIN FALLS

WHO CALLS ME? * †

BY MARY STEWART SHELDON

CHARACTERS

(*in order of appearance*)

PEDLER
UNCLE PETER, *Landlord of Tavern*
JACK DAVIS, *12—18—24—74 years in different acts*
INDIAN CHIEF *of Cherokee Tribe*
Five or more INDIAN BRAVES
INDIAN SQUAW
WOUNDED HUNTSMAN *and* FRIEND

* The incidents in the first 3 Acts have been taken from historical events, some from the life of David Crocker, whose career suggested Jack Davis.

† Where no admission is charged, this play may be produced free. Otherwise, for a fee of $5.00, written permission must be secured from Mrs. Raymond Sheldon, Chestnut Ridge Road, Mt. Kisco, N.Y.

Two Musicians *from mountains*, Old Man *and* Boy *with fiddle and flute*
Young Men *and* Women *from mountains*
Polly, *Jack's wife*
Messenger *from Washington*
Grandson Johnny
Boy *and* Girl Graduates
Darkies *with banjos, fiddles, etc.*

Time: *About 1789.*
Place: *Mountains of Tennessee.*

Act I: *Outside Tavern of Black Horse, door and large casement window to left, backdrop of mountains, trees to right. Bench at left, against wall of Tavern.*

Act II: *Deep forest, pile of stones to mark spot Indian boy was killed, to left. Near it large tree, in front of others to use for stake to tie* Jack *to.*

Scene 2: *Same forest. To represent different spot remove stones and place some wigwams at left and back.*

Act III: *Same Tavern but as this is autumn make trees brilliant.*

Act IV: *Again Tavern of Black Horse, but this time the old tavern has been replaced by fine new one with white pillars, fine sign, all painted on back drop, but real steps leading to porch in front. New bench, place this time to center right. Flower beds around Tavern, etc.*

Music: *Use any of the old song-dance tunes of the time, but there must be songs combined with the dance, and they should be gay. "Deep River" or "Who's That Calling?" to be sung by negroes at end.*

Act I

Enter Pedler *left, with pack hung by strap across shoulders. He takes it off, places it on bench, and calls—*

PEDLER. Hullo Landlord! Or whatever your name is.

UNCLE PETER. (*Coming out through door of Tavern.*) Good-day, and welcome to you, Stranger, you're the first traveler been down this road for a week. What news have you?

PEDLER. Give me some ale to moisten my tongue and I'll tell all I know. By the way, I left my horse in your barn down the hill, back there.

UNCLE PETER. That's right. (*Calls through door-way.*) Molly! A tankard of ale for a gentleman. (*Reaches into tavern, takes tankard and gives it to* PEDLER. *While he drains it,* UNCLE PETER *continues.*) Heard something a week ago about an Indian uprising, five tribes joining together to wipe us white men off the State of Tennessee. But all seems quiet here now. Have you heard aught?

PEDLER. Nothing about Indians. Heard that President Washington is having a hard time getting men who know Geography into the new Congress. Tennessee might be across the ocean for all they care. Congress makes laws for us and thinks of this State as a place where men live like panthers. (*Frightened.*) Seems to me there is a panther or something like it moving through those bushes yonder!

(*Bushes at right tremble and through them onto stage rushes* JACK. *He is dressed in ragged homespun shirt and breeches, bare-legged, no hat, hair tousled, gun in hand.*)

UNCLE PETER. Why nephew Jack, what's happened? What's the matter?

JACK. (*Excitedly.*) Uncle Peter, *Indians!* I was hunting a wild turkey on the mountains, was hidden behind a log and I saw —a file of Indians walking through the forest! They were painted red with eagle feathers in their hair, *warpath*—they were coming here! Guess they'll come to you first and I'll have time to warn Mom and Pop. You and Aunt Molly better ride off quick! (JACK *disappears.*)

UNCLE PETER. Sure we got to hurry. Say, Stranger, get on

your horse, Molly and I'll grab some stuff and go out the back door and meet you at the barn.

(*He disappears through door.* PEDLER, *terrified, has been standing crouched against wall. He now rushes off leaving pack behind. All is quiet, then from the right an* INDIAN *peers in. Seeing no one, he beckons to those behind, and a group of* INDIANS *enter. They are frightful to look at. Their bare bodies are apparently painted red,* [*red union suits!*] *striped with yellow and black. They wear fringed loin cloths, quivers of arrows and bows on backs. All wear eagle feathers stuck in hair except* CHIEF *who wears full Indian head-dress. They have tomahawks in their hands. All have painted faces and are hideous and ferocious. One carries scalps hanging from his belt, evidently just taken. They grunt and make guttural noises to imitate Indian language. Two peer stealthily through window; others glide through door.* CHIEF *goes to bench and picks up* PEDLER'S *pack, turns it over curiously and tries to open it. It is locked. The others return and exclaim,* "No one—all gone—nothing left —been warned ugh—ah—!!" *etc.* CHIEF *takes knife from his belt and slits open box. Contents fall out on bench and ground, necklaces of beads, mirrors, ribbons, two women's hoods—one white and one pink—a harmonica, etc. With exclamations of pleasure, Indians put on necklaces, ribbons and hoods—ludicrous—admire themselves in mirrors, jump about stage in glee,* CHIEF *tries to play harmonica, fails dismally, smiles with satisfaction. Some exclaim,* "Perhaps more—inside—hidden—look—find!" *They all go into Tavern, shut door.* JACK *is heard calling frantically from right;* "Uncle Peter! Uncle Peter!" *He enters, beside himself with terror and emotion, rushes to door and tries to open it, in vain.*)

JACK. Uncle Peter! Let me in! You can't have gone yet! The beasts—they scalped Mom and Dad and burned the cabin with the children in it. (*He knocks frantically, tries again to open the door, crying:*) Let me in, Uncle Peter! *Let me in!*

(*The door opens slowly from inside. An* INDIAN'S *arm comes out, his face is seen for a moment as he grabs* JACK *and pulls him in. A scream from* JACK, *and the door shuts. Window is thrown violently open from inside and* INDIANS *climb out. Others come through door, one holding* JACK *by collar of shirt, dragging him.*)

CHIEF. (*Standing in center of stage.*) This boy, he warned them, so now we punish him. I take his scalp, small one but plenty! (*With his tomahawk he makes a circle around* JACK'S *forehead and head. Guttural sounds of approval from* INDIANS. JACK *draws himself up and looks fearlessly into* CHIEF'S *eyes.* CHIEF *is furious.*) Ah— So— You have no fear? You look at me like I was—*a chicken*—ha! No take scalp here—take you to forest—put fear in those eyes—torture, fine—you see. Take him—you— Come to forest!

(CHIEF *marches out. An* INDIAN *ties* JACK'S *hands, puts rope around his waist and ties end to own belt. All march out, single file, to left.*)

Act II

Deep forest, pile of stones like cairn and on top of it a dead rabbit and two dead pheasants. Before it is figure of SQUAW *kneeling and praying. She is wrapped in dark blanket, and rocks herself back and forth, often placing head on ground, sobbing, pleading.*)

SQUAW. Great Spirit, hear me! See, I give you all I have. (*She takes off necklace of shells and places it on stones, takes off beaded moccasins and puts them there also.*) My son was strong and brave, he would have made great Chief like his uncle. Magic fire from White Men went through his heart; he lay dead, here. I make this spot yours. I pray you take care of him. Feed him with this food, show him the way. He is so young, not twelve years. I can not sleep, nor eat; I totter when I walk. Care for him and send me comfort! (*She lifts her head, listening.*) They come back from war-path. They must not see my tears.

(*She rises and totters behind trees to left. Enter* CHIEF, *others following. Two bring a slain deer swung from two small tree trunks, carried on their shoulders. Another still has* JACK *tied to him.*)

CHIEF. Here! We stop! Meant to bring Boy-With-No-Fear to camp. This is better; here, where these stones mark spot my nephew fell from magic fire, shot by White Devils. In this same spot, we bring terror to those eyes. Make fire quickly—he bothers me.

(CHIEF *folds his arms and stands immovable while* INDIANS *gather sticks and place them at foot of large tree to left. Red electric bulbs have been placed previously behind logs. As they are moved the red light shows, and when fire is lighted cold fire will blaze forth representing a terrible bonfire.* JACK *is bound tightly to tree, he is very white, but his lips are shut tightly together and he gazes at the* CHIEF *fearlessly. As preparations are made* CHIEF *talks to himself.*)

CHIEF. (*Muttering.*) No son of White Devil ever looked at me like that before. His people shot my nephew just his age. I make this boy pay for that. He shall suffer, blister, crumble into ashes. When the flames rise, those eyes shall fill with terror, that voice shall be heard screaming, soon, *now*—light the fire.—(*It blazes up.*) do you not beg for help, for water?—do you writhe in agony?—No? you *will not answer?*—

(*As the flames rise and* JACK *still looks calmly into the* CHIEF'S *eyes, the other* INDIANS *first express wonder, then admiration, but they add fuel to the fire.* CHIEF *stands mo-*

tionless. Scream is heard from bushes to left. SQUAW *rushes in and throws herself at feet of* CHIEF.)

SQUAW. Save him! Give him to me! Your brother's son was like him, my child, young and brave. This is his spirit. I prayed to Great Spirit; this is his answer, this boy. Ah, give him to me!

CHIEF. (*Motions to* INDIANS.) Take him, give him to her.

(*He bows his head while they cut ropes binding* JACK *and lift him over flames to* SQUAW. *She throws her blanket around him and, exhausted, he falls against her shoulder with his eyes shut.* CHIEF *raises head and holds up his arms toward sky.* INDIANS *kneel around him.*)

CHIEF. Great Spirit—you have spoken. This woman prayed —you answered. We listen, we keep your gift, we make this boy our own.

(*Sounds come from kneeling* INDIANS, *guttural sounds which resemble in their language our A-men.*)

CURTAIN

ACT II—SCENE 2

6 years later.
Still deep forest, wigwams, JACK *and* SQUAW *are alone together, grinding corn in small mill, pounding it in wooden bowl.* JACK *is dressed as* INDIAN, *in animal skins, cap of fur with head and ears of animal left on.*

JACKIE. Nice to have all gone on hunting trip; glad to be left on guard alone with my mother.

SQUAW. What White Devils call six years have passed since Great Spirit sent you to us, A'wah'heh. You teach me speak English but I think you speak better Cherokee than me do English. You Indian boy now. Your name A'wah'heh means Take Courage in that strange English. You brave before; you wise now. You walk through forest silent, no leaf rustle. You shoot wild duck flying, with bow and arrow; you make sounds like animals; they answer. Wake old owl now; perhaps he answer.

JACKIE. Whoo-oo-oo!

(*From distant trees an answering Whoo-oo-oo! is heard.*)

SQUAW. (*Delightedly.*) So, he sleepy, but he answer. Now wake sly fox.

(JACKIE *barks like fox and fox far away replies.*)

SQUAW. You stay here always now, you never think of White—you say no say Devils—White Skins?

JACKIE. Listen, I hear someone calling!

(*From far off a voice sounds calling* "Help! Help!" JACKIE *runs out.* SQUAW *goes on grinding.* JACKIE *returns with two white hunters. One is wounded badly in arm which is bleeding. He is half-carried in by* HUNTER *and* JACKIE. SQUAW *rises and comes to meet them.*)

JACKIE. Quick Mother. See, he bleeds.

(*They lay wounded man on skin in front of tent.* SQUAW *washes and bandages arm deftly.* JACKIE *gives him a drink of water from gourd. He opens eyes and looks around.*)

HUNTER. (*In surprise.*) You two are Indians, but you speak English. What does it mean?

JACKIE. I have lived here six years; but I came from mountains yonder. This woman is like my mother, guess I stay here alway now.

HUNTER. (*To himself.*) I wonder! (*To wounded friend.*) See, Dave, this boy and his Indian mother have saved you from bleeding to death. They speak English. Is this not the boy we need?

(*They talk together while* SQUAW *and* JACKIE *go on with the grinding. Then* HUNTER *steps toward them.*)

HUNTER. Listen, my boy, we are in great trouble. The fighting tribes of Indians, Iroquois, Crees, and others attack us every chance they get, scalping, burning and carrying away our crops and cattle. (JACKIE *starts to interrupt.*) Yes, I know they come here too and attack you Cherokees. You are a peaceful tribe generally, and want to live quietly in camp, but these red demons won't let you alone. You are not strong enough to drive them away and neither are we. But if we united, we could do it. Only there has never been anyone who speaks both the Indian and English language to make the Cherokees understand we want to be friends. Will you come back to your home in the mountains, make a truce between your people and this tribe, unite them to fight their enemies together?

JACKIE. Mother, do you understand? I can help my Tribe and help white men too! May I go?

SQUAW. Will you be a great chief there, my son?

(*All laugh.*)

WOODSMAN. Madam, he may be greater than a chief. He will keep many from bloodshed. May we take him?

JACKIE. I'll come back often, Mother, every four moons I'll come. Sometimes in the night I felt someone was calling me. It was the voice of the White Man.

WOUNDED MAN. Come now, back with us. The villagers were preparing for battle, and we came only to find the trail.

JACKIE. See, Mother, I'll leave a message for the Chief. I'll tell him why I go,—to bring friends to help him.

(*He picks up bit of birch-bark, dips brush into red paint he brings from tent, and writes rapidly, painting figures. Then he pins it with thorn to flap of tent and turns to* SQUAW. *She again throws her blanket around him, looks into his eyes.*)

SQUAW. Goodbye, A'wah'heh.

JACKIE. Goodbye, Mother, I'll be back soon.

(*He goes with* WOODSMEN, *turns to wave, disappears in*

distance. SQUAW *watches him as long as she can see him, then sinks upon ground, face buried in knees.*)

CURTAIN

ACT III

Ten years have passed.

SCENE: *Tavern of Black Horse, the same but trimmer. Window box of late flowers, tall flowers against wall. It is autumn and the trees are brilliant with red and gold. It is toward evening, but the scene is brilliantly lighted, apparently by torches either side of door and on poles to right and left. On bench near door two musicians are seated,* OLD MAN *and* BOY, *with fiddle and flute. All in this scene are dressed as woodsmen: women in homespun, barefooted. All are evidently poor, but very gay.* JACK *is a trifle better dressed. His coon-skin cap has tail hanging down behind. He wears high boots as though for riding. As curtain rises, musicians are tuning up.* UNCLE PETER *comes out of door, older and fatter, with bowl of corn-meal which he scatters on ground.*

UNCLE PETER. No room for dancing inside, boys, it's full of tables for supper. The girls are setting them now. This here meal will make the ground slippery enough for the young folks. Twenty miles some of them have ridden for this dance and will ride back at sunrise more chipper than if they had slept in their beds. Jack Davis and his wife Polly rode forty miles, and he figures on shooting a bear or two on the way home at dawn! Tune up, boys, here they come!

(*The musicians play a dance. Voices inside pick up the tune, and all come out of Tavern singing and dancing. There are as many as stage has room for, woodsmen and their wives, boys and girls. They sing and dance square dance, barn-dance, etc.* JACK *is gayest of the merry crowd.* MESsenger *appears at left. He has ridden from Washington and is dressed appropriately. He speaks with musicians who play more softly so all can hear.*)

Messenger. Is Mr. Jack Davis here? I have a letter for him from—

Jack. (*Stepping forward.*) Here I am, friend. What can I do for you?

Messenger. Mr. Davis, I've ridden all the way from the Capitol, Washington, to bring you this. (*Hands him large envelope, sealed with great red seals.*) Was told I mustn't come back without you.

(*All cluster around* Jack *as he breaks seals and opens letter, reading aloud slowly.*)

Jack. It's—it's from Mr. Jefferson, President of the United States. (*All exclaim in wonder.*) He says, "Owing to your knowledge of the State of Tennessee and your friendship with the Indians, we need you as a delegate from that State to the Congress of the United States. There will be no doubt of your election. You will sweep the State; but we must have you here at once to make plans. Please signify your acceptance by returning immediately with the messenger who brings this letter. Serious trouble is brewing with the Indians. Signed, yours with regard, Thomas Jefferson." (*Chorus of* "What, *you*, Jack?" "In Congress? What'd you do with your coon-skin cap and your gun?" "The bears would surely have a holiday!" "Why, Jack, you couldn't even read that letter a few years past. They want scholars in Congress, not hunters. We want *you* here." Jack *turns to* Polly.) Polly, what do you say?

Polly. When you came home from the State Legislature a few years ago, you swore you'd never leave home again; trees and critters were better than all the politicians in the country, you vowed.

Jack. So I did, Polly. You're right. (*Turns to* Messenger.) Sorry, friend, I can't ride with you; but step inside and have a drink on me before you go.

MESSENGER. I'll wait until dawn. They told me not to return without you.

(MESSENGER *goes inside. All dance and sing again. From right between trees* INDIANS *peer out, unseen by dancers. They draw back.*)

UNCLE PETER. (*Comes to door, beats a dishpan with big spoon, calls out.*) Supper! Wild turkeys, smoking hot. Shot by Jack Davis and donated to party!

(*All crowd in, laughing and calling, except* JACK *who is last of all. As he reaches door, call of owl is heard in woods. He wheels around swiftly and answers it* . . ."Whoo-Whoo—." *Hurries toward trees, right. Three* INDIANS *enter. He greets them delightedly.*)

JACK. Have you come for the party? Good food inside.

INDIANS. (*Shake their heads.*) No, A'wah'heh, no party; bad news, big war-path. Chief sent you this.

(*They hand him birch-bark letter on point of arrow.*)

JACK. (*Opens it and reads.*) "White Father took lands from five tribes, promised pay,—big lie. Unless money comes nothing left in Tennessee, all scalps and ashes. Awahheh go to White Father, get pay for lands, all smoke pipe of peace. Hurry! One more moon all gone."

INDIANS. (*Eagerly.*) You go? White Father send pay? What we tell Chief?

JACK. Tell him—I never forget him and Indian mother— Tell him to make tribes wait until I see White Father, the President. Tell him I ride tonight to Washington.

INDIANS. Good, fine—we tell him! (*Disappear.*)

POLLY. (*Standing in door-way.*) Jack, where are you? Why don't you come?

(*All crowd out, among them the* MESSENGER, *crying,* "What has happened? What *has* happened, Jack?" *Musicians play softly.* POLLY *goes to him and takes his hand.*

Others cluster around, anxious.)

JACK. My Indian friends just brought me this. (*Reads.*) "White Father took lands—promised pay—big lie. Unless money comes Tennessee all scalps and ashes. Go to White Father—get pay—all smoke pipe of peace. Hurry."

POLLY. (*She picks up gun from those standing against Tavern wall and hands it to him.*) Go, Jack, go at once! You—why you can save Tennessee!

MESSENGER. (*Steps forward.*) This is why I was ordered not to return without you. I have fresh horses waiting in the barn below. I'll saddle them.

(*He goes out,* JACK *embraces* POLLY, *takes gun from her, turns to go.*)

JACK. Goodbye friends, we will all meet again—somewhere.

ALL. (*Calling after him.*) Good luck, Jack,—remember us to the President! The bears and us will wait for you! Don't forget Tennessee!

CURTAIN

Act IV

Sixty years later.

SCENE: *Black Horse Tavern, but a new one painted on back drop, shining white columns, real steps to porch in front, flower-beds at sides, grand new painted sign, swinging lanterns hang from sides of porch, another on rose-twined post behind white bench to right, roses also on pillars.* JACK *is sitting on bench with his grandson* JOHNNY. JACK *is a really very old man, white beard and white hair showing below coon-skin cap, spectacles, stick beside him on which he leans heavily when he walks. Powder-horn is in belt. He is still the woodsman in spite of changed times.* JOHNNY, *in boy's clothes of period, blouse of blue with white collar and cuffs perhaps.*

JOHNNY. Granddad, tell me that story again, about the time you went bear-hunting and hung your powder-horn on a little yellow branch—

JACK. That's a good story all right; never did know who told it first. (*Takes off powder-horn and holds it up.*) You see the powder-horn was valuable because I just *had* to shoot a bear for Christmas dinner. Well, I'd hunted all day, seen the tracks of several bears, but hadn't met up with one of them by dark. So I just lay down on the mountain under a tree to sleep, and hung my powder-horn on a little yellow branch over my head. When morning came both branch and powder-horn had gone. All day I searched but when it grew dark I hadn't found it and was back at the same spot I started from the night before. The moon came up, a little crescent moon over the mountains, so close and so golden it near blinded me; and there, just where I'd hung it the night before, on the tip of the crescent moon, was my powder-horn.

JOHNNY. And you reached up and took it and that day you killed five bears, I know! I know! Now, Grandpa, tell me—

JACK. Hark! What is that?

(*A sound in the distance of* BOYS *and* GIRLS *singing.*)

JOHNNY. Oh, it's the boys and girls who graduated from school today. They stayed late to listen to an old gent—visitor in a black wrapper, talk about school of life and dull things like that. I crept out and ran here to you. Guess they're coming here too to see you and hear about bear-hunting and the alligator you rode up the river and the buffalo whose horn you blew on when—

(BOYS *and* GIRLS *dance in two by two. They are all very dressy for Graduation Exercises,* GIRLS *in full ruffled skirts, fichus and ruffles,* BOYS *in dark suits, white collars, etc. They sing as they dance in and form a circle around* JACK. *When song is finished they form a semi-circle in front of bench and sink down facing him, exclaiming,* "Oh, Uncle

Jack! Granddad! Mr. Davis! Look what we've got!" *They wave diplomas, tied with ribbon.*)

ONE GIRL. We've been told how valuable we are!

ONE BOY. Worth our weight in gold—

ANOTHER GIRL. More precious than rubies!

ANOTHER GIRL. That the world is all at our feet!

A BOY. And yet with all this treasure we haven't even enough to buy a bus ticket to Jackson.

ALL. We've been graduated all right! What next?

A GIRL. (*Springs up, a very dressy one, dances around and around singing.*) "All dressed up and nowhere to go. Heigh ho! Heigh ho!"

A BOY. My Pop says you're the greatest man who ever came from Tennessee, the best shot, the best story-teller, that you went to Congress and helped the very Indians who almost burned you alive.

ANOTHER BOY. (*Interrupting.*) That's what I want to do; hunt I mean, big game, but it's all gone now, no bears nor panthers left here, *nothing* exciting seems to be left—and what good is this anyway? (*Waves diploma scornfully.*)

JACK. Long ago (*They all gather around closer, listening eagerly.*) when I was young, I used sometimes to hear someone calling me. I heard it here. (*Places hand on heart.*) Sometimes I was sitting comfortably before the fire in the cabin and it seemed to be danger calling me to go out and shoot a bear. Sometimes a wild critter was after me and it was the nearest tree which called for safety! Once an Indian Squaw called me—and saved my life, then a hunter called me to help the Indians. I don't know what you call that Call; guess some folks name it opportunity or duty, but it's as different-sounding from those names as hearing someone grumble and listening to a bird sing at sunrise! Guess it speaks to each one in his own tongue, differently. I only know that unless you hear that Call and answer, you get kind of soft and weak.

(*Same* GIRL *who sang* "All dressed up," *etc.*)

GIRL. What does it say to *me?* What is calling me, *right now?* Tell me that, Uncle Jack?

JACK. Well, Sadie, sometimes when I hear you sing, seems like the birds or the angels must be jealous—guess Someone is calling you to use that voice of yours, train it, work over it—well you'll not be exactly an angel, but I guess you'll be famous. (*Other* BOYS *and* GIRLS *questioning,* "And me?" "And me?" "Who calls *us?*") Guess you've got to figure that out each one of you for yourselves; but because I know you so well I might help a bit. (*He takes the hand of a boy near him and examines it.*) Here, Ned, you've got what they call a surgeon's thumb; and I've seen you mighty steady when someone is hurt. Guess you'd better study at the hospital and some day—you won't save money but you'll save lives. And you— (*To another boy.*) I've seen pictures you drew when you were supposed to be studying arithmetic. They were of birds flying over the sea—seemed to hear their wings beat and felt the spray of the waves. Guess you'll hear the call to use that, to be an artist perhaps. And you others—some will hear the sea call, and will sail ships across it, through storms and danger, and see strange lands. Some will stay right at home and keep this country free. You (*He looks at a girl. She has her arm around* JOHNNY *who has rested his head on her shoulder and gone to sleep.*) You will be a good mother—best thing of all perhaps. I don't see very well now. Can't see those mountains yonder nor hear the birds sing—but you can see and hear; and when that call comes—*you follow it!* Reach for the stars —and well, perhaps you'll find your powder-horn hanging on the tip of the moon! (*All laugh and stand up.* DARKIES *had come quietly to the steps of Tavern with instruments which they played very softly while* JACK *talked. They now play a gay tune but still softly.*) Guess your mothers are calling you all now; guess they want to see those rolls of paper which mean so much to them!

(JACK *stands up and walks stiffly, leaning on cane as they surround him, and then run off calling.*)

ALL. Good night, Uncle Jack! Thank you, Mr. Davis! That was better than all the Grad Exercises!

(JOHNNY *too is led off, rubbing his eyes.* JACK *walks with difficulty to stage, left, watching them disappear. He turns and hobbles painfully back to bench, sinks down upon it. The stage has been growing darker, but a crescent moon—which appeared earlier and showed distinctly when* JACK *spoke of powder-horn on moon—is now very bright. The lanterns were lighted by the* DARKIES *before* JACK *made his last speech and now they shine out, making the stage mysteriously bright. The* DARKIES' *music was sweet and soft as* JACK *walked back to bench, but they fall asleep on steps when he has seated himself. Suddenly he rises. A light shines from left upon him. He stands perfectly straight without cane, steps forward listening, takes off spectacles.*)

JACK. What has happened? I can see—I see the mountains! And I hear, a bird's note, and—Someone is calling me— Yes! Yes! What do you say? There is more adventure ahead, the best of all? Over the river?—up the mountain?—I hear!—I come!

(*Walking like a young man, with his head high and a look of blissful expectation, he crosses the stage and walks off, toward mountains, left. As he walks the negroes who have awakened sing.*)

Deep river, my home is over Jordan,
Deep river, Lord, I want to cross over into camp ground.

CURTAIN

TO PASS OR NOT TO PASS*

By Elbridge S. Lyon

CHARACTERS

Walter, *high school senior—nineteen and large*
Horace, *high school senior—sixteen and small*
Douglas, *high school senior—average age and size*
Marge, *high school senior—just right*
Anne, *high school senior—even better*
Miss Miller, *teacher in high school*

Scene: *Biology class room, four P. M.*

Walter *is alone studying hard. Turns pages of large book. Gives deep sighs. Finally flings book down and goes to teacher's desk and works happily with microscope and other instruments. Enter* Douglas, *who watches* Walter. Douglas *shakes his head over pile of discarded books.* Walter *looks up and sees* Douglas.

Walter. Oh, hello.
Douglas. You certainly take to that toy.
Walter. A microscope is far from being a toy. It opens up an entirely new world.
Douglas. Funny how you like that and hate books.
Walter. I don't hate books.
Douglas. Why aren't you studying?
Walter. I can't seem to do it.
Douglas. I am a committee of one sent to make you stick to your books.
Walter. It's no use.
Douglas. Look here. You've got to get to work and cram.

* For permission to produce, apply to author, Chatham, N.J.

You've only got to pass this one subject to graduate with us; and, besides not wanting to see you fail, we want you to be our classmate in the alumni and be in all our reunions.

WALTER. That's swell of you; but I can't pass Biology, and you know it. The only reason I got through the other studies was that I'd had most of them all over again a second year; and, either you pals used your influence on the teachers, or the teachers didn't want a big boob like me a third year. You'll notice that all my marks are 70 or 71, which means the teachers push them up to that point. I just am no student. I hate not to graduate, for I will never get into college, and how can I ever get a job without a High School diploma?

DOUGLAS. Only Miss Miller stands in the way, and she will flunk you sure if you don't guess the right answers in the exam tomorrow.

WALTER. She's right.

DOUGLAS. She's pig-headed. Marge and Anne have been arguing with her for the last hour, and all she says is "Duty is duty!" I believe she will make it as hard as she can, too, and maybe flunk half of us.

WALTER. She has to make the test pretty stiff, or Horace will say it wasn't any exam at all.

DOUGLAS. He'll do that anyway. However hard it is, Horace will say it was a cinch.

WALTER. He is a wonder all right. Got "A" or "B" in everything for four years. Every time I got a "D," I was tickled. I had to tell my aunt that "E" meant excellent and "F" fair.

DOUGLAS. "G" was great, I suppose.

WALTER. I don't think I ever got quite that far down. Do you realize that Horace is three years younger than I am?

(*Enter* HORACE.)

DOUGLAS. Hello, Horace. How's the cranium?

WALTER. We were just talking about how much smarter you are than I am.

DOUGLAS. We were doing no such thing, not really.

HORACE. I lead the whole class, and I am the youngest member.

WALTER. That's nothing. I am the oldest and dumbest.

DOUGLAS. Quit it, will you? You mustn't talk that way.

HORACE. My father has a friend who has promised me a position in the research laboratory in the Guggenheim Foundation, if I do as well in college as I did in High.

DOUGLAS. That's swell. I wish I had the promise right now of a job in the street cleaning department or anywhere. Most of last year's grads who couldn't go to college, are still hunting work. I tell you it's tough getting a position these years.

WALTER. You bet it is.

DOUGLAS. Say, Horace, would your father give me a letter to his friend in the Guggenheim what's it?

HORACE. Why—you see—the truth is they only want extra bright minds.

WALTER. 'At-a-boy, Horace, that's telling him tactful-like!

DOUGLAS. I guess it's his goggles.

WALTER. Let's see those glasses. (*Takes them.*) Maybe I could understand some of this book. (*Takes up book.*) Wow—say can you actually read with these telescopes?

HORACE. Of course.

WALTER. Well I guess there are some advantages in NOT reading too much.

HORACE. You would have been better off if you had done more reading and less playing with all those gadgets in your cellar.

WALTER. Sure, but anyway my eyes are good. (*Returns glasses to* HORACE, *and takes up instrument from desk.*)

DOUGLAS. So are his muscles.

HORACE. From the neck down.

WALTER. Thank you. That includes the heart.

(*Enter* MARGE *and* ANNE.)

MARGE. Whose heart?

ANNE. Why aren't you working?

WALTER. We are.

ANNE. It looks like it. Where is your text book?

MARGE. Here it is, closed up.

ANNE. We sent Doug in here to make you study.

MARGE. And Horace to coach you.

WALTER. Horace has given me some sound advice.

MARGE. Well, it's a good thing we came in. The answers to the exam questions Miss Miller will ask are all in this book.

DOUGLAS. I wish I knew which ones.

ANNE. You'll pass all right, and, even if you don't, you've got enough good marks to carry you through.

MARGE. It's funny that this most living of all subjects should be so hard.

HORACE. I don't see anything difficult about it.

WALTER. It's his glasses.

ANNE. I think it's the most interesting subject there is.

WALTER. So do I.

DOUGLAS
ANNE } (*Together.*) You do?

WALTER. Certainly I do; only I have my own theories, which unfortunately don't always agree with the books.

HORACE. That's pretty good. So you know more than the books!

WALTER. Not more; but I am following some ideas in experimenting in my cellar, which might possibly prove something some day.

ANNE. And, in the meantime, you can't even graduate from High School.

HORACE. With two years in the senior class.

DOUGLAS. He'll get through O.K. if he gets 70 in this one subject tomorrow. Mr. Bleecker said so.

MARGE. Then, why in Sam Hill doesn't he plug from now till nine in the morning? We'll take turns reading to him. Come on, I'll start. (*Takes up book and sits at teacher's desk.*) Sit down, everybody. (*They take seats.*) Come here, Walter, and sit by me. Don't be so shy. How did a big fellow like you ever get so shy?

ANNE. I've been hinting at him to take me to some dance for four years.

WALTER. You have?

ANNE. You always said you had home work to do.

HORACE. Huh. Home work! Fooling with frogs and bugs and electric gadgets.

WALTER. Well, that's biology, isn't it?

MARGE. Keep quiet, everybody. Now answer this question. "How are nitrogenous chemical wastes collected in Melanoplus femurrubrum, previous to their elimination?"

HORACE. The chemical wastes—other than the carbon dioxide which is expelled through the spiracles, of course,—reach the blood by osmosis. By the same process they are conveyed to the Malphigian tubules.

MARGE. Not you, smarty. Could you have answered that, Walt?

WALTER. Not me.

MARGE. Try this one. "What are the lenticels?"

WALTER. Sorry. Never heard of it.

MARGE. Never heard of— (*Throws book down.*) What's the use?

DOUGLAS. We'll have to work on Miss Miller again.

HORACE. She is adamant.

ANNE. That is Latin or something for hard and unyielding.

DOUGLAS. Cheese it! Here she comes.

(*Enter* MISS MILLER.)

MARGE. Hello again, Miss Miller. Have you come back to your room to think up some more posers for the exam?

MISS M. What are you all doing here at this hour?

ANNE. We're trying to make Walter study. Miss Miller,

won't you promise to pass him, no matter what?

HORACE. He's had this same class two years, and he has to have a girl beg teacher to pass him.

MISS M. Horace, if you say anything like that when class is in session, I will mark you way down in deportment unbecoming a gentleman!

WALTER. Oh, don't mind him. I never did.

DOUGLAS. He's only a little boy, you know.

MARGE. Honest, Miss Miller, we want Walter to get his diploma when we do.

MISS M. You all seem pretty sure of your own selves.

DOUGLAS. You wouldn't flunk him, would you, like that dumb teacher did last year?

MISS M. It seems I have something of a surprise for you. I was in Mr. Bleecker's office a few minutes ago, and he showed me this report of the Guggenheim Foundation. Look. (*Opens magazine.*)

HORACE. Say, that picture looks like Walter.

DOUGLAS. It *is* Walter, see. (*Reads.*) "Walter A. Downs." Why, Walt, what did you do? Kill somebody?

MISS M. Let me read this to you. (*Reads.*) "Walter A. Downs, a high school student in Bockburg, Ill., has submitted to us a remarkable discovery he has made with his own crude apparatus. This discovery is a method of comparative study of blood action in invertebrates by means of filtered light rays. A great future is promised for this boy, and the Foundation has secured his services in their research department as soon as he has finished High School.

ANNE. Why, Walter—that's wonderful! No wonder you wouldn't take me out.

MARGE. What is an invertebrate?

DOUGLAS. Horace here—he's a living example.

HORACE. I am not! An invertebrate is an organism without any backbone.

DOUGLAS. That is what I said.

MISS M. Walter, why didn't you tell us all about this?

WALTER. Everybody made fun of my experiments and thought I was dumb.

DOUGLAS. And you never told us you had been offered a job with the Guggenheim thing-a-ma-bob.

WALTER. That's off. You see, they would never take me without a High School certificate.

MISS M. Well, I guess that is all right. You see, I can allow whatever mark I think best on home work, and anybody who cares enough about a subject to give up dances for a whole year and can make an impression on a great body of scientists—well, I think 98 for the year's work in Biology will be about right. And, as for you, Horace—I guess you will have to get along with a 97.

CURTAIN

POEMS

IF

By Rudyard Kipling

If you can keep your head when all about you
    Are losing theirs and blaming it on you,
If you can trust yourself when all men doubt you,
    But make allowance for their doubting too;
If you can wait and not be tired by waiting,
    Or being lied about don't deal in lies,
Or being hated don't give way to hating,
    And yet don't look too good, nor talk too wise:

If you can dream—and not make dreams your master;
    If you can think—and not make thoughts your aim,
If you can meet with Triumph and Disaster
    And treat these two impostors just the same;
If you can bear to hear the truth you've spoken
    Twisted by knaves to make a trap for fools,
Or watch the things you gave your life to, broken,
    And stoop and build 'em up with worn-out tools:

If you can make one heap of all your winnings
    And risk it on one turn of pitch-and-toss,
And lose, and start again at your beginnings
    And never breathe a word about your loss;
If you can force your heart and nerve and sinew
    To serve your turn long after they are gone,

And so hold on when there is nothing in you
    Except the will which says to them: "Hold on!"

If you can talk with crowds and keep your virtue,
    Or walk with Kings—nor lose the common touch,
If neither foes nor loving friends can hurt you,
    If all men count with you, but none too much;
If you can fill the unforgiving minute
    With sixty seconds' worth of distance run,
Yours is the Earth and everything that's in it,
    And—which is more—you'll be a Man, my son!

COURAGE

By Josephine Johnson

This is the tree that cannot be overthrown;
These are the branches that leafless can still give shade.
Here is the bud which canker may claim for its own
Yet cannot devour. Oh, this tree was made

For you—for your uttermost need, for your black despair!
Though the whirlwind bow, and the earthquake heave at its root,
It will rise in beauty and strength through the darkened air,
It will flower, it will bear fruit!

THE IDEAL

By Katharine Lee Bates

By the promise of noon's splendor in the dawn's first silvery
    gleam,
By the song of the sea that compelleth the path of the rock-
    cleaving stream,
I summon thee, recreant dreamer, to rise and follow thy dream.

In the inmost core of thy being I am a burning fire,
From thine own altar-flame kindled in the hour when souls aspire,
For know that men's prayers shall be answered, and guard thy spirit's desire.

That which thou wouldst be thou must be, that which thou shalt be thou art;
As the oak, astir in the acorn, the dull earth rendeth apart,
Lo, thou, the seed of thy longing, that breaketh and waketh the heart.

I am the cry of the night wind, startling thy traitorous sleep;
Moaning I echo thy music, and e'en while thou boastest to reap
Alien harvests, my anger resounds from the vehement deep.

I am the solitude folding thy soul in a sudden embrace.
Faint waxes the voice of thy fellow, wan the light on his face.
Life is as cloud-drift about thee alone in shelterless space.

I am the drawn sword barring the lanes thy mutinous feet
Vainly covet for greenness. Loitering pace or fleet,
Thine is the crag-path chosen. On the crest shall rest be sweet.

I am thy strong consoler, when the desolate human pain
Darkens upon thee, the azure outblotted by rush of the rain.
All thou dost cherish may perish; still shall thy quest remain.

Call me thy foe in thy passion; claim me in peace for thy friend;
Yet bethink thee by lowland and upland, wherever thou willest to wend,
I am thine Angel of Judgment; mine eyes thou must meet in the end.

THE BANKRUPT

By Mary Sinton Leitch

Some put a bullet through the head:
    He laughed and built a cottage,
And, long grown old on squab, instead
    Grows young on simple pottage.

So swift his wheels sped past a rose
    He scarce perceived it fragrant,
But now he walks and sweetly knows
    What nature gives a vagrant.

And he who told the heavy hours
    By dollars he was winning,
Now lightly counts by jasmine flowers
    Or by a spider's spinning.

THE DAY OF A THOUSAND DEATHS

By Robert Haven Schauffler

Calamity loomed in the way;
My lips went suddenly grey,
For his sword was long
And his armor, strong.
"No sword nor armor are mine," I said,
"I am but as the dead!"
But a thousand deaths I died that day
As waiting Calamity's blow I lay.

Calamity came and lifted my head.
"I am no coward," he proudly said,

"That would slink to attack
A defenceless back!
I am not Worry, the cur whose bark
Slays fools in the dark.
Not so; I fight as a well-born knight;
Nor shall you fail of the chivalrous right
To equal weapons and equal mail";
When, lo! my body was girt in steel
And a blade in my hand was bright.

Then did I feel
A tenfold might.
With a tenfold zeal
Then did I fight.
Then did I fall
With courage alight.
Deep and grievous my wounds were, all;
But none in the back, and fatal, none.
Already my confident flesh had begun,
As the clean-cutting steel withdrew, to heal.
And the pain was as naught to the pain I had felt that day
When blindly awaiting Calamity's blow I lay.

MICROCOSM

By Ernest Crosby

I split a grain of common sand
    And behold! within it lay
The vaulted universe bespanned
    By the uttermost Milky Way.

I delved in my narrow soul, and lo!
    At my being's inmost core

I saw the eternal Godhead glow
And the heavenly hosts adore.

EVENING PRAYER

By Josephine Johnson

The air was palpable with gold
Too brimming for the sky to hold
As burnished oak leaves, one by one,
Held up a mirror to the sun.
The birds above the fountain rim
Were cherubim and seraphim
Lifting translucent wings in flight
Against the radiance of light.
No smallest whisper seemed to stir
The invisible threads of gossamer
Laid on the lawn, yet rainbows ran
Shimmering, from span to span.
Midges and gnats with rise and fall
Moved to an ancient ritual
In gauzy dance. O King of Kings,
It was the hour of humble things!
The small sweet clover, magnified,
Beheld the bridegroom, was the Bride,
And every lowly plantain head
Was haloed by the glory spread!

Then, lifting high each shining sword,
The grass stood up and praised the Lord!

DUTY

By Edwin Markham

When Duty comes a-knocking at your gate,
Welcome him in; for if you bid him wait,
He will depart only to come once more
And bring seven other duties to your door.

PREPAREDNESS

By Edwin Markham

For all your days prepare,
  And meet them all alike:
When you are the anvil, bear—
  When you are the hammer, strike.

BUT, HEART, REMEMBER!

By Julia Johnson Davis

As summer lightning
  Blasts a tree,
And tears away
  All greenery,
And leaves no bud,
  No bloom, no leaf—
So can a heart
  Be stripped by grief.

The tree stands on,
  No matter how
Maimed and broken

Is each bough,
Until it gains
    What strength it can—
So must the stricken
    Heart of man.

But, heart, remember
    That the One
Who sends the bough
    Both rain and sun,
Who will not let
    It fade away,
Has strength for thee
    In thy dark day.

For though the torn
    And twisted tree
Must know a strange
    New symmetry,
It shall once more
    Have fruit to give—
O heart, remember
    This, and live!

THE QUITTER

By Robert W. Service

When you're lost in the Wild, and you're scared as a child,
    And Death looks you bang in the eye,
And you're sore as a boil, it's according to Hoyle
    To cock your revolver and . . . die.
But the code of a Man says: "Fight all you can,"
    And self-dissolution is barred.

In hunger and woe, oh, it's easy to blow. . . .
  It's the hell-served-for-breakfast that's hard.

"You're sick of the game!" Well, now, that's a shame.
  You're young and you're brave and you're bright.
"You've had a raw deal!" I know—but don't squeal,
  Buck up, do your damndest, and fight.
It's the plugging away that will win you the day,
  So don't be a piker, old pard!
Just draw on your grit; it's so easy to quit:
  It's the keeping-your-chin-up that's hard.

It's easy to cry that you're beaten—and die;
  It's easy to crawfish and crawl;
But to fight and to fight when hope's out of sight—
  Why, that's the best game of them all!
And though you come out of each gruelling bout,
  All broken and beaten and scarred,
Just have one more try—it's dead easy to die,
  It's the keeping-on-living that's hard.

THE LEVEL WAY

By Josephine Johnson

My road lies open, over level country,
    Bare as the sea.
No sudden turn, no unexpected winding,
    No mystery.

I dreamed of rugged paths to splendid summits
    Where far-flung views
Should lift my soul to heaven and recompense me
    For ache and bruise.

No heights, no dangers here, no high adventure—
   I only see
The need of greater courage still for facing
Monotony.

THE PEAK

By Mary Carolyn Davies

There's a far high trail where the pines are,
   There's a gray faint trail to the dawn,
There's a sudden hush on the hillside—
   Look! The last star's gone!
And, follow, follow, the far trail seems to say,
Follow, comrade, follow, and you'll make the peak today!

There's a steep hard trail where the stones are,
   There's a sharp crag gray at the bend;
There's a far fine mist where the road winds—
   What is at the end?
Follow, follow, the dark trail seems to say,
Follow, comrade, follow, and you'll make the peak today!

There's an unknown trail—but we'll take it.
   It's a steep hard trail—who's afraid?
There are deep sharp chasms to walk by;
   No one's hands can aid.
Follow, follow, the far trail seems to say,
Follow, comrade, follow, and you'll make the peak today!

Celebrations for Fathers' Day

PLAYS

ORCHIDS TO FATHER *

By Marion Holbrook

PLAYERS

Alfred Dingwell, *Father*
Daphne, *his daughter, about 18*
Victor, *his son, about 16*
Muriel, *Mother, his wife*
Mother Bartlett, *Grandma, his mother-in-law*
Boyle of the Bugle, *a reporter*

The scene is the Dingwell living room. The Dingwells have been married about 25 years and, for the most part, they are still getting along with their first living-room furniture. At center is a davenport or sofa with a floor lamp at left end and a coffee table in front of it. Down left center is an extremely uncomfortable straight chair. It may or may not have arms and may be one of those pieces conveniently referred to as a "transition piece," combining the worse features of several periods. Down right center is an inviting wing chair with a footstool and a floor lamp at right. There is a small desk at right; and at left, across from it, a small table on which is a telephone. These are the essentials. Bookcases or other furniture may be used up left and right center as desired. A door up right leads to the dining room and another opposite it to the entrance hall.

---

* For permission to produce, apply to the author, 50 West 8th St., New York City.

The time is about 9 o'clock in the evening. The season is spring.

DAPHNE *is seated at the right end of the sofa. There are several small bottles and manicure articles on the coffee table, and* DAPHNE *is preparing to paint her nails a deep red.* FATHER *sits at the other end of the sofa, near the lamp, absorbed in a contest. He has a writing pad on his knee. Beside him on the couch and piled on the coffee table are dictionaries and volumes of an encyclopaedia.* FATHER *is a mild-mannered man. His lips move silently as he works. Occasionally he opens a book or scribbles on the pad.* DAPHNE *gives him an impatient look.*

DAPHNE. Father, would you mind letting me sit near the light?
FATHER. What's that, Daphne?
DAPHNE. I said would you let me move over there near the light?
FATHER. Certainly. Certainly.
(*He gathers up his books with some difficulty and goes to the wing chair, placing the volumes on the floor beside him.* DAPHNE *moves her bottles to the left end of the coffee table and settles herself beside the lamp.*)
DAPHNE. How is it coming?
FATHER. Oh, very nicely. This one is quite unique. It's—it's rather good fun, you know.
(*He becomes absorbed again.* MOTHER BARTLETT *enters, right, and comes down to right end of sofa. She stands there with her knitting bag, looking a little desolate.* MOTHER BARTLETT *has been living with the Dingwells for several years and has perfected a technique for getting her own way by an exaggerated claim to self-effacement. She looks from* DAPHNE *to* FATHER, *smiling a patient, rather sad smile.*)
GRANDMA. I suppose I could go up to my room but the light up there isn't very good.

DAPHNE. I'll be through in just a moment, Grandma, and you can sit here.

GRANDMA. Oh, no, dear. Don't bother. (*Plaintively.*) It's just that my eyes aren't what they used to be and I need a good light to knit by.

FATHER. (*Suddenly conscious of the situation.*) Oh. I'm sorry, Mother Bartlett. Here. Take my chair. (*He starts gathering up his books again.*)

GRANDMA. I wouldn't think of disturbing you, Alfred.

FATHER. (*Making his way across to the straight chair.*) S'all right. (*He puts his books on the floor again and tries to squirm into a comfortable position, which is clearly impossible.*)

GRANDMA. (*Seating herself in the wing chair.*) Thank you, Alfred. (*She gets out her knitting.*) You look very industrious.

FATHER. (*Absently.*) Eh? Oh, yes. Yes.

DAPHNE. (*With good-natured scorn.*) He's working on another contest.

GRANDMA. Well, well. Another contest. Of course it's not my affair how people choose to spend their leisure hours; but I fail to see how one can become interested in contests. (*As she knits.*) Now my husband had many hobbies, too, but they were always of an improving, intellectual nature. (*To* DAPHNE.) Your grandfather was a very erudite man, my dear. I have always regretted so much that he died in the very prime of life, you might say, and deprived you and Victor of his influence.

DAPHNE. (*She is a little tired of Grandpa, too.*) Maybe he could have given Father some pointers on how to talk to important people. My face still gets red when I think of what he said to Mr. Duffy at that meeting last week, after Mother made her speech.

GRANDMA. Mr. *Horace* Duffy?

DAPHNE. Yes, the one who owns all the newspapers.

FATHER. What did I say?

DAPHNE. Oh, you just talked and talked about the Dilly

Dairy Cream Cheese contest. That's all. I'm afraid he thought you were mad.

FATHER. (*Apologetically.*) I'm sorry. I thought he was interested. In fact he gave me several good ideas. The fellow seemed to have quite a bit of talent.

GRANDMA. Talent! Ideas! What is the world coming to? Really, Alfred. (FATHER *looks as if he wanted to say something rather strong but curbs the impulse and goes back to his work.*) How well I can remember your grandfather, Daphne, sitting right there in Aunt Belle's chair (*She indicates* FATHER'S *chair.*) reading Wordsworth or Thackeray. That was his favorite chair.

FATHER. Too bad he hasn't got it now.

GRANDMA. Why, Alfred!

FATHER. (*Apologetically.*) I just mean, Mother Bartlett, that it's not a very comfortable chair, and if anyone liked it—why—it's a pity he ever had to part with it. (*Weakly.*) Of course I understand that it's a very handsome piece of furniture.

GRANDMA. I should say it is. Aunt Belle brought it back from Wadley Castle in Wales where our ancestors lived from the reign of King John. I think it was King John. Anyhow, that doesn't matter. It's a very old and valuable piece.

FATHER. Yes, I know. It ought to bring a good price when you—when you get around to selling it.

GRANDMA. Sell it! Oh, dear. Daphne. Alfred. I feel another attack coming on.

DAPHNE. (*Rising and calling with no trace of alarm in her voice.*) Victor! Vic-*tor!*

(*She picks up a magazine and fans* GRANDMA *who closes her eyes and looks very sad.* VICTOR *comes in right.* FATHER *has risen and stands by uncertainly.*)

VICTOR. Call me?

DAPHNE. Get Grandma's smelling salts.

VICTOR. Right-o.

(*He goes out and returns immediately with the bottle. He gives it to* DAPHNE, *then stands behind* GRANDMA'S *chair.* DAPHNE *moves the bottle under* GRANDMA'S *nose. She opens her eyes.*)

GRANDMA. Thank you, my dear. My dear child, never grow old. (*Glaring at* FATHER.) The world is very unkind to old people.

DAPHNE. Now, Grandma.

FATHER. I'm sorry if I said anything to upset you, Mother Bartlett.

GRANDMA. I'm sure you didn't mean to, Alfred.

VICTOR. (*Coming down to center.*) Are you O.K. now, Grandma?

GRANDMA. Yes, Victor dear. Grandma's quite all right.

(DAPHNE *and* FATHER *resume their seats.* VICTOR *approaches* FATHER.)

VICTOR. Look, Dad. About that five bucks for the dance Friday night—

FATHER. I asked you not to mention that again, Victor.

VICTOR. Aw.

FATHER. You didn't come home when you said you would last Friday.

VICTOR. I had to take Virginia home, didn't I? You can't just say to a girl—Well, so long—and leave her at a bean wagon, can you?

FATHER. Ah—no. But you didn't cut the grass this week, either.

VICTOR. Listen, Dad. I haven't had time.

FATHER. You'll have to mow it down with a sickle if you don't get busy.

VICTOR. Well, anyhow, what about the five bucks, Dad?

FATHER. I—I guess not, Victor.

VICTOR. But—gosh!

GRANDMA. (*Sweetly.*) Victor, dear.

VICTOR. (*Hopefully.*) Yes, Grandma?

GRANDMA. Where is this dance?

VICTOR. It's up at the high school gym. I've already asked Virginia. I'm in a nice spot. What'll I do when I've already asked a girl! I guess I just can't uphold the honor of the family, that's all. What's *her* family going to think of *this* family?

GRANDMA. Alfred, don't you think you could reconsider? Do you really feel that you must place Victor in such an embarrassing position?

FATHER. I think Victor can live through it.

GRANDMA. I think you're being very callous, Alfred. Young people are extremely sensitive.

VICTOR. It'll be pretty tough, having to tell Virginia that I can't take her. Of course she knows we aren't rich, but I hate to have her think my family's a tightwad.

GRANDMA. Now, Alfred, don't you think—

FATHER. (*Unable to cope any longer.*) All right, all right, all right. (*Looking disgusted, he begins to thumb through a book again.*)

VICTOR. Thanks, Grandma.

DAPHNE. Nice work, Grandma.

GRANDMA. (*Taking up her knitting with a triumphant gesture.*) Well, if your father didn't spend all his time on those puzzles and things he'd know a little more about how to manage his family. (FATHER *glowers but goes on with his work.*) Victor, go turn the porch light on for your mother. She'll be so tired.

VICTOR. (*Going off, left.*) O.K., Grandma.

DAPHNE. (*Gathering up her bottles.*) Isn't this the day she sees Senator Briggs?

GRANDMA. Either the Senator or the Governor. Fix some hot milk for her, Daphne. She probably had a hard day. (DAPHNE *goes off, right.*) Poor Muriel!

FATHER. Did you speak to me, Mother Bartlett?
GRANDMA. I was about to remark that Muriel's working much too hard lately.
FATHER. Oh, she enjoys it. Muriel couldn't live without those committees, you know.
GRANDMA. Really, Alfred. You speak as if Muriel's civic-mindedness were a mere hobby. I should think any man would be proud to have such a wife.
FATHER. I'm very proud of Muriel.

(*The front door slams and* MOTHER *is heard greeting* VICTOR *in the hall.* MOTHER *is a smart-looking woman in her forties. She has great vitality and executive ability, likes to be the center of attention and isn't above posing as a martyr before her family. The truth is that she can't bear the obscurity of being the wife of a white-collar worker, so she heads committees and substitutes good works for sables. She enters briskly behind* VICTOR. *She wears an attractive tailored costume with several orchids pinned on the left shoulder.*)

VICTOR. Here's Mom!
MOTHER. (*Coming down left center, removing hat and gloves.*) Hello, everyone!
GRANDMA. My dear, you're so late!
FATHER. (*Rising.*) Good evening, Muriel.
(MOTHER *gives* FATHER *a light kiss.*)
MOTHER. Have a hard day at the office, Alfred?
ALFRED. Just about the same as usual.
MOTHER. (*Going over and kissing* GRANDMA.) Did you take your medicine, Mother?
GRANDMA. Of course I did. Sit down, Muriel. You must be all fagged out.
MOTHER. (*Going to the sofa and sitting down.*) Oh, I'm a little tired. What a day! (FATHER *sits down and listens with polite interest.*) I had an appointment with the Superintendent of

Schools at nine o'clock. At ten-thirty I met with the nominating committee of the People's Party. Mr. Duffy is being so difficult. He doesn't approve of any of the men we want to run for mayor.

VICTOR. (*Leaning against back of sofa.*) I suppose you can't get anywhere without old Duffy, can you?

MOTHER. Hardly, Victor. He owns the *Morning Bugle* and the *Evening Call*.

GRANDMA. And did you see the Senator, dear?

MOTHER. No, not today. I had lunch with the secretary of the Chamber of Commerce. About the tree planting in Grove Street, you know. And this afternoon I drove over to Stowell with Mrs. Atherton Cook to see the Governor about the Democracy Day campaign. On the way home we stopped at several farm houses and talked with the farmers' wives about rural conditions.

ALFRED. What did they have to say?

MOTHER. (*Annoyed.*) Well, after the second stop we decided we had heard quite enough. Farmers are always so unreasonable.

DAPHNE. (*Bringing in a glass of milk on a plate.*) Had your dinner, Mother?

MOTHER. (*Taking the drink.*) Thank you, Daphne dear. Yes, I had something at the Girl Scout banquet. I had to make a speech, you know.

(DAPHNE *sits at right of sofa.* MOTHER *sips the milk.*)

VICTOR. Gee, Mom, what's the Governor like?

MOTHER. Oh, he's very charming.

VICTOR. Dad, did you ever see the Governor?

FATHER. Yep. Once.

VICTOR. At the Capital?

FATHER. No. He was in his limousine.

VICTOR. Where were you?

FATHER. Oh, I was just waiting for a traffic light.

VICTOR. Huh. You ought to get around the way Mom does.

GRANDMA. Your grandfather was one of Governor Hitchcock's most trusted friends, Victor. The men in *our* family were always very public spirited.

DAPHNE. I'll bet Grandpa was on the platform every Fourth of July!

GRANDMA. He was indeed. He was a gifted orator.

(DAPHNE *and* VICTOR *look at* FATHER *and sigh.*)

MOTHER. Alfred, what in the world are you doing with all those books?

ALFRED. Just at present I'm trying to find something to rhyme with butterscotch.

(GRANDMA *sniffs.*)

DAPHNE. With civilization going to the dogs—Father sits and does contests. Talk about Nero!

FATHER. After all, Daphne, it's an innocent pastime.

VICTOR. Innocent but sort of screwy.

(*The doorbell rings.*)

MOTHER. Answer it, will you, Victor? And if it's for me, just say I've retired. I can't face another committee member tonight.

VICTOR. (*Going out left.*) O.K., Mom.

MOTHER. (*Handing the glass to* DAPHNE.) Darling, I can't take any more.

DAPHNE. All right, Mummie. I'll take it away. (*She goes out right with the glass.*)

GRANDMA. (*Putting her knitting away.*) Well, Alfred, as I said before, it's none of my business how anyone spends his leisure but—

VICTOR. (*Entering quickly.*) It's a telegram for you, Dad!

(DAPHNE *returns as* FATHER *rises and takes the telegram.*)

FATHER. For me? (*Looking around blankly.*) Who could be sending a telegram to *me?*

MOTHER. Open it, Alfred. Open it.

(FATHER *tears it open, reads it, and staggers back against the chair, staring at it.*)

DAPHNE. (*Amused.*) You didn't win a *contest* by any chance, did you?

FATHER. (*In a rather hysterical voice.*) Yes. Yes, I did.
ALL. What?
FATHER. (*Looking around wonderingly.*) Yes. I—I won the Yummie contest.
GRANDMA. I beg your pardon?
FATHER. The Yummie contest. It's a breakfast food, you know. (MOTHER, VICTOR *and* DAPHNE *burst out laughing.*) I—I wrote the last line of a limerick. (*He fishes in an inside coat pocket and brings out several pieces of paper.*) Just a minute. Maybe I've still got my original draft. Yes. Here it is. Would you like to hear it?
VICTOR. Go ahead.
MOTHER. Of course, Alfred. Read it if you want to.
FATHER. (*Self-consciously but rather proudly.*) It goes like this—

>If you want to keep healthy and sunny
>For breakfast eat plenty of Yummie—
>It's tempting and tasty
>When meals must be hasty
>And—

This is the line I filled in, you understand.

>And, besides, it's so good for the tummy.

VICTOR. Wow! Oh, my gosh!
DAPHNE. (*Dismayed.*) Father! This won't get in the papers, will it?
FATHER. I—I don't know.
MOTHER. (*Alarmed.*) Oh, Alfred! What have you done!
GRANDMA. This is revolting!
(*The telephone rings.* VICTOR *answers it.*)
VICTOR. Hello. Yes. This is Mr. Alfred Dingwell's residence. Yes, he's here. It's for you, Dad.
FATHER. (*Answering.*) Hello. This is Alfred Dingwell speaking. Yes. Yes, I did. I won it. (MOTHER, DAPHNE *and* GRANDMA

exchange alarmed glances.) Well, I don't know that I'll have anything to say. Oh. You want it for the morning edition. Oh. He's on his way up. Well, thank you. Thank you very much. Good night.

(MOTHER *and* GRANDMA *rise and look accusingly at* FATHER *as he returns to left center.*)

MURIEL. What is this, Alfred? Who's coming here?

FATHER. It's a reporter from the *Bugle*. They—they just want me to make a statement about the contest.

ALL. Alfred! Father!

FATHER. I won't say much. Just—just enough to satisfy them, you know.

MOTHER. But Alfred, this will make a fool of me! Right in the middle of my Democracy Day campaign, too!

FATHER. I'm sorry, Muriel. I really didn't expect to win. That line just came to me and I sent it in. That's all.

(*The doorbell rings.* VICTOR *goes out left.*)

GRANDMA. I think I'm going to have another attack!

(BOYLE *of the* Bugle *enters, left, followed by* VICTOR.)

BOYLE. (*Heartily.*) Congratulations, Mr. Dingwell! I'm Boyle of the *Bugle*.

FATHER. (*Shaking hands.*) Thank you. Thank you. How do you do?

BOYLE. Well, how does it feel to win fifty thousand dollars?

(*All the family speak at once.*)

VICTOR. Hey!

MOTHER. Fifty thou—(*Her mouth just remains open.*)

DAPHNE. What!

GRANDMA. Pardon?

FATHER. (*The New Man in* FATHER *begins to emerge at this point.*) It feels fine, Boyle. It's great! Ah—pardon me. This is my wife, my mother-in-law Mrs. Mortimer Bartlett, my daughter Daphne, and my son Victor. Mr. Boyle.

(*They murmur acknowledgments, still stunned.*)

BOYLE. How do you do, folks. What a lucky family! What a break!

FATHER. (*Becoming more nonchalant with every breath.*) Sit down. Sit down.

(*Everyone is seated but* FATHER *who stands at center.* BOYLE *sits on the arm or the edge of Aunt Belle's chair.*)

BOYLE. What are you going to do with this money, Dingwell? Buy a house? Take a trip? Get a new car? Endow a home for cats?

FATHER. (*Folding his arms.*) I don't know. Haven't made up my mind.

VICTOR. If you need any help, Dad, just call on me.

BOYLE. Pretty nice for you, my lad. Pretty soft for you to have a smart man for a father.

DAPHNE. Oh, we knew Father would do something big!

MOTHER. My husband has always been a great lover of poetry, you know.

BOYLE. Ever written any verse before?

FATHER. Ah—occasionally. Just for my own amusement.

GRANDMA. My son-in-law hides his light under a bushel.

BOYLE. (*Rising.*) That so? Well, Mr. Duffy would like to know, just confidentially, you understand, how you'd feel about accepting the nomination for mayor on the People's ticket.

MOTHER. Why—why—my husband doesn't know a thing about politics, Mr. Boyle.

BOYLE. Lady, he doesn't have to know. Listen. Who's the great national hero today? The contest winner! A hundred million people dream of winning contests! Along comes a simple man of the people and by his own wits, by his own endeavor, right here at his own humble fireside, *he* writes the winning line. Why, it's terrific! A man who eats Yummie every morning for his breakfast! Everybody eats Yummie! Factory workers. Elevator boys. Street car conductors. Stenographers. The rank and file of the voters. Get it?

MOTHER. Alfred, I don't know what you ought to say.

FATHER. Well, I do! If the people call me I shall do my duty as a member of this community and a citizen of this great Democracy!

VICTOR. (*Imitating a bugle with his hands and playing a few bars from "The Stars and Stripes Forever."*) Da da *da* da da *da* da da *da*.

GRANDMA. Victor!

MOTHER AND DAPHNE. Victor!

BOYLE. That's the answer we want, Mr. Dingwell! Suppose I say that you will use your fortune for the greater happiness of your family and that you look forward to being of greater service to your fellow citizens.

FATHER. That's all right with me. And you might add that, like Thomas Jefferson, I am a firm believer in the right to life, liberty and (*Eyeing his family challengingly.*) the pursuit of happiness!

BOYLE. (*Shoving his hat further back on his head.*) Right-o!

MOTHER. Just a minute, Mr. Boyle. I know just what you're going to say next. (*She goes to the desk and gets a large photograph of* FATHER.) You're going to ask for my husband's photograph.

BOYLE. Absolutely, Mrs. Dingwell.

MOTHER. Here it is. Taken on our wedding day.

BOYLE. (*Taking it and looking at it with suppressed amusement.*) Honest Alfred Dingwell. (*Winking at* FATHER.) Good slogan. Well, see you at City Hall. (*Shakes hands with* FATHER.) Good night, sir.

FATHER. Good night, Boyle.

BOYLE. Good night, folks.

MOTHER. (*Going off left with* BOYLE *as the family respond.*) Any time you want another interview with my husband, just call me and I'll make all the arrangements.

VICTOR. (*Going up to* FATHER *with his hand out.*) Congratulations, Dad!

FATHER. (*With dignity.*) Thank you, son.

DAPHNE. (*Going to* FATHER.) Father, I think you're just wonderful.

FATHER. (*A little embarrassed.*) Well, I—I—(*Regaining his poise.*) Thank you, Daphne.

GRANDMA. (*Rising.*) I don't know what to say, Alfred.

FATHER. You don't have to say anything at all, Mother Bartlett. Isn't it my turn?

GRANDMA. (*Nervously.*) Yes, Alfred?

FATHER. Either you let me move Aunt Belle's chair up to your room tomorrow or I call in the junk man.

GRANDMA. Why, of course, Alfred. Of course. Just as you say.

MOTHER. (*Enters and goes at once to* FATHER, *giving him a hearty kiss this time.*) Alfred, I'm so proud of you. With my influence with the committee, your nomination is practically a sure thing.

VICTOR. Committee nothing! Listen, Mom, with the *Bugle* behind Dad it's in the bag right now.

MOTHER. (*Sighs, looks a little pained, and then quickly takes the orchids from her dress and pins them on* FATHER's *lapel.*) Yes. Victor's right. I think I shall retire from politics. I'll have enough to do as the wife of the Mayor.

VICTOR. And remember—plenty of mayors have been elected Governor!

DAPHNE. And lots of Governors have been made *President!*

VICTOR. Wow! (*Beginning the bugle business again and continuing until the curtains close.*) Da da *da* da da *da* da da *da*, etc.

DAPHNE. Hurrah for Father! Hurrah for Father!

(MOTHER *smiles fondly at* FATHER *who stands very straight.*)

GRANDMA. (*As the curtains close.*) Three cheers for Alfred!

ABRAHAM AND ISAAC *

(*The Brome Mystery Adapted as a Father's Day Program*)

By Grace Dorcas Ruthenburg

CAST

Abraham
Isaac
Angel
Voice of God

In this production the Brome manuscript of the mediaeval mystery has been set to music with the idea of presentation in a church as part of Father's Day services. The text has been altered somewhat to serve modern purposes, and the stage directions left fluid, to be adapted to various styles of church architecture. With the exception of the thirteenth century liturgy, SALVE SANCTA PARENS, the suggested music is all readily available in organ arrangements. If impossible to get hold of the trope indicated, almost any mediaeval liturgy will serve to set the color and period of the production at the outset. Nor is the rest of the music impervious to change.

The drama is so simple in its conception that too much effort apparent in the setting will thwart its inherent strength. Richness should be confined to voice and costume. Postures and gesture should be stylized as far as possible, though there should be nothing wooden about the inflection of the lines. As you will observe, they are extremely human.

Special lighting will prove effective in spotting the principal characters and in pointing up action. If you use lighting effects, first find out what load can be carried and plot your spots

---

* All rights reserved. Copyright applied for. No performance of this play may be given without written permission from, and payment of three dollars to Grace Dorcas Ruthenburg, 471 Park Ave., New York City.

accordingly. If possible, rig them with dimmers to cover:
1. the entrance of Abraham and follow him down the aisle, focusing on his meeting with Isaac and the first prayer,
2. the appearance of the Angel,
3. the altar, representing the voice of God and to indicate the blaze of sacrifice,
4. A fourth spot will help in picking out the ram at the right moment.

It will be necessary to allow for space behind the first spot to conceal a person, as the spot will have to be unscrewed and swung on its pivot. The other three can be attached by cables to a frog and operated from a distance. If you don't know much about wiring, get an experienced electrician to make the connections and be sure it works before you try your hand.

Costumes can follow either the traditional Biblical raiment, or better, the mediaeval conception of what was Biblical. The nearest library can show you illustrations to fifteenth century texts which will give you the right idea. Materials can just as well be inexpensive—muslin, flannel and cheesecloth can all be dyed effectively. Colors may be as fervent as you like. The Middle Ages loved rich reds, yellows and blues. You will probably, though not necessarily, want white cheesecloth for the Angel, with, say, ruby red for Abraham and a harmonizing blue for Isaac. Borders can be stenciled on. Resplendent girdles may be constructed with jewels from the dime store, though for Isaac it is better to use simply a contrasting length of cloth.

The ram is always a problem. If your pastor has no objection and you think the congregation won't, you can change "ram" to "lamb" and make it small, to be carried on Isaac's arm when the time comes. Draw the outline on unbleached muslin, allowing enough for seams. Stitch, turn, and stuff. If you don't stuff it too hard it will be more limply realistic than if you pack it tight. Cover with imitation lamb's wool, or a cast-off child's muff. Sew on buttons for eyes if you wish. If you stitch the legs on separately and weight the feet it will be more convincing.

If you feel you must have a ram, you can make it by outlining the figure on a sheet of wrapping paper and then following your outline with a skeleton of heavy wire or by making an armature of wood. Mesh in the skeleton with finer wire, leaving loops to which to attach legs, tail, and head when these are ready. Cover the wire skeleton with gummed paper or with cloth soaked in papier mâché (a mixture of newspaper soaked, squeezed, and mingled with flour-and-water paste). Carve the head, or build it in the same way with papier mâché. Carve the legs. Paint the whole thing, or cover it with material resembling ram's wool. The horns can be made of wire covered with gummed paper on papier mâché. Keep the ram out of sight as much as possible. Only his horns need show to convince the audience he is there. A live ram is too unpredictable to use, and an artificial one is apt to tickle the credulity of the onlookers and destroy the real beauty and solemnity of the drama's mood.

The fagots are easy enough. They can be concealed behind the lectern if the Angel speaks from it, or if there is no natural hiding place for properties, a box can be covered with a bit of tapestry or velvet and used boldly and stylistically as a repository.

The lamp to light the altar fire should be a wick in a receptacle. You may be able to find a bronze saucer that will serve, or add to it with papier mâché and paint it to resemble a mediaeval lamp. If you leave a lighter beside it, Abraham can ignite it as he stoops to pick it up with the fagots. If you think this is too risky, it can simply be carried aloft as frank make-believe. If you do use a lighted wick in oil, be sure the gadget is absolutely foolproof. You don't want to be setting the church on fire.

Be sure all the audience is seated before the drama begins. Where you use the church aisles as part of the production, it is ruinous to have spectators swishing to their seats after the thing has begun. If there are any late arrivals, have the ushers hold them in the vestibule at least until after the appearance of the Angel.

Not all churches are equipped to be darkened during the daytime. It is quite possible to go ahead without altering the natural light, but it is more effective if you can, to darken the church auditorium while the Choir sings: *Salve sancta parens.*

This old trope, dating from around 1300, is one of a few which have survived with four parts fairly intact. It can be found in "The Worcester MS, with Mediaeval Harmony of the 13th and 14th Centuries," Don Anselm Hughes, published by The Plainsong and Mediaeval Music Society, Nashdom Abbey, Burnham Bucks, England, 1928. If this is not available, use some other mediaeval liturgy which seems appropriate. The play dates from the first half of the fifteenth century, so you would be justified in using almost any music composed before 1600, as it was probably played all during its own century and well into the next.

As the music dies away, ABRAHAM'S *voice can be heard. If a spotlight is used, it should be trained on the door in the rear of the church through which* ABRAHAM *is to enter. From here on, the organ provides a background to the spoken dialogue as indicated in the left margin:*

Organ: VOICE OF ABRAHAM.
Bach: Prelude
No. 8 from   (*Outside.*)
"The Well-
Tempered   Father of Heaven, omnipotent,
Clavichord"   With all my heart to thee I call.

(Abraham enters alone, making his way to the front of the church during the next twelve lines.)

Thou hast given me both land and rent,
And my livelihood thou hast to me sent.
I thank thee greatly evermore for all.

First of the earth thou madest Adam,
    And Eve also to be his wife;
All other creatures from these two came:
And now thou hast granted me, Abraham,
    Here in this land to lead my life.

In mine age thou hast granted me this
    That with me should dwell this young child dear.
I love nothing so much, ywis,
    Except thine own self, dear Father of Bliss,

(He joins ISAAC *at the front of the church.)*

As my own sweet son, my Isaac here.

(Putting his arm about ISAAC'S *shoulders.)*

I have divers children more, I know,
    But I love them not half so well as he.
This fair sweet child he doth cherish me so,
In every place wherever I go,
    That no affliction may trouble me.

Organ:
Prayer
from "Der
Freischütz"

*(*ABRAHAM *and* ISAAC *mount the pulpit and kneel. If there is no higher level in the church on which the* ANGEL *can appear, you may want to introduce a platform lower than the pulpit but one which will raise the kneeling figures to*

a height where they can be seen by the congregation.)

And therefore, Father of Heaven, I thee pray
    For his health and also for his grace.
Now, Lord, keep him both night and day,
That never affliction nor terror may
    Come to my child in any place.

Now, Thou that didst form everything,
    My prayers I make to Thee,
For this day my tender offering
    Here must I give to Thee.
Ah, Lord God, Almighty King,
    What kind will be to Thee most fain?
If I had thereof true knowing,
    It should be done with might and main
        Full soon by me!

Organ:
"Unfold,
Ye Portals
Everlasting"

(They remain bowed in prayer while THE VOICE OF GOD *is heard off. If possible, a vivid light can shine on the altar during the following speech.)*

VOICE OF GOD.

Mine angel, hie thee on thy way!
    To dark earth shalt thou swiftly speed.
Abraham's faith I would essay,
    Whether my commands he heed.

Say I command him that he take
    His young son Isaac whom he loveth so,
And with his blood that he sacrifice make
    If my friendship he would have and know.

Show him the way unto the hill
    Where that his sacrifice shall fall.

I shall essay now his good will,
    Whether he love me before all.
Let earth example take from him,
    My commandments how they shall keep.

    (*The light on the altar vanishes. The* ANGEL *appears at a point above the kneeling* ABRAHAM *and* ISAAC. *Just where depends on the church: either in the pulpit, the choir balcony, or in a window of the clerestory. The higher, the more dramatic.*)

Organ:
Bach:
Passion according to St. Matthew
"Even Break, Thou Loving Heart"

ANGEL.

Abraham, Abraham, be at rest!

    (ABRAHAM *rises wonderingly and moves slowly in the direction of the* ANGEL. ISAAC, *unaware of the* ANGEL'S *presence, continues to kneel.*)

Our Lord commandeth thee to take
Isaac, thy young son that thou lovest best
    And with his blood that thou sacrifice make.

    (ABRAHAM *stops short.*)

Into the Land of Vision do thou go
    And offer thy child unto thy Lord:
I shall thee lead and show also.
    To God's bidding, Abraham, give accord.

ABRAHAM.

Welcome to me be my Lord's command!
And his behest I will not withstand—
Yet Isaac, my young son, I ween,
    A full dear child to me hath been!

Were God so pleased, I were liefer rid
   Of all the good that I have, he gave,
Than that Isaac, my son, were discomforted,
   So God in Heaven my soul may save!

No thing on earth so much love I bore,
   And now mine own child must I kill!
Ah, Lord God, my conscience is troubled sore,
And yet, my dear Lord, I dread me the more
   To begrudge anything against thy will.

I love my child as my life,
   But yet I love my God much more thereto,
For though my heart should make any strife,
Yet will I not spare for child or wife,
   But do as my Lord hath bid me do!

Ah, Father of Heaven, to thee I kneel.
A hard death my son shall feel,
   For to honor Thee, Lord, withal!

ANGEL.

Abraham, Abraham, this is well said,
   And all these decrees look thou obey!
But in thy heart be nothing dismayed.

ABRAHAM.

Nay, nay, forsooth! I hold me well paid
   To please my God the best I may.

For though my heart be in heaviness set,
   The blood of my own dear son to see,
Yet will I not withhold my debt,
But Isaac, my son, I will go get
   And come as fast as ever may be.

(*The* ANGEL *vanishes.* ABRAHAM *turns blindly in the direction of* ISAAC.)

Now, Isaac, my own son dear,
    Where art thou, child! Speak to me.

ISAAC.

    (*Lifting his head.*)

My fair sweet father, I am here
    And make my prayers dutifully.

ABRAHAM.

    (*Beckoning.*)

Rise up, my child, and fast come hither—

    (ISAAC *comes quickly and confidingly.* ABRAHAM *lays his hand on the boy's head.*)

My gentle bairn that art so wise,
For we too, child, must go together
    And unto my Lord make sacrifice.

ISAAC.

I am full ready, my father. Lo!
    Given to your hands, I stand right here,
And whatsoever ye bid me do, even so
    It shall be done with glad cheer,
        Full well and fine!

ABRAHAM.

Ah, Isaac, mine own son so dear,
    God's blessing I give thee, and mine.

    (*Taking fagots and laying them on* ISAAC'S *shoulder.*)

Hold this fagot upon thy back

(*Picking up lamp.*)

And I myself here fire shall bring.

Isaac.

Father, all this here will I pack;
I am full fain to do your bidding.

Abraham.

Ah, Lord of Heaven, my hands I wring,
This child's words wound like death my heart!

(*Starting toward altar.*)

Now, Isaac, son, go we on our way
Unto yon mount with might and main.

Isaac.

(*Following.*)

Let us go, my dear father, as fast as I may—
To follow you I am full fain,
Although I be slender.

Abraham.

Ah, Lord, my heart breaketh in twain,
This child's words, they be so tender!

(*They mount to altar.*)

Ah, Isaac, son, anon lay it there;
No longer upon thy back it hold,
For I must make ready prayer
To honor my Lord God as I was told.

Isaac.

(*Taking his father's hand.*)

Lo, father, meet and true it is,
To cheer you, always I draw me near,

But, father, I marvel sore at this,
 Why it is that ye make this heavy cheer,

   (*Looking about him with the first tinge of fear.*)

And also, father, ever more fear I—
 Where is your quick beast that ye should kill?
Both fire and wood we have ready by,
 But quick beast have we none on this hill.

A quick beast, I know well, slain must be,
 Your sacrifice to make.

ABRAHAM.

   (*After a pause during which he draws sword from beside altar.*)

Dread thee not, my child, I counsel thee.
Our Lord will unto this place send me
 Some manner of beast to take
  By his sweet command.

<small>Organ:
Bach:
Passion according to St. Matthew

"The End Is Come"</small>

ISAAC.

Yea, father, but my heart beginneth to quake
 To see that sharp sword in your hand!
Why bear ye your sword drawn so?
 Of your countenance I have much wonder!

ABRAHAM.

Ah, Father of Heaven, so great is my woe,
 This child here breaks my heart in sunder!

ISAAC.

Tell me, my dear father, ere that ye cease—
 Bear ye your sword thus drawn for me?

ABRAHAM.

Ah, Isaac, sweet son, peace! peace!
   For in sooth thou breakest my heart in three!

ISAAC.

Now, truly, father, on somewhat ye think
   That ye mourn thus more and more.

ABRAHAM.

Ah, Lord of Heaven, let thy grace down sink,
   For my heart was never half so sore!

ISAAC.

I pray you, father, let me know the truth,
   Whether I shall have any harm or no.

ABRAHAM.

Not yet may I tell thee, sweet son, in sooth,
   My heart is now so full of woe.

ISAAC.

Dear father, I pray you, hide it not from me,
   But some of your thought tell ye me, your son.

ABRAHAM.

Ah, Isaac, Isaac, I must kill thee.

ISAAC.

   (*In a low voice.*)

Kill me, father? Alas, what have I done?

If in aught I have trespassed against you, God knows
   With a rod you may make me full mild—
But with your sharp sword kill me not,
   For in truth, father, I am but a child!

ABRAHAM.

I am full sorry, son, thy blood to spill,
  But truly, my child, it is not as I please.

ISAAC.

  (*Retreating from his father.*)

Now I would to God my mother were here on this
    hill!
  She would kneel for me on both her knees
    To save my life.
And since that my mother is not here,
Change your look, I pray you, father dear,
  And kill me not with your knife!

ABRAHAM.

Forsooth, my son, save I thee kill,
  I should grieve God right sore, I fear.
It is his commandment and also his will
  That I should do this same deed here.
He commanded me, son, for certain
  To make my sacrifice with thy blood.

ISAAC.

  (*After a pause.*)

And is it God's will that I should be slain?

ABRAHAM.

  (*Also pausing, barely able to speak.*)

Yea, truly, Isaac, my son so good,
  And therefore my hands I wring!

  (ISAAC *turns his back to* ABRAHAM, *who stands bowed with grief. He walks apart. A*

Organ:
Grieg:
Peer Gynt Suite:
"Aase's Death"

pause for a count of ten, and the boy comes back, speaking in an older, more subdued voice, with a maturity he has not shown until now.)

ISAAC.

Now, father, against my Lord's decree,
 I will never murmur, loud or still.
He might have sent me a better destiny
 If it had been his will.

ABRAHAM.

Forsooth, son, save this deed I did
 In grievous displeasure our Lord would be.

ISAAC.

 (*Tenderly.*)

Nay, nay, father, God forbid
 That ever ye should grieve him for me!
Ye have other children, not a few,
 Which ye should love well in natural kind.

 (*Going close to his father.*)

I pray you, father, no more your grief renew,
For if I am once dead and gone from you,
 I shall soon be out of your mind.

Therefore do our Lord's bidding,
 And when I am dead, then pray for me.
But, good father, tell ye my mother nothing;
Say that I am in another country dwelling.

ABRAHAM.

Ah, Isaac, Isaac, blessed mayest thou be!

 (*Covering his face.*)

My heart in anguish beginneth to rise
To see the blood of thy blessed body!

ISAAC.

(*Taking his father's hands in his.*)

Father, since it may be no other wise,
Let it pass over, as well as I.

But, father, ere I go unto my death,
I pray you bless me with your hand.

ABRAHAM.

(*Raising his hand as* ISAAC *kneels.*)

Now, Isaac, with all my breath,
  My blessing I give thee upon this land,
  And, verily, God's thereto with this.
Isaac, Isaac, son, rise up and stand,
  Thy fair sweet mouth that I may kiss.

(*He kisses* ISAAC.)

ISAAC.

(*Returning the kiss.*)

Now farewell, father, with soft word
  Greet well my mother as may accord.

ABRAHAM.

Son, thy words make me to weep full sore—
Now, my dear son Isaac, speak no more.

(*He turns* ISAAC *so that the boy's back is toward him.*)

ISAAC.

Ah, my own dear father, wherefore?
  We shall speak here together so little while.

And since that I must needs be dead,
   Yet, my dear father, to you I pray,
Smite but few strokes at my head
   And make an end as soon as ye may!

ABRAHAM.

   (Taking the boy's girdle.)

I must bind thy hands with thong
   Although thou be never so mild—

ISAAC.

Ah, father! I have done ye no wrong!

ABRAHAM.

So thou should'st not resist, my child!

ISAAC.

   (Extending his hands behind him.)

Organ:
Chopin:
Funeral March

Nay, father, I'll not hinder you.
   Do on, for all of me, your will.
The purpose to which ye have set you
   For God's love, hold it steadfast still.

I am full sorry this day to die,
   But yet I wish not my God to grieve.
But, father, I pray you evermore,
   Nothing unto my mother tell.
If she knew it, she would weep full sore,
   For she loveth me, father, in truth, full **well**,
   May God's blessing with her be!

Now farewell, my mother so sweet,
We two are like no more to meet.

ABRAHAM.

> (*Finishing with the thong.*)

Ah, son, my son, thou makest my heart to beat
And with thy words thou doth anguish me!

ISAAC.

I am sorry, sweet father, to grieve you truly;
I cry you mercy for what I have done!
And for all trespass I did you unduly,
Forgive me, dear father, all I have done.

ABRAHAM.

Thou hast been to me a child full good.
But in truth, child, though I mourn
Never so fast,
Yet must I needs here at the last
In this place shed all thy blood.

Therefore, my dear son, here shalt thou lie.
Unto my work I must proceed.
In truth, I as lief were myself should die
If God would be pleased with my deed.

ISAAC.

> (*Kneeling at the altar, his head thrown back.*)

Ah, mercy, father! mourn ye no more.
Your weeping maketh my own heart sore.
Your kerchief, father, about mine eyes wind.

ABRAHAM.

So I shall, sweetest of all my kind.

Organ:	ISAAC.
Chopin:	Now still, good father, have this in mind,
Funeral March	And smite me not often with your sharp sword, But hastily that it be sped!

(ABRAHAM *binds his eyes.*)

ABRAHAM.

Now farewell, my child so full of grace!

ISAAC.

Ah, father, father, turn downward my face!

(ABRAHAM *changes the boy's position so that his head is bowed on the altar.*)

Lord, receive me into Thy hand!

ABRAHAM.

Lo, now is the time come for sure
    That my sword into his neck shall bite.
Ah, Lord, my heart may not this endure.
    I may not find it in my heart to smite!

My heart is not equal thereunto!
    Yet fain would I work my Lord's will,
    But this young innocent lieth so still
    I may not find it in my heart him to kill.
O Father of Heaven, what shall I do?

ISAAC.

Father, heartily I pray you, let me be slain,
    Let me not wait thus till it be done.

ABRAHAM.

Now, my heart, why wouldst thou not break in twain?
    Receive the stroke, my own dear son.

(ABRAHAM *lifts the sword. The* ANGEL *appears.*)

Sharp break in music
Slight pause
Handel:
Xerxes: Largo
Organ.

ANGEL.

Hold!
I am an angel, as thou mayest soon see,
That from heaven to thee is sent.
Our Lord a hundred times thanketh thee
For the keeping of his commandment.
He knoweth thy will and also thine heart,
That thou fearest him above everything,
And to ease of their heaviness a part,
A fair ram yonder I did bring.
Lo! among the briars he standeth tied.

(*A spot can pick up the ram at this point. The lighting does away with the necessity of smuggling the ram into position with possibly humorous effect.*)

Now, Abraham, amend thy mood,
For Isaac, thy young son, here by thy side
This day shall not shed his blood.
Go make thy sacrifice with yon ram.
Now farewell, blessed Abraham,
For unto heaven I now go home.

ABRAHAM.

Organ:
Priests' March from Athalia

(*Following a few steps in the direction the* ANGEL *has taken, his arms upraised.*)

Ah, Lord, I thank thee for thy great grace.
Now I am eased in divers wise.

(*Turning to* ISAAC.)

Arise up, Isaac, my dear son, arise!

Isaac.

Ah, mercy, father, why do ye not smite?
  Ah, smite on, father, once with your knife!

Abraham.

  (*Removing the blindfold and bonds.*)

Peace, my sweet son, let your heart be light,
  For our Lord of Heaven hath granted thy life
    By his angel now,
That thou shalt not die this day, son, truly.

Isaac.

Ah, father, full glad then were I
  If only then this tale were truth!

Abraham.

A hundred times, my son fair as the sky!
  With joy let me kiss thy mouth forsooth!

Isaac.

Ah, my dear father Abraham,
  Will not God be wroth that we do thus?

Abraham.

No, no, surely, my sweet son! for yon same ram
  He hath sent hither down to us.

Yon beast shall die here in thy stead,
  In honor of our Lord, alone!
Go fetch him hither, my child, indeed.

Isaac.

  (*A jubilant child again.*)

Father, I will go catch him by the head,
  And bring yon beast with me anon.

(*He goes toward ram.*)

Ah, sheep, sheep, blessed may thou be!
   That ever thou wert sent down hither!
Thou shalt this day die for me
In worship of the Holy Trinity.
   Now come fast and go we together,
      To my father quick hie!
Though thou be never so gentle and good,
Yet I had liefer thou shouldst shed thy blood,
   In sooth, sheep, than I!
   (*Brings ram to* ABRAHAM.)
Lo, father, I have brought here, full smart,
   This gentle sheep, and him to you I give,
But, Lord God, I thank thee with all my heart,
   For I am glad that I shall live,
      And kiss again once my dear mother!

ABRAHAM.

Now be right merry, my sweet child,
For this quick beast that is so mild
   Here I shall offer before all other.

ISAAC.

   (*Bending to the altar.*)

And I will fast begin to blow,
   This fire shall burn a full good speed.
   (*Turning quickly to study his father's face.*)
But, father, if I stoop down low,
Ye will not kill me with your sword, I trow?

ABRAHAM.

   (*A little shamefaced.*)

No, to fear, sweet son, thou hast surely no need.
   My mourning is past!

Isaac.

> (*Looking nervously at the sword with which* Abraham *is making sacrifice of the ram.*)

Yea, but I would rather that sword were in a fire indeed,
For, father, it maketh me full sore aghast!

Abraham.

> (*Kneeling with* Isaac.)

Now, Lord God of Heaven in Trinity,
Almighty God Omnipotent,
My offering I make in worship of thee,
    And with this quick beast I thee present.
    Lord, receive thou my intent,
As Thou art God and ground of our grace!

Choir:
Seven fold Amen

> (Abraham *and* Isaac *continue to kneel during the Choir's "Amen." At its conclusion,* God *speaks.*)

Voice of God.

> (*Off. The light blazes up on the altar as He speaks.*)

Abraham, Abraham, well mayest thou speed,
    And Isaac, thy young son, thee by!
Truly, Abraham, for this deed,
    I shall multiply of you both the seed
As thick as stars be in the sky.
    Both of greater and less,
And as thick as the sand is in the sea,
So thick multiplied your seed shall be,
    This grant I you for your goodness.

Organ:

Triumphal March from "Judas Maccabeus"

(*The light vanishes from the altar.* ABRAHAM *and* ISAAC *rise as the organ bursts into the Triumphal March from "Judas Maccabeus." They make their way down the aisle as they speak.*)

ISAAC.

Ah, father, I thank our Lord heartily
That so well my wit hath served me
   The Lord God more than my death to fear.

ABRAHAM.

   (*Putting his arm around the boy's shoulders.*)

Why, dear worthy son, wert thou frighted so?

ISAAC.

By my faith, yea, father—If aught I know
   I was never so afraid before.

   (*Looking fearfully over his shoulder.*)

   As I have been on yonder hill!
But by my faith, father, I swear
I will nevermore come there,
   Except it be against my will!

ABRAHAM.

Yea, come on, my own sweet son, even so,
And homeward fast now let us go.

ISAAC.

By my faith, father, thereto I agree!
I had never such good will to go home
   And to speak with my dear mother!

ABRAHAM.

Now go we forth, my blessed son.

ISAAC.

I assent, father, and let us go,
For by my troth, once home, why then
I would never go out like this again. . . .

    (*They go out as the choir begins "He So Loved the World."*)

Organ and Choir:

"God So Loved the World," from Stainer's "Crucifixion"

POEMS

PATERNITY

By William Rose Benét

Not only women dream the future's child
Or children, though such deep desire they bear
For all the rich rewards of motherhood,
They smile in travail; though each girl ungrown
Who sings her dolls uncertain lullabies
Sees infant faces, feels soft arms that cling,
Hears deep within the nursery of her heart
A medley of small mirth adorable,
And, as she grows, mothers all things she loves,
Lacking the little head against her breast
And yearning for it, when she cannot know
Wherefore she yearns. Yet sometimes to a man,
Roughest and sternest though he be of men,
Shocked into strength and pondering, from his young
Exuberance and easy joy, there comes
A longing that convulses all his soul;
And, standing in the wind against some dawn's
Prospect of racing cloud and lightening sky,
Or hard-beset in battle with the world
Deep in the city's stridence, or at pause
Before some new-discovered truth of life,
Unwittingly his hands go out to touch,
Hold off, and scan the youth of him that was,
Thrill to that brighter youth it is decreed

Each father shall inherit from his son.
And, if his hands grope blindly, so his heart,
To hear a young voice at his shoulder speak,
Know young, elastic strides beside his own,
Resolve the problems of an unsullied heart
Flaming to his for counsel. I, scarce-grown
Into my manhood, hovering, hovering still
Over my boyhood (as the gravest, oldest
Of men doth yet, or is no man of men),
Felt my heart tense, and but a noon ago
Strove in quick torture—for no woman's arms,
No woman's eyes, but for a questioning voice
Beside me, and a sturdy little step
In rhythm with mine. A phantom face looked up,
Trusting, round-eyed, alive with curious joy;
And all my being yearned: My son! My son!

FATHER'S LETTER

By Eugene Field

I'm going to write a letter to our oldest boy who went
Out West last spring to practice law and run for president;
I'll tell him all the gossip I guess he'd like to hear,
For he hasn't seen the home folks for going on a year!
Most generally it's Marthy does the writing, but as she
Is suffering with a felon, why the job devolves on me—
So, when the supper things are done and put away tonight,
I'll draw my boots and shed my coat and settle down to write.

I'll tell him crops are looking up, with prospects big for corn,
That, fooling with the barnyard gate, the off-ox hurt his horn;
That the Templar Lodge is doing well—Tim Bennet joined
 last week

When the prohibition candidate for Congress came to speak;
That the old gray woodchuck's living still down in the pasture
    lot,
A-wondering what's become of Little William, like as not!
Oh yes, there's lots of pleasant things and no bad news to tell,
Except that old Bill Graves was sick, but now he's up and well.

Cy Cooper says (but I'll not pass my word that it is so,
For Cy he is some punkins on spinning yarns, you know),
He says that since the freshet, the pickerel are so thick
In Baker's pond you can wade in and kill 'em with a stick!
The Hubbard girls are teaching school, and Widow Cutler's
    Bill
Has taken Ed Baxter's place in Luther Eastman's mill,
Old Deacon Skinner's dog licked Deacon Howard's dog last
    week,
And now there are two lambkins in one flock that will not
    speak.

The yellow rooster froze his feet, a-wadin' through the snow,
And now he leans agin the fence when he starts in to crow;
The chestnut colt that was so skittish when he went away—
I've broke him to the sulky and I drive him every day!
We've got pink window curtains for the front spare room up-
    stairs,
And Lizzie's made new covers for the parlor lounge and chairs;
We've roofed the barn and braced the elm that has the hang-
    bird's nest—
Oh, there's been lots of changes since our William went out
    West!

Old Uncle Enos Packard is getting mighty gay—
He gave Miss Susan Birchard a peach the other day!
His late lamented Sarah hain't been buried nigh a year,

So his purring 'round Miss Susan causes criticism here.
At the donation party, the minister opined
That, if he'd half suspicioned what was coming he'd resigned;
For, though they brought him slippers like he was a centipede,
His pantry was depleted by the consequential feed!

These are the things I'll write him—our boy that's in the West;
And I'll tell him how we miss him—his mother and the rest;
Why, we never have an apple pie that Mother doesn't say:
"He liked it so— I wish that he could have a piece today."
I'll tell him we are prospering, and hope he is the same—
That we hope he'll have no trouble getting on to wealth and fame;
And just before I write "Good-by from Father and the rest"
I'll say that "Mother sends her love" and that will please him best.

For when *I* went away from home, the weekly news I heard
Was nothing to the tenderness I found in that one word—
The sacred name of Mother—why, even now as then,
The thought brings back the saintly face, the gracious love again;
And in my bosom seems to come a peace that is divine,
As if an angel spirit communed awhile with mine;
And one man's heart is strengthened by the message from above,
The earth seems nearer heaven when "Mother sends her love."

THE TOYS

By Coventry Patmore

My little Son, who looked from thoughtful eyes,
And moved and spoke in quiet grown-up wise,

Having my law the seventh time disobeyed,
I struck him, and dismissed
With hard words and unkissed,
—His Mother, who was patient, being dead.
Then, fearing lest his grief should hinder sleep,
I visited his bed,
But found him slumbering deep,
With darkened eyelids, and their lashes yet
From his late sobbing wet.
And I, with moan,
Kissing away his tears, left others of my own;
For, on a table drawn beside his head,
He had put, within his reach,
A box of counters and a red-veined stone,
A piece of glass abraded by the beach,
And six or seven shells,
A bottle with bluebells,
And two French copper coins, ranged there with careful art,
To comfort his sad heart.
So when that night I prayed
To God, I wept, and said:
Ah, when at last we lie with trancèd breath,
Not vexing Thee in death,
And Thou rememberest of what toys
We made our joys,
How weakly understood
Thy great commanded good,
Then, fatherly not less
Than I, whom Thou hast moulded from the clay,
Thou'lt leave Thy wrath, and say:
"I will be sorry for their childishness."

MAGIC FIRE

By Robert Haven Schauffler

A candle suddenly pierced the night
Where our young curlyhead lay sleeping.
He woke, half dazzled by the light;
Then we saw creeping
Into the mystery of those sleep-dimmed eyes
The dawn of deep surprise,
As he beheld the draught-blown flicker leaping.

He crowed and clapped his hands in ecstasy
And held them forth to capture
And to caress that thing of rapture.
Thereat, in the exuberance of his pleasure,
Swaying he rose and trod a rude, instinctive measure.
So, on the earthen floor
Of his primæval dwelling,
Might dance a stone-age man in Labrador.

And then, as we
Watched our light-drunken boy
And felt his gaiety upwelling,
Faintly we seemed to hear
Vibrating down the ages, wild and clear,
Reverberations of the primal joy
Our savage fathers knew when first
Into a bleak and groping world there came,
And on their bodies beat,
The power and glory of Promethean heat,
And on their spirits burst
The magic flower of flame;
And life surged half a heaven higher

As man began his awed, ecstatic dance
Around that new-born radiance,
His first home fire.

From IN MEMORIAM

By Alfred, Lord Tennyson

How many a father have I seen,
  A sober man, among his boys,
  Whose youth was full of foolish noise,
Who wears his manhood hale and green:

And dare we to this fancy give,
  That had the wild oat not been sown,
  The soil, left barren, scarce had grown
To grain by which a man may live?

Or, if we held the doctrine sound
  For life outliving heats of youth,
  Yet who would preach it as a truth
To those that eddy round and round?

Hold thou the good: define it well:
  For fear divine Philosophy
  Should push beyond her mark, and be
Procuress to the Lords of Hell.

From TINTERN ABBEY

By William Wordsworth

That best portion of a good man's life,
His little nameless, unremembered acts
Of kindness and of love.

CHILD'S PLAY

By Mildred Focht

On the grass sat Two-years-old:
Through the leaves a spot of gold
Danced upon her small dark head.
Two-years-old was very still;
Only to herself she said
In the way that children will,
Something in a chanting round,
Fascinated by the sound.

Curiously I strained my ears:
Then I could not see for tears.
What the baby said was this,
Making of the words a play:
"He is dead, my father is,
  Dead and gone away;
He is dead, my father is,
  Dead and gone away."

From THE FIRESIDE

By Nathaniel Cotton

If solid happiness we prize,
Within our breast this jewel lies;
  And they are fools who roam:
The world has nothing to bestow;
From our own selves our joys must flow,
  And that dear hut,—our home.

From TO DR. BLACKLOCK

By Robert Burns

To make a happy fire-side clime
  To weans and wife,
That's the true pathos and sublime
  Of human life.

From CHRISTABEL

By Samuel Taylor Coleridge

A little child, a limber elf,
Singing, dancing to itself,
A fairy thing with red round cheeks
That always finds, and never seeks,
Makes such a vision to the sight
As fills a father's eyes with light;
And pleasures flow in so thick and fast
Upon his heart, that he at last
Must needs express his love's excess
With words of unmeant bitterness.

WISHES FOR MY SON

(Born on St. Cecilia's Day, 1922)

By Thomas MacDonagh

Now, my son, is life for you,
And I wish you joy of it,—
Joy of power in all you do,
Deeper passion, better wit

Than I had who had enough,
Quicker life and length thereof,
More of every gift but love.

Love I have beyond all men,
Love that now you share with me—
What have I to wish you then
But that you be good and free,
And that God to you may give
Grace in stronger days to live?

For I wish you more than I
Ever knew of glorious deed,
Though no rapture passed me by
That an eager heart could heed,
Though I followed heights and sought
Things the sequel never brought:

Wild and perilous holy things
Flaming with a martyr's blood,
And the joy that laughs and sings
Where a foe must be withstood,
Joy of headlong happy chance
Leading on the battle dance.

But I found no enemy,
No man in a world of wrong,
That Christ's word of charity
Did not render clean and strong—
Who was I to judge my kind,
Blindest groper of the blind?

God to you may give the sight
And the clear undoubting strength,

Wars to knit for single right,
Freedom's war to knit at length,
And to win, through wrath and strife,
To the sequel of my life.

But for you, so small and young,
Born on St. Cecilia's Day,
I in more harmonious song
Now for nearer joys should pray—
Simple joys: the natural growth
Of your childhood and your youth,
Courage, innocence, and truth:

These for you, so small and young,
In your hand and heart and tongue.

GROWTH

By Helen Welshimer

He can not be a child forever, God,
Who walks my way, hand fast within my hand.
Nor would I have him stay a little boy.
Instead, I pray that some day he may stand
With body tall and strong and arrow-straight,
With clear eyes looking bravely at a task.
But more than that his body finds its height,
And that his step is light and free, I ask

That he may keep the sturdiness of heart
He has today, and that his soul may grow
In stature as his body waxes strong,
Until the little lad whom I love so

Will come to know brawn does not make a man.
Maturity goes deeper—after all
A gallant body does not matter much
Unless the soul it houses can grow tall.

ESSAYS

FATHERS AS PALS
By James Peter Warbasse

"Father, when will you be able to come and go sailing with us?" breathlessly called my seven-year-old enthusiast.

"When I'm through my work," I answered him simply.

"That will be never," I heard him say disappointedly.

Before very long he came upstairs again, with his friend Frankie, this time with a sea gull in his arms. It had a broken wing.

"Dad, can't you put a splint on it like you did when Mother broke her arm?"

I did. Two earnest boys watched the surgical act. Relieved, they departed with their gull.

We can share the absorbing interests of our children. We can set aside our work. We can participate in their play. But is that being a pal? Are not pals equals? Must there not be a similarity of interests as well as equality of power between pals? Can fathers really be pals with their children?

The talk about a man being just a larger kind of boy sounds well, but no father acts as if it were a fact. How can a father be the pal of a person to whom he is a high authority?

Parents want to guide, influence, correct, and generally engineer the affairs of children, for the reason that parents regard themselves as superior and because the desire to dominate is innate in the human character. The grownup wants his own liberty, but he really does not want his child to have liberty.

Every child grows up with the recollection of coercions—recent or remote. He resents having been thwarted in the attainment of his desires. Why should he be made to put on a muffler when his mother feels a draft? Why should he be made to go to school, to bed, to dancing class in violation of his liberties? A child's idea of a grownup is a bossy person who tells others what to do.

On the other hand, the child has a sense of security in the knowledge that someone is watching over him, taking care of him. He has a private god of his own who is essentially concerned with his welfare. He finds a certain pride also in this relation. When a boy boasts that his father is bigger than the moon, he is indulging in a sort of lunacy which is characteristic not only of children but of many others to whom such ideas give comfort.

It would be wonderfully good for us if our children would honestly tell us what kind of pals they think we are, or whether they think of us as pals at all.

I once asked a father: "Why do you want to be the pal of your son?" The dreadful answer was: "To do him good." He was a real evangelist with his son. He was more concerned about trying to make a certain kind of character out of him than he was in associating with him for the sheer joy of companionship. The mother, too, was quite the same. "Go with son this afternoon," she said to her husband, "it is so good for him to be with you." The father starts off with the boy, carrying in his breast the exalted passion to be a noble example. He tries to illustrate the high qualities of character which he would like to see his son develop. He tries to exemplify to the boy the great virtues—punctuality, honesty, prudence, resourcefulness, kindness, observation, and use of correct language. All this he covers with the misty garment of a careless comradeship with the boy.

Once when a father held up as a horrible example to his boys a man who was an idler, who preferred loafing and smoking and sailing boats and wasting his time generally to good hard work, his blue-eyed, golden-haired son looked up at him when he had finished his vivid story of this idler's bad end and said, "That suits me; that's just what I'd like to do, Daddy." Children big and little see through us older folk and our poses.

I do not depreciate the moralities one jot. I am for them; I should like to see them grow and thrive in our youth. However, if I were a boy going off for a day of recreation, the last sort of person in the world I should want to take with me would be a person who hoped to do me good. He might be successful as a pest, but not as a pal.

But there is another side—a very different side of the picture. There is a relation between the father and children which may hold for each of them something even better than palship. It is a relation which acknowledges the differences between them. Each recognizes certain superiorities in the other and each accepts in a spirit of friendly charity certain deficiencies.

Such a relation between a father and his children is based on a foundation of mutual consideration. Kindness and modesty are the materials out of which real understanding is built. Sincerity and affection closely cement this structure.

I have often had a youngster hurl himself into my arms from a height, or swing himself to my grasp, at the imminent peril of his life, because he had confidence in me, a confidence that he would never repose in a pal. I was recognized as something reliable, trustworthy and staunch. He knew I was there to be depended upon. This is not palship; it is something more.

On the other hand, I overheard a son of mine saying to a group of his pals proudly, "My sister can stunt any of you fellows." The confidence he had in his sister's skill was that between equals. The confidence he has in his father is that which one places in superiors.

Children frankly recognize their equals and their superiors in school, or in any matching of strength, skill or wits. They just as honestly respect the real superiority of their fathers. They evaluate this knowledge and experience. We parents do not need to place ourselves on a pedestal. Children know our real worth.

I have enjoyed the satisfaction of being more than a pal. I was once the expert. I taught my six fellows a multitude of tricks: to swim, sail, dive, ride, skate, ski, play tennis, live in the woods—to do a lot of things. Now, as I find myself surpassed one by one in these fields, I recognize them as the experts, more proficient than I. And this I admit with satisfaction.

I do not regret that they seek pals among those more like themselves in age and skill. For me the important fact remains that I have never stopped doing these things with them, and we both still find joy in them together.

The same differences exist between father and sons in the realm of the intellect. The important thing for a father is to be honest with himself and his children.

FOR FATHERS ONLY

By Benjamin H. Carroll

One of fatherhood's chief pleasures, I anticipated before the birth of our first child, would be to rush home from business every evening for an hour's romp with the baby before his bedtime.

It was with considerable shock that I discovered, within a few months after the arrival of the son of whom I was so proud, that this anticipated pleasure quickly reached satiation point, by which time father was confronted with one of his first problems of parenthood: baby was monopolizing all of his leisure hours at home, with obvious detriment to both baby and father. Babies undeniably are the most fascinating creatures in the world but, when one doesn't give you an opportunity to draw a deep breath without howling for more attention, his charm begins to wear a bit thin. And my son rapidly reached the stage where he demanded that father portray all of the acts of a three-ring circus, with a few of the more strenuous sideshows as added attractions, as his daily measure of amusement. If father sat down puffing, baby would use him as a sort of gymnasium apparatus on which to do acrobatics, most of them being performed with his feet in his hapless parent's face.

This in itself was a fairly serious problem for a father whose nerves are frequently frayed by an exhausting day at the office and certainly not soothed by an hour of such strenuous romping. But there was the more important problem presented by the fact that my son, having no playmates of his own age and encouraged by my own short-sightedness, was becoming entirely dependent on me for his amusement.

I had seen the undesirable result of such a situation develop in the home of a friend, father of a boy four years older than my son. When this child was at the toddling stage, I had observed with somewhat sentimental envy how he gleefully forced his father to romp by the hour, demanding his complete attention. This must be great fun, I thought, until the child's demands on his father's time became so insistent that any deviation from the daily schedule brought on a tantrum and father was reduced to sneaking from the house every morning in order to prevent a display of temper.

Let sweet sentiment be hanged, I decided brutally, when it dawned on me that my own son was rapidly developing the same desire to monopolize all of my spare time. Something should be done about this problem in its early stages, for the sake of both my son and myself. For my son's because he was acquiring all his knowledge of play from an adult, with no encouragement to develop his ability to play alone or with other children; and my increasing irritability because of the demands on my time, might eventually lead him to regard his father as a grouch who had little or no interest in him. For my own sake, because I realized I was becoming increasingly susceptible to irritation.

Solution of the problem was not easy to find, however, and

before I had succeeded in developing one which I thought would prove workable, circumstances accidentally eliminated a major part of the cause: first, the arrival of our second baby; second, our removal to a neighborhood where there are several children of our son's age. With the aid of these factors, it became a relatively simple matter to complete the cure of the "father complex" my son was acquiring and, more important, to prevent its occurrence with the second child. Baby sister's advent diverted considerable attention from Johnny and now I am careful to see that neither child gets a larger share of my attention. His natural interest in and fondness for the baby has been encouraged with the result that there have been few instances when he has shown resentment at being compelled to share father's attentions with her.

Gradually, I discouraged what had become a daily ceremony of greeting me on my arrival home, the sound of the car in the drive being the signal for the beginning of the day's fun for Johnny. Now my greeting is more casual and divided equally between Johnny and his sister. The next step was to hang out the "welcome" sign for all the children in the neighborhood and our lawn has become their play headquarters, to Johnny's great delight. Frequently he is too absorbed in fascinating play to do more than hurriedly return my greeting when I arrive home in the evening.

We have given our son toys with which he can do things—fitted blocks, sand-box, hammer and nails, and velocipede. They have proved excellent substitutes for the acrobatic games we used to play. Not only does he play alone when he is indoors on rainy days but he has learned to share his toys, without adult prompting, with the children who gather in the yard on sunny days. The program is rounded out with a special treat once or twice each week. Johnny is taken along when father goes to town in the car on an errand or is taken for a ride about the neighborhood in his coaster wagon. Recently we have begun including sister in these excursions.

Needless to say, Johnny enjoys these outings doubly because father's undivided attention is not lavished on him so frequently. The result is that I'm working at the part-time job of being a father with all the enthusiasm and pleasure I had anticipated but I'm no longer an unwilling, full-time slave to my son.

FATHER'S DAY

Editorial in *Woman's Home Companion*

"Don't try to surprise me—just give me what I want and that will be surprise enough." So ran a cartoon of husband to wife in a metropolitan newspaper. An echo of regret for man's neglect upon the hearth sounds too in a recent letter from a COMPANION reader:

"I really think the fathers make more sacrifices than mothers do and nothing is thought of it. I must be truthful and say the same thing happens in my own family. I get lots more attention than he does and I do feel so sorry about it for every day is Mother's Day in our home. It isn't that the children do not love their father as much, but he really discourages gifts to him and they rather neglect him."

This wise and fond wife urges us to try to work up more sentiment for Father's Day. But we do not feel that is the solution, for it has always seemed to us unwise to make an annual and exceptional event of what should be everyday sentiment. It's like going to church once a year, telling the truth once a year, speaking kindly to your child once a year. The happiest parents are those whose children manifest affection and friendly regard and respect in all those ways of daily life that add up to such a tremendous total. Father's day and Mother's day should both be every day like the weather—not once a year like taxes.

FOR FATHERS ONLY

By Ethel Kawin

Father seems to be coming into his own these days so far as sharing the fun along with the responsibilities of bringing up children. Gone are the days when child training was considered entirely "mother's job." It is now generally conceded that fathers have an important rôle to play in the family drama. Yet many fathers—and some mothers—still feel that when the children are very little, in babyhood and young childhood, father's influence is hardly needed, that it is only as children grow older and become more companionable that father can be expected to take much of an interest in them.

A recent study conducted by the Behavior Research Fund at the Institute for Juvenile Research has important data to bring to bear here. The study concerned social adjustment in two hundred and fifty children of preschool age and it uncovered many interesting points. For instance, it was found quite possible to group the children—who ranged in age from about two to seven years—into youngsters who were socially well adjusted in their relationships to other children outside their own families, children who presented problems of social adjustment in such relationships, and children who were neither outstandingly well adjusted nor unadjusted. By means of this study it was hoped to discover, if possible, what are the elements in the make-up of the child himself, in his environment, or in his experience and training, which help him or hinder him in adjusting happily to his fellows. Sex, age, general physical condition, and intelligence of each child were, of course, taken into account. In regard to the family situation, the number of children was considered, the child's place in the family and his relationships to his brothers and sisters. As to his parents, attention was given to their ages, the amount of education they had had, and their national origins.

The social and economic situation of each family was analyzed through such facts as the occupation of the father, the family's financial dependence or independence, and the type of living quarters which they had.

Less concrete qualities of family background were also given consideration, such as the relationship of the father to the children, his attitudes toward them, and the agreement between the parents in regard to child training. Attention was also given to the amount of previous opportunity the child had had for play with other children, the age at which he had entered a nursery school or kindergarten, and any personality and behavior problems other than those of social behavior.

It seemed that any or all of these items listed above might conceivably be related to whether or not a young child gets on well socially with his playmates. But results seemed to indicate that the only factors which appear to be significantly related to the social adjustment of a young child are the intelligence of the child, the social-economic status of the family as represented by the occupation of the father, *the relationship of the father to the child and his attitudes toward the child,* and the agreement of the parents in regard to child training.

To find that the father's relationships and attitudes are significant factors in the small child's adjustment to other children is especially impressive in view of the fact that so few of the other nineteen items considered appear to be significant to the child's social adjustment.

What type of father-child relationship, you may ask, appears to help the child in his ability to get on with other children? The attitudes of the fathers in the cases studied were grouped under three types: "Father present in home but seldom sees children"; "Father has 'negative' attitude"; "Father shows 'positive' interest in children." There were also other cases in which the father was not present in the home (being either dead or away), and also cases in which the child was living away from his parents, either with relatives or in an institution.

"Father present but seldom sees children" included fathers who were absent from town for long periods of time, or fathers who reached home late and did not see much of their children. In other words, they were fathers who did not seem to play a very vital rôle in the lives of their young children. "Father has 'negative' attitude" included fathers who were reported by their wives as "not wanting to have the children around," or those who "prefer not to be bothered" with the youngsters; and in that group were even some fathers who seemed to show open dislike for their children. Fathers who "show a positive interest," however, were fathers who regularly spent some time with the children, played with them, helped put them to bed, or who took them out frequently for walks and other recreation.

Information regarding the relationship of the father to the child was necessarily based, to a considerable extent, on the mothers' statements, since there was not always opportunity to make contact with the fathers themselves. In many instances, however, those engaged in the study did meet the father, observed him in the home with his children, or heard reports of him from others who were members of the household or had some close relationship to the family. Frequently conversations with the child himself revealed, openly or by subtle implication, interesting and unsuspected aspects of the father-child relationship. Although one realizes that most fathers are also deeply interested in the welfare of their children, by a surprising number of intelligent fathers the care of the child, during the preschool years at least, is considered the mother's responsibility. They hope *later* to be companionable with their boys and girls, but—to be quite frank—they feel a bit "foolish" when they try to descend to the level of the preschool child's play. Mothers in discussing family situations reveal these paternal attitudes in various ways.

For example: "Suburban life does have its drawbacks," says

Mrs. White. "Mr. White is a very busy attorney; he rarely gets home much before the children's bedtime, and of course Saturday afternoons and Sundays he does like his golf. He says some day the boys will be old enough to go round the links with him, but meanwhile he considers that their weekend recreation is my job."

Fortunately, however, there are many instances where the father appears to have a very vital relationship to his youngster. Mothers often say, "We have a good many pleasant social contacts, but we don't go out to dinner more than two or three evenings a week. My husband says he has too little time with the children; he likes to read to them for a bit and put them to bed himself frequently." Then there are many fathers like the daddy who helps his four-year-old son to construct a tower of blocks that is just a little too difficult for the child to master by himself, or plays a game with his three-year-old daughter.

Turning again to the results of the study—it was found that among the fifty children who got along especially well with other children, there were *none* whose fathers showed "negative" attitudes toward their children. These well-adjusted children also had a very much higher percentage of fathers who showed a "positive" interest in them than did the one hundred children who presented problems in their social relationships, and a somewhat higher percentage than did the hundred whose social behavior was neither especially good nor bad. The children who were socially difficult had a larger proportion of fathers who were "absent or dead," and of fathers who were "present, but seldom sees child" than did the other children. In other words, his father's attitude toward him apparently has much to do with a youngster's social success.

One cannot, of course, help wondering why a father's relationship to his child and his agreements with his wife in regard to the child's training should affect the child's ability to get on well with playmates. On this point one can only conjecture, but here is what seems a logical explanation. One of the essential foundations for the successful adjustment of any human being is that he or she have a feeling of security. Very young children must have their feeling of security supplied from outside themselves; it comes to them chiefly from the affectionate care and protection of parents who provide for their children's needs in these early years when youngsters cannot protect and care for themselves. It also seems reasonable that parents must present a "united front" to the child, if they want him to feel secure.

It seems evident that the youngster who feels that his father is both a kindly protector and a friend can face the world with equanimity. He isn't afraid of his playmates, nor does he have to bolster up any feeling of insecurity by dominating them. Therefore, he gets on socially—other things being equal.

But of course other things aren't always equal. The study cited shows that at least three other factors play a rôle—parental agreement on questions of child training, occupation of father (as an index of the social and economic status of the family), and the intelligence of the child himself. In other words, this study indicates that a young child's social adjustment is related to a group of factors that are found in the child's own make-up and his life-situation.

To sum up—the mere fact that a child is intelligent will probably not mean that his adjustment to other children will be good. But if he possesses intelligence, also comes from a family of good social background, and has a father who spends considerable time with him and has constructive attitudes toward him, the chances that the child will get on well with his fellows are excellent.

Celebrations for Hallowe'en

PLAYS

MYSTERY AT HALLOWE'EN *

By Margaret Parsons

CAST

Mrs. Morris
Sidney Morris
Ruth Morris
Ann
Bill
Jack
Howard
Jane
Rachel
Marjorie
Helen
David
Myron
Frank Hastings

SCENE: *Dining or living room in Morris home on Hallowe'en, a few minutes before 8 o'clock. There are Hallowe'en decorations of orange and black paper, streamers, black cats, etc. Doors center leading to another room and down right leading to hall. Down left is table or sideboard on which are cups and*

---

* This play may be presented by amateur actors upon payment of $4 for each performance if admission is charged, or of $2 for each performance if no admission is charged, to be sent on or before the day of the performance to (Mrs.) Margaret Parsons, 6 Leicester Street, Auburn, Mass.

saucers to be used later. Up left is mantel (or table) on which is an ivory elephant or some similar small art object. Divan left, and six or seven chairs left and back. Down left are two chairs and a tabouret on which is a cigarette box of silver or other valuable material. The telephone is in the back room, with a long cord so it can be brought on.

COSTUMES: *All are in fancy dress costumes suitable for a Hallowe'en party, except* MRS. MORRIS *and* FRANK HASTINGS. RUTH *and* SID *have costumes not too incongruous with the playlet they are to stage as part of their mystery game.* ANN *is dressed as a gypsy,* BILL *and* JACK *as bums. There should be a witch and a spook among the guests. They carry noise makers and those paper toys which unroll as one blows them.*

NOTE: *It is of utmost importance that the tone of the play should be kept light and jolly, with Hallowe'en merriment and with laughs always near the surface. There is not a serious note until* ANN *unmasks.*

Curtain rises on an empty stage. RUTH *in costume enters with tray containing Hallowe'en paper napkins and two dozen silver spoons, goes to table down left and starts arranging them. Enter* MRS. MORRIS *with dish of candy which she sets on mantel or table upper right.*

MRS. MORRIS. How are you getting along, Ruth?

RUTH. Fine. Everything is about ready.

MRS. MORRIS. Why don't you bring in those spoons later when you are ready to serve?

RUTH. Oh, they have to be here now. We are using them for a game.

MRS. MORRIS. Dear me, don't get rough with them. You know they are rather handsome spoons and I'd hate to have anything happen to them. They were a wedding present from Aunt Emmeline.

RUTH. Don't worry, Mother dear, we're not going to black our faces with them. It's for a mystery game Sid and I have planned. We think it will be a good ice-breaker, because the guests don't all know each other.

MRS. MORRIS. No, I suppose not.

RUTH. You see, Sid is bringing a couple of fellows from college; and there are some of my high school friends and two or three from the church crowd.

MRS. MORRIS. What's your mystery ice-breaker?

RUTH. It's sort of like that old game of murder we used to play; only we've worked it out a little further. Hallowe'en is just the time for mystery and gruesomeness. We've made up a sort of play where a fellow comes in and steals the silver spoons and then there's a murder, all in these two rooms. Every one trails around and sees what he can, and then a policeman asks them questions. They'll all be masked so they'll have to keep their wits about them.

MRS. MORRIS. That ought to go well. Where is Sid now? (*Starts towards door right.*)

RUTH. He had a date to meet Jack before the party and tell him just what to do. Jack's to be the bum. Sid should be back soon.

MRS. MORRIS. (*At door.*) Here he is now. Hello, Sid. Ruth's in here. (*Exit right.*)

SID. (*Entering right.*) Hello, Sis. Got everything fixed.

RUTH. Fine. Is Jack all set as the bum?

SID. Yes, and Howard's got a real policeman's uniform—isn't that swell?

RUTH. Do they know what to do?

SID. Sure; I took Jack into the lunch cart and explained to him all about the stunt over a cup of coffee and some pie. He'll be all right. How's everything?

RUTH. O.K. Ann is coming as a gypsy and is going to tell fortunes later.

SID. Fine. Say, Ann's so keen on mystery stories, she'll like this mystery stunt.

RUTH. Yeh, she'll love it. (*Bell.*) There they are. Quick. Put your mask on. Here, wait a minute, I've got one for you. (*Picks up a couple of masks from table, fastens* SID's *on and then her own. Enter* MYRON, DAVID, MARJORIE *and* HELEN *right, all in costumes and masks, making a great noise and shooting off their various toys and noise makers.*) Good gracious, I don't know one of you. You're tall enough to be Helen, but I'm not sure.

(*Change line to fit girl.*)

SID. (*At door.*) Here are some more.

(*The rest come on. This scene should be carefully rehearsed and should be very spirited. They are talking, laughing, joking, cutting up, trying to play tricks on each other and they give the impression of general hilarity. After a few minutes,* RUTH *is seen passing out some cards to them, and* SID *gives each a pencil. They quiet down as they look at cards and gradually find seats and go to work.* ANN *and* BILL *are in the two chairs down right, so that we hear their conversation, without hearing that of the other groups.*)

DAVID. Can we take off our masks?

RUTH. Don't you dare. Not for a while.

MARJORIE. My thinker won't work in a mask.

BILL. (*To* ANN.) Jees, some intelligence test!

ANN. Isn't it? I've got the third. (*Writes.*)

BILL. More'n I hev. Say, what's your rig? Gypsy?

ANN. Yes, I'm going to tell fortunes later. You're good as a bum. I noticed the way you slouched in: it was just right.

BILL. (*Perplexed.*) Right? Oh, yes, I get you. Say, will yer tell me fortune? (*Holds out hand.*) What do yer see in that mitt? Plenty of brass?

ANN. (*Looking at it carefully.*) Yes. Brass, and adventure, and here's the love-line—oh, my!

Sid. Here, you two holding hands over in the corner, get on to your job; we're going to collect those cards in a few minutes.

Ann. Oh, all right. Now let's see, the fifth—oh, I've got it.

Bill. Say, can't he give a guy no peace? And you was doin' swell with me fortune.

Ann. Oh, well, I'll finish it later.

Bill. Jees, I think you're a neat little trick. Why, I've paid good dough to dames that make out they know what's comin' and they're flops compared to you.

Ann. I think you're wonderful, too.

Bill. (*Rising to the bait.*) You do?

Ann. Yes, I do. Most fellows would start talking like a bum, and then they'd keep slipping right out of character. But you stay in.

Bill. You've said it. When I sets out to be a bum, I'm a bum.

Ruth. How are you coming? Are you through?

Four or Five. (*Together.*) No!

Marjorie. Where'd you ever think up these? I can't get half of them.

David. Give us more time, will you?

Ruth. Well, all right, keep them until after we do the next stunt.

Helen. Good. I'll need mine all the evening at the rate I'm going.

Ruth. We're going to give you a little mystery scene now, because we don't want everything too plain on Hallowe'en.

Myron. I haven't found anything plain yet—including my partner here.

(*All laugh.*)

Ruth. We're going to test you out as detectives. Come here.

(*Beckoning to* Sid. *He and* Ruth *go into a huddle.*)

Ann. Oh, I just love detective games.

Bill. Don't tell me a swell skirt like you's keen on crime.

ANN. Absolutely. I read every mystery story I can get hold of. I solve most of them, too.

BILL. Aw g'long.

ANN. Yes, I do. That is if the solution is logical. I have a boy friend, too, who's terrible keen. He's an insurance investigator. But he does a lot of private detective work on the side.

BILL. (*Casually.*) That so? Is he here tonight?

ANN. Oh, no, he's older than most of this crowd. Say, I've got to go get my handkerchief. I left it in my coat pocket.

BILL. Where's yer coat? I'll git it for yer. I noticed some girls' coats in the hall when I come in.

ANN. Oh, no, those belong here. Ours are in one of the bedrooms.

BILL. Where's that? Upstairs?

ANN. Yes, but don't bother.

(*Exit right.* BILL *doesn't rise.*)

RUTH. Now we're going to be a young married couple and this is our house. You watch everything we do. You can follow us about if you want to.

HELEN. All over the house?

RUTH. No, just in this room and that one and the hall. (*Points to door center.*)

JANE. Can we unmask?

SID. No, you keep your masks on. You'll have to spot us by our clothes.

(*All are now seated facing table left where* SID *and* RUTH *are.*)

DAVID. Can we take notes?

RUTH. If you want to.

(ANN *comes back and resumes her seat.*)

SID. Well, here I am, little sweetie. (*Chucking her under the chin.*) Long day at the office and all that. Hope dinner's nearly ready. Biscuits not burned.

(*All snicker.*)

RUTH. It's a wonderful dinner, dearie. I can hardly wait to feed it to you.

SID. Well, it's nearly six: let's eat.

RUTH. O.K. (*Knock at door right.*) Who's that?

SID. Hope it's not company.

RUTH. With only two chops and me in my house dress.

SID. I'll go see. (*Goes to door.*) Come in.

JACK. (*As bum slouches in.*) Hello.

SID. Hello, what do you want here?

RUTH. I think you have the wrong house.

JACK. Wrong nothing. (*Produces note and hands it to him.*) Is that your monicker or ain't it—Mr. William McPherson.

SID. That's mine, all right. (*Reads it.*)

RUTH. (*In whisper to* SID.) Why, how could he know your name?

(JACK *looks around room.*)

SID. Dear me, this is from my old friend Danny Darling. I used to know him in Troy. He says to treat this—this gentleman kindly, as he's his uncle's gardener's godson—

RUTH. Kindly? But what does he want?

JACK. (*Rough.*) I want somethin' to eat. That's what I want.

SID. Oh, yes, yes, of course. What can you do for him?

RUTH. Me for him?

SID. Yes, yes, a ham sandwich—

JACK. (*Ugly.*) With mustard—

SID. And a cup of coffee—

JACK. With cream.

RUTH. Well, I'll see what I can find—(*Exit center.*)

SID. Now, my good man, if you'll just sit down—(*Telephone rings three times.*)—excuse me a minute, that's my ring. (*Exit center.*)

ANN. (*To* BILL.) Three rings. Remember that. They're sure to ask it.

BILL. (*Picking up silver cigarette box.*) Have a cig?

(*Looks curiously at box before setting it back.* ANN *watches him.* JACK *looks around room searchingly. His eye lights on the two piles of spoons. He picks up one pile and puts it into pocket.* RUTH *appears at center door.*)

RUTH. Oh, here you are. Your lunch is ready. Come right in here.

(*Both exit center.*)

RACHEL. Let's follow them.

JANE. Come on, then.

(*They all pile pell mell through center door, leaving stage empty. Enter* BILL *right. Takes cigarette box and puts it into pocket. Stealthily goes to mantel or table up center. Takes off ivory elephant or similar object and slips it into other pocket. Enter* JACK *center. Followed by* RACHEL *and* MYRON.)

MYRON. What's he up to now?

RACHEL. He's given the rest the slip. Let's follow him.

BILL. (*Picking spoons off table.*) Quick. Here's the rest of the spoons. Gimme your bunch too.

JACK. Why, who are you?

BILL. I'm yer pal. Don't yer know all crooks in books have pals? I'm it. Sid told me to pal up with yer—

JACK. Oh, all right then. I didn't understand that part of it.

(*Hands him spoons, which he pockets.*)

BILL. Now when they frisk yer, yer won't have nothin'.

JACK. Say, I'm supposed to pull off a murder in there, and I'm stuck. I don't know just how to go about it and I've forgotten what Sid said.

BILL. Come on, I'll show yer.

(*They exit center.*)

MYRON. There, the rest didn't get that pal business at all.

RACHEL. That ought to give us some points on them. Come on, let's not miss the murder.

MYRON. Okie Doke. (*Starts towards door.*) And did you see

the tall one (*Or short one.*) pick up that elephant?

(*Exit center. Shriek offstage center. Then great hullaballoo of voices. Enter* ANN *center. Goes around room noticing what has disappeared. Knock right.*)

ANN. Come in.

(*Enter* HOWARD, *who in his policeman's uniform and mask has been at party since its beginning, but went out when game began.*)

HOWARD. Good evening. I'm Officer Sherlock Holmes. I hear there has been a crime committed here.

ANN. (*Shaking hands.*) How do you do, Mr. Holmes? This is indeed an honor. And how is dear Dr. Watson?

HOWARD. Oh, that little shrimp. I'm tired of him. I polished him off with a dose of chloroform—

ANN. (*Pretending to be shocked.*) Not permanent, I hope—

HOWARD. Oh, no, nicely calculated to last through this evening. Now where's the corpse of this case?

ANN. In there, but I understand they're bringing him in here.

MYRON. (*Offstage.*) Easy there, easy. Don't jounce him.

DAVID. Jounce him well, I say; he deserves it.

(*Enter* MYRON *and* DAVID *carrying* SID. *Lay him on davenport. Others follow, except* BILL, *and group around.*)

HOWARD. I take charge of this case from now on. All be seated, and no one is to leave the room until I give him written permission. (*To* DAVID.) You shouldn't have touched the body. Don't you know *anything*?

RUTH. But it was my doing. He looked *so* uncomfortable on the floor.

(*Everybody laughs.*)

HOWARD. Uncomfortable, my eye!

(JACK *starts to slink out right.*)

RACHEL. Hey, there's the murderer. Catch him.

(HOWARD *strides over, grabs him by collar and brings him back.*)

HOWARD. You stay there. (*Stands him against wall.*) Now I want you all to tell me the whole story just as it happened.

RUTH. (*Wailing.*) Oh, my poor dear husband! How can I live without you?

HOWARD. (*Patting her on back.*) There, there, Madam, be calm, be calm.

MARJORIE. Guess you wouldn't be calm, Cop, if your husband had been bumped off under your very nose.

HOWARD. (*Sternly.*) Madam, I shall commit you for contempt of court. (*Bangs on table.*) Hereafter, I want all of you to address me as *Mr.* Cop. *I must have respect.*

RACHEL. Please, Mr. Cop, I want a drink of water.

HOWARD. Come, come, we must get on with our case. I want something stronger than water, but I'm not going to get it and *neither are you.*

DAVID. Take that.

(NOTE: *Keep this all very light in spirit of fun.*)

HOWARD. Now answer my questions and no *irrelevancies.* At what time did this— (*Pointing to* JACK.) this creature enter the house?

JANE. A few minutes before six.

HOWARD. How do you know?

JANE. Somebody said so.

MARJORIE. Sid said so.

HOWARD. Very good. What did he want?

HELEN. A free feed. He had an introduction from an old friend in Syracuse.

JANE. In Utica.

HELEN. No, it was Syracuse. I particularly noticed.

JANE. But I know it was Utica, because I used to know a girl who lived there, so I remember.

HELEN. Syracuse.

JANE. Utica.

HOWARD. Ladies, ladies—does anyone else know?

DAVID. ⎫
ANN.   ⎬ It was Troy!
MYRON. ⎭
HOWARD. (*Writing.*) Troy wins.
JANE. Oh, well, I have a friend in Troy, too.
HOWARD. Did he get the feed?
MARJORIE. The wife went to get him a ham sandwich—
HELEN. With mustard—
MARJORIE. And the telephone rang—
ANN. It rang three times. He said that was his ring.
MARJORIE. So the husband went to answer it—
HOWARD. Leaving him alone here?
JANE. Yes, and he swiped the spoons off that table.
HOWARD. All of them?
JANE. No, half of them. He took one pile and left the other.
HOWARD. Show me the other. That will be exhibit A.

(JANE *looks for them.*)

JANE. Why, I can't find them. They aren't here.
RUTH. Oh, I'll find them. (*Looks.*) Why, you're right, they *aren't* here.
RACHEL. Oh, go on looking. But when you give up, *we'll* tell you where they are.
HOWARD. Search him, boys.

(DAVID *and* MYRON *search him with great gusto.*)

HOWARD. What do you find?
DAVID. Nothing but one purse—
MYRON. One handkerchief—
DAVID. One jackknife—
MYRON. One pawnshop ticket—
JACK. (*Indignantly.*) It isn't.

(*Everyone laughs.*)

MYRON. My mistake. It's an old parking ticket. He must have slipped his car away while no one was looking.

(*All laugh.*)

HOWARD. Then he has disposed of the spoons somewhere. Perhaps he hid them.

(DAVID *and* HELEN *begin looking for them.*)

RUTH. (*To* JANE, *down left.*) Gee, this game's going over slick! Jack's putting in stuff I never even thought of, like getting rid of the spoons.

HOWARD. Did anyone see him hide the spoons?

RACHEL. Do we get extra credit if we tell what he did with them?

RUTH. You certainly do. Who's we?

MYRON. Rachel and I. We know what he did with them.

HOWARD. Tell us, then.

MYRON. Sure. He gave his spoons to his pal, who had already taken the others.

RUTH. What pal?

RACHEL. Why, the other fellow who was dressed like a bum.

ANN. Where is he now?

MYRON. He must be hiding. Come on, Rachel, let's find him! May we go look, Officer?

HOWARD. Certainly. Now, while they are gone, let's get on to the murder.

(MYRON *and* RACHEL *go off right.*)

HELEN. Well, he demanded money of the husband and the husband refused—

DAVID. So he picked up a paper cutter and stabbed him in the heart—

HELEN. I thought it was in the neck—

HOWARD. (*Impatiently.*) Well, which was it? Which was it?

MARJORIE. Ask the corpse.

SID. (*Lifting his head, in hoarse stage whisper.*) It was the gizzard.

(*All laugh. Enter* MYRON *and* RACHEL *center.*)

MYRON. What's the joke?

RACHEL. We can't find him anywhere.

ANN. (*Coming forward.*) We're having lots of fun, but my private opinion is that this has got beyond the game stage. I think it's serious. I think there's been a real crime committed here tonight. *I* think we ought to unmask. (*Does so.*)

DAVID. So it's Ann Leland, our own little detective fan! We might have known it.

ANN. You can make fun of me if you want to, but this game isn't so funny as it started out to be.

(*All unmask.*)

SID. (*Sitting up.*) What do you mean, Ann?

ANN. Well, who *was* that rough guy? Tell me that.

SID. I don't know. He must be some friend of Ruth's. I didn't know him.

RUTH. But I didn't recognize him either, Sid. I noticed him and thought he was one of your college friends.

ANN. I'd lay money on it he never went to *any* college.

SID. What *are* you hinting at, Ann?

ANN. Well, I think he's a real criminal.

SID. Don't go melodramatic, Ann.

ANN. All right, all right, laugh at me. But who was he?

RUTH. Well, we don't seem to know. I see everyone I invited here.

(MRS. MORRIS *comes to door right and stands looking in.*)

SID. So do I. But that doesn't make him a criminal, Ann. Lots of fellows think it's smart to crash a party.

ANN. All the same, I ask you who is he and where is he and where are your two dozen silver spoons.

MRS. MORRIS. (*Coming forward.*) My silver spoons! Are they gone?

RUTH. It's just a game, Mother. At least we hope it is—

RACHEL. And where's that ivory elephant the other bum slipped into his pocket?

SID. Gee, is that gone too?

ANN. (*Looking at tabouret.*) Yes, and where's that silver

cigarette box that was on this table? I saw him examine that keenly when he offered me a cigarette.

DAVID. (*Grabbing one pocket after another.*) Gosh!

ALL. (*Turn towards him, saying.*) What's the matter? You lost something? etc., etc.

DAVID. My wallet is gone. And I had nine dollars in it.

(*Exit* HELEN *right.*)

SID. But you didn't have it out.

ANN. That bird could pick pockets, or I miss my guess.

RUTH. But this is terrible, to invite you to our house and then have one of our guests pick your pockets.

MARJORIE. Only he apparently wasn't a guest.

ANN. And it looks as though you'd lost the most, Ruth.

MRS. MORRIS. Those are fine old spoons. What can I ever tell Aunt Emmeline?

MARJORIE. Shouldn't we call the police?

SID. I suppose so. But we've so little to go on. We don't know his name and we haven't even seen his face. Would you recognize him, Ann?

ANN. I'd know his voice. I'm sure he wasn't disguising it.

HELEN. (*At center door.*) Girls!

(*All turn as she stands there in distress.*)

MARJORIE. What is it?

HELEN. I went for my compact a while ago and it wasn't there. I thought I must have left it at home, although I seem to remember bringing it. But I've just looked again, and there's not a pocket book on the bed with our things.

JANE. Oh dear, I had the bag Uncle Gerald brought me from Paris!

ANN. When I said I was going to get my handkerchief, he offered to go, and pumped me as to where the girls' coats were.

JANE. Well, if you were so smart and suspected so much, it seems as though you might have done something about it.

ANN. Perhaps I did.

SID. But what *could* she have done? After all, one doesn't accuse a fellow guest of being a pickpocket. Don't be silly, Jane.

HOWARD. Personally, I think Ann's not so goofy as we all make out by teasing her so. Maybe she does know a clue when she sees one.

(*Telephone.* SID *goes to door center.*)

ANN. (*Rising.*) That may be for me, Sid. I'm expecting a call.

MARJORIE. More mystery!

SID. (*Back at door with telephone.*) You're right, Ann, it's for you. Here, I'll bring it in—unless it's private.

ANN. Not at all. (*Takes telephone.*) Hello. Is that you, Frank? . . . Well, what about him? . . . You did? . . . He was? . . . Where are they now? . . . Bring them over here. . . . Yes, we'll be waiting. . . . And you'll certainly be welcome. . . . All right, goodbye.

(*All ask questions at once.*)

HELEN. Who was it?

DAVID. Have they caught him?

MARJORIE. Tell us about it.

(*Etc., etc. the rest ad lib.*)

HOWARD. Just a minute. Just a minute. I'm still conducting this investigation. What's it all about?

ANN. Well, I'll tell you. I did do something about it, Jane, when I suspected there was something phoney about him.

JANE. I'm sorry. Of course you would.

DAVID. But what made you suspect?

ANN. Two things. First his hand when I read his palm. It just didn't look like any college boy's hand that I'd ever—

MYRON. That you'd ever held before.

(*All laugh.*)

SID. Don't interrupt. I want to hear.

ANN. The second thing that made me suspicious was the way he talked. At first I just thought he put it on to go with the bum's outfit he had on. But he was too good.

HELEN. Too good? What do you mean?

ANN. Why, he never slipped out of character. You know, if you've talked good grammar all your life, it's a real effort to use bad, and an occasional "I did it" or "I saw it" will slip by, but not with him. The bad grammar came too easy not to be natural.

SID. You *are* keen, Ann.

MARJORIE. But what did you *do?*

ANN. When I pretended to go for a handkerchief, I called up Frank Hastings. You know he is working up a business as an independent insurance investigator, and he's awfully keen on detective work. He has an idea of sometime having his own bureau which would handle both lines. Well, I asked him if he was doing anything and he said no. So I told him how suspicious I thought this man was and suggested he hang around the house awhile and see if anything happened. I had a hunch the fellow'd leave before we unmasked.

DAVID. And did he?

ANN. Yes, Frank saw him slink away and trailed him. Then Frank picked up a policeman who recognized him as a fellow they've been suspicious of for a long time, but they haven't been able to get anything definite on him. He has the reputation of being a slick pickpocket.

DAVID. (*Patting his empty pocket.*) I'll say he is.

ANN. So he went right to the bus station and found out when the next bus out of town was leaving.

MYRON. Apparently his game was to get to another town and cash in on his loot before they began to look for it here.

MRS. MORRIS. But where is he now? If he once pawns those spoons, they may be melted and we'll never get them back. I've heard that's what they do.

ANN. No, they arrested him as he was getting on the bus and Frank's headed here to see what we recognize.

JANE. I hope he still has my Paris bag!

HELEN. But how did this bird know about our mystery game?

SID. That's what I can't figure out. Did you tell anyone, Ruth?

RUTH. Not a soul. Did you?

SID. Only Jack and Howard here.

JACK. I've an idea.

SID. What is it?

JACK. Do you remember that guy who was having coffee in the lunch cart?

SID. Sure.

JACK. Wasn't he about the build of this one?

SID. That's so, he was. He didn't seem to pay any attention to us, but he stayed until after we left.

JACK. Yes, and come to think of it, he was just finishing his coffee when we got there. I noticed it. And then he took another cup and a third.

SID. Yes, I remember the fellow who was serving us said: "Hungry tonight, Bill, ain't you?"

ANN. And Bill's the name Frank mentioned over the telephone.

SID. That's how he knew. And he even heard you tell me how you were going to dress so that he copied it.

JACK. And you said we were going to keep our masks on until after the mystery stunt.

ANN. He certainly had his nerve with him.

SID. Yes, he took a long chance, but he'd have got away with it if it hadn't been for you, Ann.

DAVID. Yes, he'd have been headed for New Haven or Boston by this time with my nine dollars.

(*Doorbell.*)

SID. That must be Frank now. I'll let him in. (*Exit right.*)

RUTH. Well, I was looking for a little mystery to liven up

the party, but I got more than I bargained for.

HELEN. It sure was a good ice-breaker, Ruth.

MARJORIE. Yes, I feel as if we'd all known each other for ever and ever, after this.

(*Enter* FRANK *and* SID *right*.)

MYRON. Hello, Frank.

MRS. MORRIS. We're certainly glad to see you, Mr. Hastings. Did you find the spoons?

FRANK. We did.

ANN. Nobly done.

FRANK. (*Opening bag.*) This may be a Hallowe'en party, but I'm playing Santa Claus.

DAVID. Hope you've my nine dollars in your pack, Santy.

FRANK. Here are the spoons, Mrs. Morris. Two dozen, I believe.

MRS. MORRIS. Then they're all here. (*Taking them.*)

FRANK. (*Holding up bag.*) And this?

JANE. My Paris bag!

FRANK. (*Taking out a handful of bags and compacts.*) You girls did quite well for him. (*They all take their own with exclamations of relief.*) And here's a cigarette box, and this ivory elephant, and a gold thimble—

MRS. MORRIS. Why, that's mine! He must have picked it out of my basket as he went by. He's a sly one.

JANE. He certainly is.

DAVID. But where's my wallet? Don't tell me he spent my money before you got him!

FRANK. Oh, no, that's in my pocket. Here. (*Gives him wallet.*)

DAVID. Oh, thanks. We certainly do thank you a lot.

SID. Yes, you should get a reward.

FRANK. Thanks, but I already have one.

ANN. What is it, Frank?

FRANK. I've been trying for some time to stand in well with

the police department, because I am more than a little interested in this private detective work. And they're putting me in their records for the work I've done rounding up Bill Banning. It means a lot to me. They've promised to call on me again.

MYRON. I'll say that you and Ann work pretty well together.

HELEN. Yes, you team up very neatly as detectives.

FRANK. That's not the only way we intend to team up together.

MYRON. And what's the meaning of that cryptic remark?

MRS. MORRIS. It wouldn't take any very keen detective to fathom that. And I do think it's pretty fine.

(*Comes down between the two and takes a hand of each in hers and then puts them together.*)

ANN. We've been planning to announce our engagement as soon as Frank's prospects looked a little brighter.

SID. And it's taken Ruth's goofy mystery game to give him a break.

ANN. That and Bill Banning. Let's give credit where credit is due.

SID. Pretty swell, Frank. (*Shaking his hand.*)

RUTH. And I did so want a real surprise for my party.

(*Everybody congratulates the two as*)

THE CURTAIN FALLS

GRANDMA BERRY'S SHEET-AND-PILLOW-CASE PARTY *

By Jean Milne Gower

CHARACTERS

Grandma Berry
Alice Berry, *17 years*
Jack Berry, *19 years*
Billy Berry, *10 years*
Kathleen Hoyt
Jim Joslin
Anna Cole
George Kane
Virginia Wright
Bobby Green
Banker Obadiah Danks
Gerald Danks, *his son*
Dinah Deuteronomy Johnson, *Voice of Mystery*

Time: *Hallowe'en.*

Scene: *Old-fashioned sitting-room of the Berry farmhouse. Cut-outs in black depicting the usual figures of Hallowe'en lore—witches on broom-sticks, owls, bristling cats, etc., backgrounded by the drab faded wall-paper—give the desired atmosphere of mysterious possibilities. Aside from a few occasional chairs, there is no furniture except a three-fold screen which stands near the door down-stage, right, which leads into the entrance hall. Across the room, slightly up-stage, left, a tub of floating apples stands near an open door into the big kitchen. An old-time gramophone, plainly visible, stands just inside, droning*

---

* For permission to produce, $5.00 must be sent to Mrs. John H. Gower, 56 West 70th Street, New York City, N.Y. Special terms will be granted to small groups.

out a weird sort of march as the guests enter, right, from where they have left their wraps in hall. They are met by the family who file in solemnly from the kitchen. They do not speak, however, as a mysterious and sepulchral voice from some unseen source warns them that some frightful doom awaits anyone who betrays his identity to another. They present a grim and ghostly appearance in their sheets, safety-pinned into loose gowns, and with pillow-cases making peaked caps over identical squares of white muslin through which eye-holes have been cut.

VOICE OF MYSTERY. Listen careful, all yo' Spook folkses, to whut the great an' aspired *VOICE* gwyne tell yo'-all! Yo' is all fo'bid by th' ORACLE o' MYST'RY to speak or peek or let any oth' SPOOK know who you is. Iffen yo' do, yo' incurs th' BLACK DOOM—so be it, AMEN. (SPOOKS *groan in unison, with here and there a giggle.*) NOW, choose yo' partners an' march dignified roun' dis-here room three times, den fix yo'-selfs fo' one figure in de ol' Virginny Reel, an' turn yo' rattlin' bones loose like how yo' done when yo' was on dis t'rest'al globe.

(GRANDMA BERRY, *in her ghost costume, has changed the record on gramophone. The dancers get under way, much impeded by their garments but manage to do most of the necessary things, prompted by* VOICE OF MYSTERY *who calls out occasional directions—* "Geml'man on de right, s'loot lady on de lef'."—"Balance to de Ghostes on de far end o' de line."— "Dosey-do' in de middle wid yo' backs to each oder," *and so on, as suggested by director.*)

BILLY. (*Who because of his smallness and special antics has been making himself particularly obvious throughout proceedings, turns a somersault just as the dance is finishing up, and lands down stage close to the footlights and addresses the audience in a stage whisper through cupped hands.*) I think this is a fool way of spendin' Hallowe'en. I'd a sight ruther be takin' off gates, wouldn't you?

VOICE OF MYSTERY. (*Ominously.*) 'Pears lak I heared somebody whusperin'! Any pusson 'at even whuspers is gwine get caught by dat BLACK DOOM whut I done tol' 'bout, ef he don' look out. (*Clock is heard striking in kitchen.*) Ah reckon ol' Pa Time's tellin' yo' Spookses it's nine o'clock an' they's doughnuts an' cider in de pantry so yo'-all can exit out into the kitchen fru de lef'-hand do' opposite to de right-han' do' wha' yo' entered in. Dey's a nice wood flo' out dere wha' you'all can practise up on dis new fangled jazz-swing stuff mortals is goin' crazy 'bout, an' you can dance till yo' etheral—what-yo'-call-it?—'billiments fall off. Yo' caint *take* 'em off, though, nor tell who you is till de clock strikes twelve. Beware! De VOICE OB MYSTERY is done spoke.

(*The ghosts follow directions with creditable dignity, except for* BILLY, *who does an impromptu cake-walk at the end of the procession, and makes a longnose at the audience as he exits and nearly collides with his grandmother, who is changing the record to a modern number. She gives him a more or less playful smack on the portion of his anatomy which Nature has indicated for such chastisement, then re-enters the sitting-room and closes the kitchen door and locks it.*)

GRANDMA BERRY. It's safe now, Dinah; you can come out.

DINAH. (*Emerging from behind screen and fanning herself with her megaphone.*) Did ah done the Voice o' Myst'ry lak yo' wanted it, Mis' Berry?

GRANDMA BERRY. Marvellously, Dinah. No one could have made it more convincing. I'll warrant they're all shaking in their shoes this minute.

DINAH. Ah's guessin' they's doin' some peekin' along wid eatin' they doughnuts an' drinkin' they cider—an' Ah'll bet they's some speakin' goin' on too. Ah bettah hurry in an' give 'em some mo' Doom-stuff.

GRANDMA BERRY. I don't think it will be necessary to rub it

in any more. The novelty of a sheet and pillow-case party has given them a sort of fancy-dress feeling. It was no novelty in my young days, and still it was fun. Suppose we move this tub of apples further away from the door for fear someone may tumble in?

DINAH. Yas 'um. But first Ah'll hide mah meggerphone behind the screen so'st dey'll never cotch on 'bout de Voice. An' Ah'll hang up this Witch o' Endor sign for de fortune-teller booth.

GRANDMA BERRY. Fine. I'd forgotten about that part, and as I have to be the Witch, it should have been uppermost in my mind—but so many things have happened.

(DINAH *hangs up the sign and joins* GRANDMA BERRY, *and they move tub. Enter from entrance hall, right, a tall Ghost. Seeing the two women busy near the opposite door, he slips behind the screen.*)

DINAH. Ah thought, ma'am, yo' seemed awful worried 'bout something. Kin Ah help yo' somehow? Yo' bin so good to Sambo an' me when we was down an' out.

GRANDMA BERRY. You've repaid that over and over, Dinah. I don't know what I'd have done after my son's death five years ago, if it hadn't been for your loyalty.

DINAH. Us didn't do nothin'. We was glad to live where we was treated lak white folks. Yo'-all sure had moughty bad luck—Billy's Ma dyin' when he was borned, an' then his Pa, leavin' you with three kids to bring up—an' you've brung 'em up grand—Miss Alice an' Marse Jackie doin' so fine in town at the Agercultural College an' all.

GRANDMA BERRY. (*Sinking wearily into one of the small chairs and motioning toward another near by.*) Dinah, sit down a minute. I've got to talk to someone or I'm afraid I'll break down and spoil the vacation for Alice and Jack. I've known things were pretty shaky for a long time, but I'd hoped to get an extension on my note at the bank; but Mr. Danks says it's impossible—

DINAH. (*Indignantly.*) Dat long-nosed, skinflintical ol' thing, ridin' round in his shiny cyar w'en quality folks lak yo'-all ride in a rickety ol' buggy wi' lil' Don archin' he naick an' liftin' he feet so dainty-like—

GRANDMA BERRY. Don— Oh, I'd almost forgotten him— We *couldn't* give up faithful old Donnie! I think you are wrong about Mr. Danks— He's just the manager of the bank, and things are in an awful way—they have to consider their investors first. Perhaps, though, he'll think of some way we can keep Donnie and a few of our little treasures, even if the farm has to go. He's always seemed interested in our family.

DINAH. Well, Ah hopes yo're right, Ma'am, but mos' folks says he's harder'n nails. He's got a moughty nice boy though, Marse Gerald—no stuck-uppiness about dat boy iffen he do go to de swelles' college in de United States. An' *has* he got a crush on yo' gal Alice! Oh, boy! He ain't got eyes for nobody else when she's roun'.

GRANDMA BERRY. Nonsense, Dinah. You're imagining things. They are good friends, of course, but I'm sure Alice hasn't any special interest there and, besides, the Danks family will fly much higher for a wife for their son when marrying time comes. (*Rising.*) Well, I suppose we must go out and help make the party a success; though from the sound it seems to be going well. It certainly was an inspiration my digging up out of the musty past this old idea for a frolic. When Alice wrote to ask could she bring a couple of friends from the Agricultural College and give a little party, my heart sank. Though I didn't know then that we were at the end of the rope and would have to give up the farm,—still the refreshments worried me.

DINAH. (*Putting her chair against the wall.*) Yo'd plumb fo'got ouah cidah bar'll an' ol' Aunt Dinah's fried-cakes an' a few mo' things we can spring on them town folks 'at won't cost nothin'. Hi, yi, yi, yi, us done put somepin' ovah tha'!

GRANDMA BERRY. And I'm glad we thought to have the guests dress at home so they needn't see our worn-out sheets.

DINAH. Saves me a right smart lot o' laundryin' too.

GRANDMA BERRY. (*Glancing wistfully around the witch-decorated walls.*) At least we are leaving unusual murals for our successors. I wonder what sort of people they'll think have been living here.

DINAH. (*Grimly.*) An' Ah'm wonderin' whut 'at nice Danks boy's gwine think w'en he fin's out whut dirt he's Pa's done yo-all—an' w'en he fin' th' gal he loves caint go back to college— (*Wipes her eyes on corner of her apron.*)

GRANDMA BERRY. Nonsense, Dinah dear! Cheer up! Banker Danks simply adores his only son and Alice is too good a sport ever to let him know his father was in any way to blame—which I really don't think he was. Besides, she and Jack can probably work their way through the rest of their college course; you, Sambo and I can run a doughnut stand and Billy can sell newspapers. We'll all stick together and something's sure to turn up.

DINAH. Mebbe some meracle'll up an' happen—wid all dese yere sperits 'round.

GRANDMA BERRY. That's so, Dinah. Although tonight is celebrated as a sort of pagan festival, tomorrow is the Feast of All Saints when the *real* spirits of the *blest* are all about us. We will all go to church, and who knows what blessing may come in answer to our prayers?

DINAH. (*Devoutly.*) Yo'-all sho' deserve God's blessin', Amen. (*Turning to door.*) Now Ah reckon Ah better be gittin' back on mah job in de pantry.

GRANDMA BERRY. (*Adjusting her mask.*) And I'd better turn back into a ghost and see how things are going.

(*They open the door into the kitchen and close it after them. As the door closes,* BANKER DANKS *in ghostly attire, but without mask, emerges from behind screen. He looks* about nervously, takes a note-book from his pocket, writes a short note and tears out the sheet.)

BANKER DANKS. (*Aloud to himself.*) Where can I put it? (*Noticing the megaphone as he peers around screen.*) That's it! I'll put it in the megaphone. They'll probably not use it again tonight. Gerald must *never* know I—

(*Enter stealthily from right,* GERALD DANKS. *He is in dinner jacket and carries over his arm a sheet and pillowcase. He stares in amazement at his father who is placing the megaphone behind the screen.*)

GERALD. (*Joining him near screen.*) DAD! Well, I'll be hanged! What the dickens are you doing in that rig? And whose body are you hiding? "The Witch of Endor"? What goes *on* here! Have you been burying widows and children or burning up witches?

BANKER DANKS. (*Glancing round in great confusion.*) Sh-h-h-h— I was just going to hide the megaphone—so—so that people wouldn't blow it. They make me nervous, you know— Got to get out— (*Hurries toward door, down stage, right, mumbling to himself.*) Mustn't know how near—

GERALD. (*Following and detaining him.*) Dad! What's the matter with you? Do you feel all right?

BANKER DANKS. Of course, Son, only I've got to get home. Mother'll be worrying—

GERALD. Mother! Doesn't she know where you are?

BANKER DANKS. No. You see she ran across the street to sit a while with Aunt Hattie. Then your wire came to say your train was in a wash-out and when I saw your sheet and pillowcase all spread out on your bed, with the safety-pins and mask ready, it kinda made me homesick for old times. Mother'd never understand—being city-bred—so I—

GERALD. (*Slapping him on the back.*) You old skeesiks, you! Running out on the Mater! And now I know what happened to my ghost outfit. I had to grab anything I could find in the linen closet and I quite forgot pins and a mask.

BANKER DANKS. But how'd you get here, son?

GERALD. (*Grinning.*) Hitch-hiked. Held up an old guy with a high-powered car and bribed him to break the traffic laws. But, say, Dad, if you really do want to escape without busting any banking traditions and getting onto the front page to outrage Mum's sense of the proprieties, why don't you peel out of that outfit and let me climb in—mask, pins and all?

BANKER DANKS. (*Relieved, acts on suggestion and drops his disguise on floor.*) That's the ticket. I'll just slip into the hall, put on my overcoat and vanish, while you join that crazy bunch in the kitchen, and they'll never know the difference. Lucky we're about the same height.

GERALD. (*Dragging up a chair to middle of room and placing his own sheet and pillow-case on it while he struggles to adjust the other ones.*) Now, Dad, you'd better beat it while the beating's good. I'll never give you away, old pal, even if it's ever discovered that you've murdered the Witch of Endor and concealed the remains in a megaphone.

BANKER DANKS. (*Backing out through the door, right, with a queer expression on his long-nosed, wrinkled face.*) I may have to hold you to that some day, son.

(*He exits and closes the door softly just as the opposite door from kitchen opens and* ALICE *enters. She pauses and regards the half-costumed* GERALD *with amazement, as she pushes back her own mask and closes the door before speaking.*)

ALICE. Why, Gerald Danks, what in creation are you doing? I thought I saw a tall lanky spook sneaking out through the scullery but I never guessed it was you—in fact I haven't been able to spot you all the evening—

GERALD. (*Roaring with laughter.*) Haven't you, darling? That's queer, I've been with you every minute of the day— whirling toward you, I mean, in the spirit—

ALICE. Do be sensible. And hurry; they'll miss us. And don't make such a noise!

GERALD. Then come, Honey, and help me into this darned thing again—there was a pin sticking me or something, and I seem to have grown younger and thinner so it's too loose.

ALICE. (*Puzzled.*) Younger? And thinner? Any reflection on Dinah's doughnuts?

GERALD. Gosh, has she made doughnuts? Lead me to 'em. (*Realising his error.*) I mean lead me to some more of 'em.

ALICE. (*Impatient.*) You sound like a Gracie Allen broadcast, Gerry. What's the matter with you? (*Discovering the second sheet and pillow-case on chair.*) And why on earth did you bring two sheets and pillow-cases?

GERALD. (*With impressive dignity.*) I always take *two* sheets and pillow-cases to a party for fear *one* would make me sick.

ALICE. (*Regarding him worriedly.*) Gerry dear, are you sure you're feeling all right?

GERALD. Of course. If I felt any better we'd have to send for a doctor and an ambulance.

ALICE. You—you're sure you haven't been taking—but, no, you haven't had anything but cider.

GERALD. (*Indignant.*) Cider! You wrong me. I haven't had a taste of that demoralizing beverage since I went east to the University.

(*Enter* BILLY, *right.*)

BILLY. (*Righteously shocked.*) Why, Alice Berry an' Gerald Danks, you've looked at each other an' talked to each other an' gone an' broke the spell.

GERALD. You're the young divil that's broken the spell, eh, Alice? We *were* having quite a spell, weren't we?

ALICE. I'm not sure what we were having—or why.

BILLY. Anyhow you've started the awful doom the VOICE OF MYSTERY talked about.

(*Enter,* GRANDMA BERRY *right. Other masked faces ap-*

pear behind her in the doorway.)

GRANDMA BERRY. (*Lifting her mask.*) Well, it looks as though at least two of the Berry family have smashed the Sheet-and-Pillow-case Spook tradition so I'll join them and share the predicted doom.

(*Enter* JACK BERRY *tripping over his sheet.*)

JACK. Guess I'll have to stand by the rest of the Berries— (*Putting his arm around his grandmother.*) They're a tough bunch to beat—excuse my modesty—and I'm with 'em—sink or swim. Here goes my "etheral 'billiments" as Voice of Mystery called 'em. (*He strips off his sheet and pillow-case and speaks to the others gathered at the door.*) Come on in, folks; the water's fine!

(*Enter guests chattering and disposing themselves around the room, taking off their costumes and using short sentences or exclamations as suggested by director of play*—"Good riddance!"—"Thank Fortune!" *etc.*)

BILLY. (*Rolling his garments into a ball and binding it with his mask and a safety-pin.*) Let's play football! Let's play football!

(*He picks it up and hurls it toward the open kitchen door and hits* DINAH *in the tummy as she is about to enter.*)

DINAH. (*Advancing in wrath.*) Yo' Marse Billy, yo'! Jes' fo' dat yo' gwine get busy an' he'p me pick up de fambly an' houseguess' beddin' an' chuck em' in de hamper. (*To the others.*) An' yo' local folkses fold up yo' own things an' rest 'em wid yo' wrops in de hall. (*Grumbling to herself.*) Ah ain't honin' to do no launderin' fo' de neighbors.

GRANDMA BERRY. Why, Dinah, I'm surprised at you—

JACK. Yes, Dinah, this "ain't the way we brung you up." You sound like a Topsy that "jes' growed."

DINAH. (*Weakening.*) Quit yo' clownin', Marse Jackie, an' he'p me an' Marse Billy clean up dis mess. Ev'body git a move on!

(*General activity as directed.*)

BILLY. (*Slowly joining them.*) Have a heart!

KATHLEEN. You come help me, Billy. Dinah's right; we have made a frightful mess and she must be tired out, making all our delicious eats and helping with this perfectly spiffy party. We never had anything like this in town, did we, Anna?

ANNA. Never. Maybe that's why we were such untidy, rambunctious spooks—sort of amateurs—

JIM. And maybe that's why we local boys had the edge on you college folks. We showed some class—especially me.

GEORGE. Oh yeah! Suppose you show some action an' help me fold up this darn sheet. It's about a mile square. I guess Ma musta used the double-bedest one she could find.

JIM. (*Flapping a corner of the sheet helplessly.*) What'll I do?

GEORGE. Gosh, Jim, you're a wash-out! I pity your wife.

JACK. Didn't know he had one. (*Coming to help* GEORGE.)

JIM. No more did I—but that's a detail that can be remedied,—eh, Kathleen?

KATHLEEN. Is this a proposal or a joke?

VIRGINIA. (*From across the room near hall door.*) Who's getting proposed to?

ANNA. We don't know. Kathleen is trying to find out. Trust her!

JACK. (*Crossing to* VIRGINIA.) And how's our little local belle getting along? Can I help?

VIRGINIA. Idiot! Yes, you can help if you want to. Just fold 'em any way and we'll "rest" 'em with my "wrops" in the hall. Isn't Dinah a scream?

JACK. A bully old scream. I get sort of homesick for the bunch of you down at college.

VIRGINIA. We miss you too—and Alice. Still, we hear you're both doing fine. One of your professors told Dad that you've got a better future than any of the students because you have imagination and concentration and—

JACK. Bunk! I'm about the average, I guess. Still, I am determined to help Gran make a model place of Berry Farm. Alice is majoring in home economics to help make a bang-up go of it. Just you wait and see.

VIRGINIA. (*Significantly.*) Perhaps Alice should be majoring in modern banking.

JACK. It does sort of look that way. If she falls down on us, how are you on domestic economics, Ginny?

VIRGINIA. I'm not exactly an expert but—but—well, I'm not quite such a dumb Dora as I look.

JACK. Dumb? Gosh, I bet you'd turn out a wiz, honey.

(*Exeunt into hall with their ghost-wrappings.*)

GRANDMA BERRY. Now that the room's in order, why don't you girls try the magic stunt of going backwards down the cellar stairs with your mirrors and see how they tally with the fortune the WITCH OF ENDOR has in store for you.

GIRLS. Hurrah! We're ready for anything. Let's go. Where's my vanity case mirror?

(VIRGINIA *and* JACK *re-enter from hall.*)

VIRGINIA. Wait, girls, I'm coming. I want to see what lucky man looks in my glass.

JACK. (*To boys huddled up-stage over a pack of cards on floor.*) What superstitious geese girls are! We boys don't need to break our necks down cellar stairs to find our good fortunes. Let's try the cards for luck.

DINAH. (*Marching to the kitchen door, her arms full of linen.*) Come on, gals. Follow me an' Ah'll git yo' candles. Watch out an' don't snag them purty clo'ses yo' done got on. They may be some splinters on de stairs.

(*They all exit into the kitchen except* ALICE.)

ALICE. (*Pausing and calling after them.*) I'll be along in a minute.

GERALD. (*Catching hold of her hand.*) Why do you go,

darling, when everything's settled for us? It is, isn't it?

ALICE. (*Trying to escape.*) Oh, Gerald—I don't know—I don't know—

GRANDMA BERRY. (*Crossing from screen where she has been inspecting her Witch booth.*) You don't know what, child?

GERALD. Look here, Mrs. Berry, I've just been asking Alice if she'll marry me. You like me, don't you?

GRANDMA BERRY. Why yes, Gerry, I like you very much, but I'm afraid I am a little too old to marry you, and Alice is much too young—she's got to finish her course at the Agricultural College. Maybe we'd all better wait a bit.

GERALD. (*Solemnly.*) I'll wait all my life if I have to.

ALICE. This is the craziest proposal I ever heard of—but maybe—well, I'll see you later. (*Exit* ALICE *through the kitchen door.*)

BILLY. (*Who has been bobbing for apples in the tub upstage, right, points his finger at* GERALD *and chants in the well-known taunting manner of small boys.*) Gerry's got a gur-rul, Gerry's got a gur-rul, Gerry's got a gur-rul, (*ad lib.*)

GERALD. Mrs. Berry, do you mind if I choke that infant?

GRANDMA BERRY. You have provocation, but— (*To* BILLY.) You're forgetting you're a host, Billy, and must be polite.

BILLY. (*Continuing the same chant.*) Got to entertain 'em, Gerry an' his gur-rul—

JACK. (*Rising and starting after him.*) You shut up or I'll throw you into the garden to eat worms.

(BILLY, *continuing his chant, dodges round the screen. Enter* DINAH *right.*)

DINAH. Ah want all yo' boys should come out an' move de kitchen-table an' de dinin'-room one along de wall fo' de banquetty-buffetty whut we-all gwine have aftah de mystic Witch o' Endor done deliver' her pernostifications. When de gals gits back frum de cellar, dey'll do de prittyin' up wid posies an' sich.

BOYS. (*Except* BILLY, *enter kitchen saying.*) O.K.—Sure!

What orders? etc.

DINAH. (*Directing through open door.*) Along dat wall, thar. Move de chairs ovah. Ah'll be in t'rectly when I done res' mah han' whut Ah strained liftin' things. (*To* GRANDMA BERRY *as she closes door.*) Ah done tol' dat whopper to git 'em out so's Ah kin he'p yo' into yo' Witch togs. (*She pulls an old Oriental sort of kimono from under her apron.*) Dat sho' ought to knock 'em, didn't it?

GRANDMA BERRY. It's wonderful, Dinah. Thank you. It ought to cheer me up, but I do feel very tired and as though we were dancing on top of a volcano. However, when I get on that terrible mask which I've hidden behind the screen, nobody will guess.

DINAH. Jes' keep yo' faith boilin' an' mebbe dat meracle'll happen.

(*With a whoop enter from behind screen,* BILLY *wearing the mask.*)

BILLY. (*Waving the megaphone in time to his monotonous chant.*) I'm the Witch of Endor, I'm the Witch of Endor, (*ad lib.*)

DINAH. Yo'll sho' wish yo' was w'en Ah cotches ye! (*She chases him and finally catches him but as she does so he blows a blast through the megaphone and a paper flies out and falls at his grandmother's feet.*) Ah gwine lock yo' up in de hall closet, Marse Billy, whar yo' caint give away no secrets.

(DINAH *fulfills her promise and when they are in the hall* GRANDMA BERRY *picks up the note written by* BANKER DANKS *earlier in the evening. She puts on her spectacles and reads the superscription, then breaks the stamp-paper which closes it and reads the contents with wonder and incredulity on her face. Enter* DINAH *puffing from her tussle with* BILLY.)

DINAH. Ah done tole dat young ramscalion he'd git no supper effen we heared a peep outen him— (*Observing* GRANDMA BERRY.) Why, Ma'am, whut done happen?

GRANDMA BERRY. Dinah, a wonderful thing has occurred. When Billy blew through the megaphone, this piece of paper fell at my feet. Listen while I read you what is written on it.

DINAH. Ah—Ah feel kinda creepy— (*She glances around nervously.*) lak they was somepin happenin'.

GRANDMA BERRY. Something *has* happened. This note addressed to me and sealed with narrow strips of stamp-paper was mysteriously left in that megaphone sometime this evening. Here's what is written: "Dear Mrs. Berry: I have decided to take up your note myself tomorrow, and you may redeem it whenever it is convenient. Yours faithfully, John Danks."

DINAH. Glory be!—but is yo' sho' it ain't no joke?—

GRANDMA BERRY. It is in Mr. Danks' own hand-writing. It's genuine I know—and isn't it too wonderful?—I can hardly speak, there's so much in my heart.

DINAH. Th' meracle's done happened. De blessed sperits is hoverin' 'roun' ouah haids.—Glory hallelujah!

GRANDMA BERRY. Yes. The hour of the Feast of All Saints is very near.

DINAH. (*Suddenly practical.*) Lawdy me, I plumb fo'got. Yo'all bettah climb into yo' Witch things an' git behind de screen while I turn Marse Billy loose an' 'nounce to de udders dat de Oracle am on de job.

(GRANDMA BERRY *adjusts her kimono and mask as she goes toward the screen. Then before entering she turns and says through her weird disguise.*)

GRANDMA BERRY. It is strange how near the sublime is to the ridiculous in this old world of ours.

(*Enter* DINAH *and* BILLY *right as the others enter left.*)

DINAH. (*With a sweeping gesture toward the screen, announces with gusto.*) Ladies an' Gen'elmen, de WITCH o' ENDOR am in her cave.

BILLY. (*Turning and leering at the audience.*) I bet it's jest Gran wearin' my mask. (*He grabs up the megaphone as the cur-*

tain falls and the familiar cadence of his chant is heard to new words.) I bet it is jest Granny—I bet it is jest Granny— (*Etc. ad lib.*)

CURTAIN

FLAMES OF HALLOWE'EN * †

By Mary Stewart Sheldon

CHARACTERS

Guardians
- Bird-House
- Scarecrow
- Dogwood Tree
- Tulip Tree
- Statue of Faun

Maggie, *young Scotch nurse*
Bobbie, *aged 9*
Jean, *aged 7*
Susie, *aged 5*
Chief Witch

Horrors
- Other Witches
- Goblins
- Toads ⎫ These may be actors, or made from card-
- Snakes ⎭ board
- Murderers (*Skeletons*)

Time: *October 31st, this year.*
Place: *Somewhere in Scotland.*

---

* Fires to drive away the evil spirits which were abroad Hallowe'en were lighted many hundreds of years ago, and may still be found blazing that night in the north of Scotland.

† Where no admission is charged, this play may be produced free. Otherwise, for a fee of $5.00, written permission must be secured from Mrs. Raymond Sheldon, Chestnut Ridge Road, Mt. Kisco, N.Y.

Act 1: *Outside of House—late afternoon.*
Act 2: *Scotch Moor-Night.*
Act 3: *Same scene as Act 1—Dawn.*

DIRECTIONS: Actors who take parts of Guardians must be costumed as realistically as possible. Trees can be made of painted muslin for trunks, with branches above actors' heads. They look and breathe through faces painted on trunks, dog face on Dogwood, nymph with very red lips on Tulip Tree. In Bird-house actor looks through his post and carries a real bird-house above his head. All carry flash-lights which, when turned on, illumine the masks. In Bird-house light streams besides through bird holes. Scarecrow also carries a flash; but when turned off faces are not conspicuous. Faun wears faun's costume of gray-green to imitate weathered bronze. His face is also painted and his ears beneath his cap are pointed. Maggie wears light blue nurse's dress with cap and apron. Children are dressed in country clothes appropriate to their ages.

The rails of fence have faces painted on them, which look like knot-holes when not lighted from inside. Electric bulbs are placed there attached to wires which can be operated off stage. Bell, hanging one side of Door, has laughing face painted on it, which only shows when bulb within is turned on.

Witches and other Horrors wear appropriate costumes, are painted to look as frightful as possible. The Witches' cats have red and green eyes which gleam when witch turns flash on from inside. The others also carry flash-lights, concealed, to illumine their hideous masks. Murderers carry clanking gallows' chains. Their faces and hands are skeletons, and they make much noise by swinging chains and rattling bones of hands for rhythm of dance.

Cold Fire must be used plentifully in second act to represent bonfires, and flash-lights had better be purchased wholesale. Punk can be used for sparks of fire-fly and for glow-worm.

Act I

Outside of House. Only window and front door show.

There is a bench between them. Front right TULIP TREE, *front left* DOGWOOD, *right center* BIRD-HOUSE, *right of center of stage, pool around which low circle of stones stands only high enough to be seen by audience. It must be strong enough to support* FAUN *who stands upon it and also, later,* MAGGIE. *It is covered with climbing roses.* FAUN *stands in any position in which he can keep practically immovable—a statue. Across the back is the rail-fence separating garden from cornfield, which is painted on back-drop with corn-sheaves.* SCARECROW *stands just behind fence, left.*

MAGGIE. (*Comes through door, rings bell, calls.*) Supper! Supper! Where can those bairns be now? Perhaps it is forgetting they are that this is Hallowe'en, and when the sun sets—Ah, when the last beam fades, witches and goblins and horrors will be in the air. I must keep them close to this home garden tonight. Only kindness can enter *here*. Is that not so? (*She looks around garden and lights gleam from the Guardians, bell, and rails.*) What is happening? I can almost see the souls of our friends, almost hear their voices. If only the Faun would show me his spirit! Ah, never will I dream of marrying the gardener lad while this beautiful one makes my heart leap just to look at him. (FAUN *moves slightly, stretches out his hand to* MAGGIE, *who runs forward and takes it.*) Oh my wonderful one, my love, is it only at Hallowe'en I can see you alive? I would rather be a statue forever standing beside you than—ah, the children!

(*Gay voices of children are heard at right beyond fence.* MAGGIE *runs back to doorway, lights fade,* FAUN *stands as before. Children climb over fence, each carrying a pumpkin.*)

BOBBIE. See, Maggie!

Susie. Look at these wonderful pumpkins.

Jean. Won't they make perfect goblins?

Maggie. Indeed and indeed, never did I see finer ones! Come in to supper and we'll cut faces on them.

(*Children run in,* Maggie *stands a moment at door. Lights flash and* Faun *kisses his hand to her. She kisses hers back and goes into house. Guardians come very much alive. Not only do lights gleam, but they all move.* Faun *takes dancing steps around pool,* Trees *walk forward,* Scarecrow *climbs fence,* Bird-house *walks importantly to center.*)

Bird-house. Stop dancing, Faun, we have a terrible matter to deal with tonight.

Scarecrow. I know, I can see from where I generally stand. The stream between us and the moor is dried up! Do you folks know what that means?

Trees. Are you sure?

Bird-house. Of course *I* am sure. That's why all my bird-boarders drink from the stupid pool here instead of flying to the stream.

Faun. Don't be rude about the pool, it reflects my image, it is beautiful.

Dogwood Tree. Don't fight, *please;* this is a horrible matter. The stream is dried up. Its running water kept out the witches and Horrors who could not cross it; and now—

Tulip Tree. Oh dear, oh dear! What shall we do? This garden and the house will be filled with the Horrors, the children will be murdered in their beds, the ghouls will suck their blood, and we—

Scarecrow. I'm an ugly fellow, I know; but beside those ghosts of murderers I'm a beauty, I who scare even the crows.

Bird-house. (*Mournfully.*) The Evil Things will eat the birds; the children will be ill; their parents will fight; and we—we'll never be anything again but *things.* Our spirits will be dead.

FAUN. I have an idea! We all know the Horrors can't cross running water. We can't fill the stream, but there is something else. They can't cross fire either. In the good old days, people built bonfires around their farms to keep them safe. But now even Maggie doesn't know that, and she is the smartest one in the house.

BIRD-HOUSE. (*Jumping around clumsily for joy.*) I know, I know! (*He takes hands from post where they were apparently part of the wood, lifts them to shelf around bird-house, and picks up seed there.*) Do you see this seed? It's fern-seed. It's magic. Even Maggie knows that if a human puts it on his eyelids tonight he can see spirits. We'll get the children to try it. They will see and hear us. We'll tell them about the fires. They'll light them on the moor, and we'll all be saved! Hurrah! Hurrah!

(*He lumbers around clumsily, trying to dance for joy, but is stopped by* SCARECROW'S *scorn.*)

SCARECROW. Very fine! They would see and hear us and the *Horrors too*. They would be terrified, and they can't light bonfires. They would each have to light one, and only Maggie is allowed to use matches. Besides, it would take magic flames, not ordinary fires lighted by matches, to drive off the Horrors who have burrowed for years in the moor. Where would the children find magic in time?

(*All this while the fence-rails and bell have been blinking away at a great rate.*)

FAUN. (*Dances around.*) Magic isn't hard to get, not for children nor for Maggie. I'll help her, too. Hush, here they come.

(*Lights go out and all resume places as children come out, each carrying a lighted pumpkin. They turn their backs on garden as they place pumpkins on bench. While they do this,* MAGGIE *steps toward* FAUN, *holding out her hand. He points to* BIRD-HOUSE, *who bows before her to show what is on his shelf, takes some fern-seed from it and holds it out to her. She looks at it curiously and asks—"Fern-seed?"— He bows again.* FAUN *points at it and at children, placing his hands on his eyes to show her what he means. As children turn, figures are motionless again.*)

MAGGIE. Children, listen! There are spirits all around us, in everything, although we can't always see nor hear them.

JEAN. I know—I hear the trees whisper often.

SUSIE. I saw the Faun dance once.

BOBBIE. The Scarecrow is one of my best friends. He taught me to jump the fence.

(SCARECROW *puts thumbs in arm-holes and proudly waves his hands.*)

MAGGIE. Well, tonight, if you put this fern-seed on your eyelids, you'll see and hear still more. Our friends here have something special to tell us. I don't understand, but here's the seed.

(*She puts it on each child's eyelids and brushes her own. All the lights gleam. The Guardians cluster around trying to talk all at once. Children show their delighted amusement.*)

SCARECROW. Shut up, you fellows, let the Bird-house talk. He's the oldest.

DOGWOOD TREE. (*Aside.*) But not the smartest, bow-bow.

BIRD-HOUSE. I'm very sorry that the first time you see me I have something perfectly terrible to tell you. On Hallowe'en not only friends like us, but the Horrors—witches, goblins, murderous ghosts—walk around. We have always been safe from them here because there is a stream between us and the moor where they meet tonight, and the Horrors can't cross running water. But this summer the stream has dried up and the ghastly spirits can rush across. You are all in deadly danger. There is only one hope—

SCARECROW. You see, they can't cross fire either, magic fire, not lighted by man-made matches.

FAUN. If each of you can light a different fire, with flames so brilliant that the Horrors will be driven away, you can save your parents, yourselves and us. From what now could you light such fires?

JEAN. I'll take a fire-fly. (*Catches one.*)

SUSIE. I'll find a glow-worm. (*Picks one up.*)

BOBBIE. I don't know what I can find, but I can jump pretty high. I might find something in the air.

MAGGIE. Faun, dear Faun, will you help me? There is something called ecstasy. Will it light a fire?

FAUN. Come, we will see. Have courage!

SCARECROW. You must not be afraid, any of you, though it will be *awful*,—worse than anything you can imagine.

TREES. We're ready; we'll stand this side of the stream.

MAGGIE. Come, bairnies, the Faun and I will go first—

(*Exeunt everyone.*)

CURTAIN

ACT II

Scotch Moor.
Night, thunder and lightning.
There are low bushes and stunted trees at left, and back, at right, bed of dried-up stream. On back-drop, heavy clouds. It is dark; but light enough to see figures mysteriously.

WITCH. (*Enters from left back, seated on broom-stick, cat on shoulder. She mutters at first; but voice gradually rises to shriek.*) Come, my darlings, my beauties! Creep and crawl, horrors and hateful, slimy and sinful, mean and murderous! Bring your poisons, your stings, your strangling hands! Come! Come!

(*She waves broomstick. More* WITCHES *enter, dance around her on broomsticks. Cats' eyes flash. They chant.*)

From the mudholes of the snakes,
From the slime where black toads dwell,
From the gallows where they hung
Murderous bones, this chorus swell!
Come! Come!

(*From left, back and front, enter horrible* SNAKES, TOADS, *slimy creatures, black* GOBLINS *and last the ghastly* MURDERERS' SKELETONS, *clanking chains, etc.*)

CHIEF WITCH. Are you all here?

CHORUS. Ay, ay! All ready! Dripping with horror. Bursting with hate!

CHIEF WITCH. The time has come. For hundreds of Hallowe'ens we have waited. The stream is dried up, stupid humans today never think of fire to keep us out. We'll hop and crawl and fly across the stream bed.

SECOND WITCH. We'll murder all who try to stop us!

THIRD WITCH. We'll poison, bleed and choke them!

ALL. We'll trample the farm and garden, kill the Guardians, creep into the house, bring horrors and hatred to everyone!

(*Chorus of assent, accompanied by hisses, clanking of chains, bones rattling. All dance grotesquely. Thunder peals, lightning flashes. Scene is horrible.* FAUN, MAGGIE, CHILDREN *and* GUARDIANS *peek out from front right, unperceived.*)

CHIEF WITCH. (*Screaming above din.*) Before we start our devil's work, let us gather poison berries and deadly nightshade!

(*They sweep out, left.* GUARDIANS *only peek out, but* FAUN, MAGGIE *and* CHILDREN *enter.* FAUN *throws small white feather into air, blows upon it, it flies left.*)

FAUN. That means the winds will help us. Jean, do you dare run to the other side before the Horrors come back? Bobbie, stand in front, next to her. Susie, you'd better stay near us, and

Maggie and I will guard the stream-bed.

JEAN. I'm *awfully* scared, but I won't tell. (*Goes to left front.*)

BOBBIE. If I had a dagger I would feel better; but I haven't even a spark to light a fire with. (*Another flash of lightning, very near this time.*) Ah! Glad I learned to climb that fence. (*He springs up and apparently catches bit of lightning in his hand. He and both girls now hold spark of fire in readiness. In a flash of lightning* MAGGIE *and* FAUN *are illumined, they hold hands, kiss. A light springs out above their heads.* MAGGIE *grasps it. Thus each of the four stands in readiness when* HORRORS *rush back, holding red and purple berries on branches above their heads. They howl, shriek, career around stage.*) Now! Now! (*He lights bushes near him. They blaze out, and* HORRORS *rush wailing to left front where* JEAN *also sets bushes on fire, and* HORRORS *scream—*"To the Stream-bed!" *As they reach there* MAGGIE *has lighted all the bushes along it, and with wild wails of fear and fury the* HORRORS *dash across stage in a long line and disappear at extreme left. With lighted torches— or branches—in their hands* CHILDREN *and* MAGGIE *meet in center with* FAUN, *and* GUARDIANS *who now join them. Sounds of the disappearing* HORRORS *grow gradually dimmer.* BOBBIE *holds up his hand.*) Hark!

(*From the right comes a* "Cock-a-doo-dul-doo!")

CURTAIN

Act III

Same scene as Act I. Outside of House. Daybreak.

GUARDIANS, *except* FAUN, *are standing in their places as at beginning of play.*

SCARECROW. What a night! I'm tuckered out, glad to rest for another year.

DOGWOOD TREE. Bow-wow! Now I can put my buds quietly to sleep until the spring.

TULIP TREE. And I can admire my lovely dried tulips in peace.

BIRD-HOUSE. And I can feed the birds again, but *not* with fern-seed. Here come the blessed children!

(*Enter three children. They run to look at Pumpkins which still flicker on bench.*)

SUSIE. There are the nice old Pumpkins, still burning.

JEAN. They didn't help us a bit, did they?

BOBBIE. We thought they looked like goblins until last night; but now we know what real Horrors are.

SUSIE. I'm afraid I'll dream of them.

JEAN. Then dream of how we drove them away!

BOBBIE. Where's the Faun? The pool looks strange without him.

(*Sound of singing comes from left and children turn, watching* MAGGIE *and* FAUN, *who enter hand in hand singing a gay Scotch song. They dance gracefully around stage while children watch, and* GUARDIANS *show lights, but do not move.* FAUN *springs upon wall around pool and* MAGGIE *stands beside him in attitude of dancing nymph.*)

SUSIE. Why, Maggie!

JEAN. Aren't you going to be our nurse any more?

BOBBIE. Are you going to live there?

MAGGIE. (*Laughing, and stepping off wall.*) Bairns, you don't need a nurse any more; you know that not only these Guardians are your friends but all the trees of the forest, the winds and the fire. I want to be a statue, so I can stay on this wall beside my chosen One forever. I'll be watching you and every Hallowe'en we'll have a party together. Until then—

(FAUN *steps off wall, takes* MAGGIE'S *hand. She springs back on wall with him. They hold their clasped hands high. Light is thrown upon her, making her also look like statue of weathered bronze. The stage has been growing lighter and, as they raise hands, sunlight fills the garden. Voices of parents are heard calling*—"Children! Breakfast! Where are you?")

JEAN. I'm the oldest girl, so I'll ring the bell in Maggie's place.

(*She rings bell. Two girls go into house.* BOBBIE *stands outside at door.*)

BOBBIE. Good old Guardians, that was a fine night's work. Without your help we wouldn't be here now, eating breakfast and having fun. Thank you, friends!

(*He waves at them and each bows, salutes, waves, or kisses his hand back.*)

GUARDIANS. We thank *you*, Bobbie. You were glorious! Remember the lightning!

BOBBIE. I'll never forget it, nor the Flames of Hallowe'en. (*He goes in.*)

CURTAIN

THE CLAY GNOME *

(*A Farce*)

BY MIRJANE STRONG

CHARACTERS

THE GNOME
TITTERMOUSE ⎫
FLITTERBAT ⎪
LITTLE-PITCHER ⎬ *Elves*
OWLER ⎪
FIDGET ⎭
RABBIT

---

* All rights reserved. No performance of this play may be given without permission from, and payment of royalty of five dollars to, Mirjane Strong, 835 South Sheridan Road, Highland Park, Illinois.

The scene is a green bank by a brook on a summer morning. The motionless GNOME *is sitting on a stump, his fishing pole extended over the bank of the brook. At the right,* TITTERMOUSE, FLITTERBAT *and* LITTLE-PITCHER *are regarding him with some concern and discussing the situation among themselves, in whispers.—The elves are quick and frisky like young goats.*

TITTERMOUSE. (*Addressing* THE GNOME *indignantly*.) Pardon me!—This happens to be *our* fishing place! (THE GNOME *does not move, being made of clay.*) I say—this is *our* fishing place!

FLITTERBAT. (*Dancing around the other side of* THE GNOME.) Has a witch got your tongue?

LITTLE-PITCHER. (*To* TITTERMOUSE.) What's the matter with him?

TITTERMOUSE. Maybe he's deaf—(*Going close to* THE GNOME *and shouting into his ear.*) I say! This is *our* fishing place.

(FLITTERBAT *dances up and shouts into the other ear.*)

FLITTERBAT. Heigh! (*He starts to shake* THE GNOME *by the arm, and darts back in amazement.*) Feel him! (TITTERMOUSE *puts out a cautious finger and pokes* THE GNOME. *He and* FLITTERBAT *exchange significant glances.*) Come here, Little-Pitcher—you with the big ears—(*He motions.*) come and have a feel.

(LITTLE-PITCHER *walks all around* THE GNOME, *peering at him suspiciously, and then gives him a quick cautious poke in the stomach.*)

LITTLE-PITCHER. (*Wide-eyed.*) Why, he's been turned to stone!

TITTERMOUSE. Someone has cast a spell on him, that's what!

FLITTERBAT. Bouncing Blizzards! I believe you're right! The poor old chap's enchanted.

LITTLE-PITCHER. (*Excited.*) Do you really think so?
TITTERMOUSE. Not a doubt.
LITTLE-PITCHER. (*Importantly.*) I know a disenchantment! I learned it in school. I'm going to work it—watch me!
TITTERMOUSE. Pooh! You couldn't do it—a little elf like you.
LITTLE-PITCHER. You just watch me! (*The others nudge each other and wink.*) This is the way it goes—(*He tries to remember. The other two elves giggle.*) I know!—

    Roll-a-ma-rig, roll-a-ma-rice
    Skip a magic circle thrice,
(*He skips around* THE GNOME, *first to the left, then to the right, then to the left again.*)
    The spell is broken in a trice!
(*He waits triumphantly for* THE GNOME *to move. Nothing happens. The others laugh shrilly.*)
FLITTERBAT. (*Scornfully.*) That's no good—that's baby stuff. Let me try. I know a real one! (*He reaches into his pocket.*) I've got the tooth of a Jubjub!
TITTERMOUSE. That's not so much.
FLITTERBAT. Oh, it isn't, isn't it? Just you watch! (*He stands in front of* THE GNOME *and rubs his charm vigorously, chanting.*)

    Mimble-jimble
    Mumble-jumble
    Rub and rerub
    Tooth of Jubjub.

(FLITTERBAT *and* LITTLE-PITCHER *wait expectantly.* TITTERMOUSE *feigns scornful indifference, but glances over his shoulder to see if anything is happening. Nothing is.*)
TITTERMOUSE. Now, let *me* do it! (*He sweeps them aside.*)
FLITTERBAT. Bet you can't.
TITTERMOUSE. (*Importantly.*) You don't know what I've got. (*He takes something from his shoe.*)

LITTLE-PITCHER. (*Edging closer.*) What *have* you got, Tittermouse? (TITTERMOUSE *gives him a peek at what he is concealing between his hands.*) Ohhhhh! Are they real?

TITTERMOUSE. Of course they're real! You have to keep them in your shoe.

FLITTERBAT. (*Consumed with curiosity but appearing indifferent.*) What is it?

LITTLE-PITCHER. (*Awed.*) The whiskers of a Runcible cat!

FLITTERBAT. (*Coming over to see.*) Are they crimson?

TITTERMOUSE. Of course!

FLITTERBAT. Where did you get them?

TITTERMOUSE. I found them.

FLITTERBAT. That ought to do it, then.—Do you know the charm?

TITTERMOUSE. Of course! (*Carefully he sticks the whiskers in* THE GNOME'S *cap and they all crowd around excitedly.*)
  Boggie woggle, boggie woggle,
  Snickery, snackery
(*He flings his hands suddenly in* THE GNOME'S *face.*)
  Skilikabooch!
(OWLER *has appeared from the right, unseen by the other elves. He is a venerable old elf with a squeaky voice.*)

OWLER. What do you think you're up to?

(*The young elves jump. Then they all talk at once.*)

LITTLE-PITCHER. We're doing disenchantments!

TITTERMOUSE. The Runcible cat's whiskers don't work!

FLITTERBAT. This gnome's been turned to stone!

OWLER. (*Hobbling forward with the aid of his stick.*) Hold your rabbits, hold your rabbits! One at a time. What's this all about? (*They all start to speak again.* OWLER *holds up his hand—sternly.*) Flitterbat, perhaps you can explain this excitement?

(TITTERMOUSE *hastily replaces the whiskers in his shoe.*)

FLITTERBAT. Well, you see, this gnome has been turned to stone.

OWLER. (*Looking critically at* THE GNOME.) What makes you think so?

TITTERMOUSE. (*Impatiently.*) Why, all you have to do is feel of him to know—

(OWLER *has been staring disapprovingly at* TITTERMOUSE *during this interruption.*)

OWLER. Tittermouse—be silent! (*He raps* TITTERMOUSE *on the head with his stick.* TITTERMOUSE *tries to speak but no sound comes.*) Now, Flitterbat, perhaps we can continue our conversation without interruption. (*He goes over to* THE GNOME *and examines him.* LITTLE-PITCHER *is keeping his hand clapped over his mouth, so that he will not displease* OWLER; *but, alas, in his excitement, he skips into the old elf.* OWLER *shakes his head hopelessly and taps* LITTLE-PITCHER *on the head with his stick.*) Little-Pitcher, stay where you are!

(LITTLE-PITCHER *is rooted to the spot. He and* TITTERMOUSE *gesture hopelessly at each other.* TITTERMOUSE *tries vainly to speak and* LITTLE-PITCHER *to move his legs.*)

OWLER. (*Poking* THE GNOME *with his stick.*) Humph! This is no gnome. It never was a gnome. It's made of clay.

FLITTERBAT. Clay?

OWLER. Yes, clay. (*He pokes the stump.*) This stump is made of clay, too. It was made by humans and put out here.

FLITTERBAT. Why? (*He examines the stump curiously.*)

OWLER. Well, Flitterbat, I'm an old elf and I know many things; but I don't know why humans do the queer things they do. I must be on my way.

(*He starts to hobble off, left.* LITTLE-PITCHER *and* TITTERMOUSE *are much concerned.*)

LITTLE-PITCHER. Please, Owler—!

(TITTERMOUSE *plucks at his sleeve.* OWLER *turns, a little annoyed.*)

OWLER. Oh—you two. Yes, yes. (*He taps* TITTERMOUSE *on the head with his stick.*) You may speak, Tittermouse.

TITTERMOUSE. (*Meekly.*) Thank you, Owler.

OWLER. (*Tapping* LITTLE-PITCHER.) You may move, Little-Pitcher.

LITTLE-PITCHER. (*Leaping about.*) Thank you, Owler!

OWLER. (*Amused but trying to be gruff.*) Out of my way, now—out of my way.

(OWLER *goes off. The others examine* THE GNOME *again.*)

TITTERMOUSE. So that's why our charms didn't work.

LITTLE-PITCHER. I knew there wasn't anything wrong with my charm!

FLITTERBAT. (*Poking* THE GNOME.) Just an old clay gnome. —Well, let's get our poles and go fishing.

TITTERMOUSE. Yes, let's go fishing.

LITTLE-PITCHER. I'm going to catch that big silver fish today!

(*They go off right. After a moment* FIDGET *comes sauntering in from the opposite direction, putting a feather in his jaunty, red cap.*)

FIDGET. (*Barely glancing at* THE GNOME.) Hello, Gnome. (*He continues to work with the feather. Receiving no answer he glances at* THE GNOME *again and says louder.*) I said, hello, Gnome.—Not very sociable, are you? (*Puzzled, he walks around to look at* THE GNOME's *face.*) What's the matter with you? (*He peers closely at the figure, then feels of him.*) Pooh! You're only clay.

(*He starts to saunter on—then looking back at* THE GNOME, *he notices that their clothes are similar and his face lights up with an idea. He looks around quickly to make sure no one is coming—then he runs to* THE GNOME *and tries unsuccessfully to pull him off the stump. Then he examines the stump, laughs triumphantly and begins to tug at the stump, which he can move with* THE GNOME *on it. He pulls it off the stage left and comes running back, giggling and looking about to make sure he has not been detected. Then he seats himself on another stump near where* THE GNOME *was placed. He runs off to get* THE GNOME'S *fishing pole and returns, again seating himself on the stump. Suddenly he feels his chin, critically—no beard. He looks around for something he can use.* RABBIT *comes skipping in from the right, whistling gaily to himself.*)

FIDGET. Hello, Rabbit.

RABBIT. (*Startled, then reassured.*) Hello, Elf.

(*He skips on, whistling.* FIDGET *studies the fluffy tail, speculatively.*)

FIDGET. Oh, Rabbit—

RABBIT. (*Again startled.*) Yes, Elf?

FIDGET. (*Getting up from the stump and coming over to* RABBIT.) I'd like to borrow your tail for a few minutes.

(RABBIT *looks at his tail.*)

RABBIT. (*Dubiously.*) Well—if you won't keep it long— (*He tries to take it off.*) I can't seem to unfasten it—can you do it? (*He turns his back to* FIDGET *and leans over.*)

FIDGET. Oh, I can do it. (*He unfastens the tail and holds it up, delighted.*) Thank you, Rabbit. I won't want it long.

RABBIT. You're welcome. I'll get it later.—Goodbye, Elf.

(*He hops off, looking over his shoulder at where his tail was.* FIDGET *is trying the tail as a beard.*)

FIDGET. (*After a while.*) Oh, goodbye, Rabbit.

(RABBIT *is again startled and runs off left.*)

RABBIT. (*Over his shoulder.*) Goodbye, Elf.

(FIDGET *reaches over the bank, appears to put water on his chin, sticks the tail on and wobbles his face to make sure the beard will stay on. He capers about, delighted with the result. Then, hearing a sound, he leaps onto the stump and sits motionless in the position of* THE GNOME. TITTER-

MOUSE, FLITTERBAT *and* LITTLE-PITCHER *come in from the right, with their fishing poles over their shoulders and sit on the bank,* LITTLE-PITCHER *next to* FIDGET, *and* TITTERMOUSE *next to him.*)

LITTLE-PITCHER. Bet you I catch the first fish!

TITTERMOUSE. I hope that big silver one is hungry today.

FLITTERBAT. (*Putting a worm on his line.*) Here's a nice slick, juicy one for you, Silver. (*He throws his line in.*)

TITTERMOUSE. (*Looking at* FIDGET.) You know, that gnome doesn't look a bit real to me now. I'm surprised we were fooled before.

FLITTERBAT. No, you can see from here that he's just made of clay.

LITTLE-PITCHER. (*Excitedly.*) I've got something! I've got something!— (*He pulls up his line.*) Oh, now I haven't.

TITTERMOUSE. (*Nudging him.*) Don't make so much noise!

(*They all sit in silence for a few moments, during which* FIDGET *stealthily reaches over with his pole and knocks* FLITTERBAT'S *cap off.*)

FLITTERBAT. (*Indignantly to* LITTLE-PITCHER.) Hey! What's the idea?

TITTERMOUSE. What's the matter with *you!*

FLITTERBAT. (*Recovering his cap.*) Big ears, over there, knocked my cap off.

LITTLE-PITCHER. Who? Me?

FLITTERBAT. Don't be funny— I saw you.

LITTLE-PITCHER. (*Indignantly.*) I didn't do a thing. Besides how could I, way over here?

FLITTERBAT. You did it with your fishing pole. I saw it.

TITTERMOUSE. (*Jabbing both of them.*) Keep still, you two! You're scaring all the fish.

(FIDGET *can scarcely control his amusement.*)

LITTLE-PITCHER. I *have* got a bite this time! (*He jumps up and tugs at his line.*) It must be the big silver one! (*The others get excited.*) Look!

(LITTLE-PITCHER *hoists into the air an old boot. His face falls. The others shriek with laughter.*)

FLITTERBAT. It's a big one all right, Little-Pitcher.

TITTERMOUSE. It thought the worm was a shoe-string!

(LITTLE-PITCHER *untangles his line and throws the shoe aside.*)

LITTLE-PITCHER. (*Grinning.*) I got the first catch, anyway.

TITTERMOUSE. You'll catch something else if you don't keep still.

(*They all fish silently again.* FIDGET *reaches over behind and jabs* TITTERMOUSE *in the back.*)

TITTERMOUSE. Cut it out, Flitterbat!

FLITTERBAT. Who's been yelling about keeping still?—I didn't do a thing!

TITTERMOUSE. I suppose you didn't jab me in the back just now!

FLITTERBAT. I certainly didn't! I had both hands on my pole.

LITTLE-PITCHER. So did I.

TITTERMOUSE. (*Glaring from one to the other.*) Well, all I can say is, don't let it happen again!

(FIDGET *is almost splitting when* RABBIT *comes in from the left and going quietly up to* FIDGET, *clears his throat to attract his attention.* FIDGET *looks down and gestures impatiently for* RABBIT *to go away.* RABBIT *hesitates and finally goes off with an unhappy expression on his face.* FIDGET *reaches over and tweaks one of* LITTLE-PITCHER's *long ears.*)

LITTLE-PITCHER. (*Holding the ear.*) Tittermouse, you leave my ears alone!

TITTERMOUSE. I didn't touch your ears!

LITTLE-PITCHER. You did too! You tweaked this one just now!

TITTERMOUSE. (*Exasperated.*) Say, what do you think I'm doing? Fishing or tweaking? Flitterbat probably did it. He's the playful one! He just jabbed me in the back.

FLITTERBAT. (*Heatedly.*) I did not jab you in the back! But I bet you were the one who knocked my cap off!

LITTLE-PITCHER. (*Jumping up and down.*) I *have* got a fish this time! And it's the big silver one—I saw it. (TITTERMOUSE *and* FLITTERBAT *forget their quarrel and jump up too.*) Look!

(LITTLE-PITCHER *hoists into the air a big, bright tin can.* TITTERMOUSE *and* FLITTERBAT *shriek with laughter.* FIDGET *can no longer control himself. He doubles up with amusement.*)

TITTERMOUSE. (*Suddenly pointing.*) Look! Look at the gnome! I saw it move.

FLITTERBAT. Don't be—

LITTLE-PITCHER. It is moving!

(FIDGET'S *shoulders are shaking with laughter.* RABBIT *looks in apprehensively.*)

TITTERMOUSE. It's Fidget!

LITTLE-PITCHER. Fidget?

(FLITTERBAT *pulls off the beard and throws it on the ground.* RABBIT *wrings his paws in dismay.*)

FLITTERBAT. So it is!

TITTERMOUSE. So he's the one!

LITTLE-PITCHER. So he's the one!

FLITTERBAT. Duck him!

(*With one accord they dump the howling* FIDGET *over the bank into the brook—then laughing excitedly, they run off, looking back to see if he is pursuing them.* FIDGET *does not emerge.* RABBIT *comes over, ruefully picks up his mistreated tail, brushes it off and puts it back on the proper place. Then he peers over the bank.*)

RABBIT. Are you there?

(*He is startled by a burst of mirth from the unseen* FIDGET,

who slowly appears above the bank, grinning broadly.)
FIDGET. (*Giggling.*) Rabbit—
RABBIT. Yes?
FIDGET. (*Triumphantly.*) I got their fish! (*He holds the big silver fish aloft by its tail.*)

THE CURTAIN FALLS ON HIS LAUGHTER *

BRE'R RABBIT AND THE GHOSTS †

(*A one-act play for Hallowe'en*)

BY BERTHA NATHAN

CHARACTERS

BRE'R RABBIT
SUSIE COTTON TAIL RABBIT, *his wife*
MARTIN PETER RABBIT, *a son*
BUNNY BALL RABBIT, *another son*
GOOD FAIRY
ONE GHOST
ANOTHER GHOST
EZEKUAL, *a little colored boy*
AL, FRED, *two white boys*
NICODEMUS, *white mule*
ONE PUMPKIN
ANOTHER PUMPKIN
OWL, *voice off-stage*

PLACE: *A clearing in the woods.*
TIME: *Hallowe'en. Around midnight.*

---

* If there is no curtain, FIDGET can run off the stage to the others, RABBIT following after.
† For permission to produce, consult the author, 130 East 39th St., New York City.

Costumes

Rabbits: *They wear one-piece sleeping suits. They must all have hoods and tails. The sleeves must all be sewed across so the hands do not show.*

Good Fairy: *Long full skirt of crepe paper or cheese cloth in a pastel color. Silver wand with a star on end or use a small flash light attached to wand. Silver or gold ribbon to bind hair.*

Ghosts: *One-piece white or gray sleeping suits with hoods. Painted symbols of skeletons and cross-bones on robes and markings on masks. They wear large white gloves.*

Boys: *All wear every-day clothes.*

Mule: *White sleeping suit with a mule mask or hood and tail.*

Pumpkins: *Short flare skirts of orange crepe paper. Full bodice with cape effect, trimmed with green leaves at throat. Small tight green caps with stem at top. They stand in back of umbrellas covered with orange paper. The head, nose and mouth and hair of a jack o' lantern should be marked on them in black paper.*

Owl: *A painted owl should be hung in a tree or pasted to the back drop on the opposite side of the stage from the mound.*

Setting

Back drop of leaves and trees or plain dark curtain. Some sort of a mound to resemble earth at either left or right stage, back. A large-sized piece of dark green or brown material may be draped over some bulky objects; with a small ladder in back of the mound, where it can not be seen by the audience.

A big, full moon suspended on a wire or two. It may be made of orange paper pasted to the outside of a pie-pan. Or, better still, use thin paper wired and put an electric bulb in back of it, to be lighted at mid-night.

The only other properties needed are one very large-sized handkerchief and two small rope lassoes.

The Story

There seems to be a generally accepted folk belief that the left hind foot of a graveyard rabbit caught at midnight, on Hallowe'en, by a cross-eyed colored boy riding on a white mule brings the best luck of all.

So, Bre'r Rabbit, in order to save his family, asks help of the good fairy who, along with the witches, ghosts, and goblins appear on Hallowe'en.

This Good Fairy sends two small ghosts—having no large ghosts at this season of the year—and for good measure throws in two pumpkins. Needless to say, the boys are completely routed and the rabbits save their feet.

Suggested Music

Rabbit Dance .... Cshebogar
Hungarian Folk Dance
Ghosts .... The Parade of the Wooden Soldiers
La Chauve Souris
or
Funeral March of a Marionette
Pumpkins .... Pizzicati
Sylvia
or
Glow Worm

The length of the production varies according to the dance numbers introduced.

The RABBITS *come on together from right or left back.* SUSIE COTTON TAIL *is hanging on the* BRE'R RABBIT'S *arm with one hand, and crying into a large handkerchief held in the other hand. The other two are hanging on to the arm of* BRE'R RABBIT *and* SUSIE COTTON TAIL.

BRE'R RABBIT.
We are a pair of rabbits,
And we are not for sale.
My name is Bre'r Rabbit;
And this: Susie Cotton Tail.
Now this our son is Martin Paul
And the other one is Bunny Ball.

(*The two little* RABBITS *go over to the other side of the stage and play leap frog or tumble about together.* BRE'R RABBIT *tries to comfort* SUSIE.)

BRE'R RABBIT. There! There! Susie Cotton Tail! Stop crying so hard, nothing has happened *yet*, you know.

SUSIE. I know but something *might* happen. You never can tell.

BRE'R RABBIT. Yes, but if you cry so much now you won't be able to cry any more if anything should happen. And then think how badly you would feel. Why that would disgrace our whole family. That would be dreadful.

SUSIE. (*Drying her eyes.*) Yes, I guess you are right. I never thought of that. Well, perhaps I had better stop. (*She gives one final, long sob, then dries her eyes and lays handkerchief on the mound of earth to dry.*)

(RABBITS *dance together. Any music in* ¾ *or* ⁴⁄₄ *time. Join hands and form circle. One and three bend forward; two and four pull back. Repeat. Drop on hands and toes. Extend feet backward. Wag left foot, right foot, left hand, right hand. Wag head up, down, and around. Repeat. Hop up and turn in place. Stamp 4 times, arms folded high. Repeat circle.*)

(SUSIE *takes up her handkerchief and starts to cry again just as the* GOOD FAIRY *appears on the mound.*)

GOOD FAIRY. Why are you so sad, Susie Cotton Tail?

RABBITS. (*All chant together, and shake their heads.*)

PLAYS

                BECAUSE
                Tonight is Hallowe'en!
                Tonight is Hallowe'en!
                Tonight is Hallowe'en!
                (*Look around right and left.*)
                Has anybody seen
                Has anybody seen
                (*Hands cupping mouths.*)
                Any mortals hereabout?

GOOD FAIRY. And do you fear them, little Rabbits?
BRE'R RABBIT.   Yes indeed! We do.
                For we are grave-yard rabbits,
                And mortals love us well.
                But on Hallowe'en night
                I've heard them tell
                They crave our left hind feet.
BOTH LITTLE RABBITS. (*Sadly shaking their heads.*)
                They crave our left hind feet.
GOOD FAIRY. But why? Can they run about on your feet?
SUSIE.   These mortals have strange ways,
                They celebrate queer days
                Like Hallowe'en.
                And on this day, these mortals say
                They will be mean.
BRE'R RABBIT.   (*Beckons all the* RABBITS *to come close to his side.*)
                They'll catch a rabbit
                By his left hind leg.
                And even though he may beg
                They will not let him go;
                Until they have this charm to keep.
                And at this charm they'll often peep
                And keep it just to show.

GOOD FAIRY. Yes! Yes! But what do they do with it? Get on with your story. I have not the night to waste listening.

SUSIE. Some use it for a powder puff.
As if our feet were made to scuff
Some lady's face.

BRE'R RABBIT. Men put it in their vest.
Of luck, they say, it brings the best,
And helps them win the race.

GOOD FAIRY. But how can your feet bring good luck? I do not yet understand. Be quick.

BRE'R RABBIT. We know not, Fairy Queen:
Except that mortals mean
They have no sense.

GOOD FAIRY. And now, little Rabbits, you have told me the sad story, what can I do to help you?

(*All the* RABBITS *kneel in a semi-circle, partly facing the* FAIRY *and partly facing the audience.*)

BRE'R RABBIT. (*Hands clasped together in front, head on hands.*) Could you not give us a very large ghost to scare these mortals off?

GOOD FAIRY. Now you know very well, Bre'r Rabbit, that at this time of the year, I have no very large ghosts.

(SUSIE *pulls at* BRE'R RABBIT *to catch his attention, then whispers in his ear.*)

BRE'R RABBIT. Well then, could you not give us two small ones instead?

GOOD FAIRY. Yes, that I can do.

RABBITS. (*All link arms and walk or hop about on one foot. They chant as they hop.*)

Thanks, kind Fairy, we were feeling pretty scary;
For we need our left hind feet to walk upon.
Now if we had three or more!
But with one, it can't be done.
Oh! No! No!

Good Fairy. Enough. (*Claps her hands.*) I will help you. (*Points to* Owl *in the tree.*) Call the ghosts for me.

Off Stage Call. O–O–O–O–O–O
OW–OW–OW–OW–OW
U–U–U–U–U–U

(Ghosts *come on and dance any dance, clog or eccentric dance they know. Or do a dance such as the "Balloon Dance."*)

Ghosts. What are your wishes, Good Fairy?

Good Fairy. Do you know what night this is?

Ghosts. We do. 'Tis Hallowe'en.

Good Fairy. Do you know the Rabbits' fate unless you intervene?

Ghosts. We do.

Good Fairy. Can we count on you to help? I have a plan.

(*Each* Ghost *puts right hand on heart of other; left hand on own head. Inside feet together, outside feet crossed over each other in front.*)

Ghosts. We promise. (*Snap into position. Each bows the other's head with right hand.*)

Good Fairy. (*Claps her hands.*) Bring on two pumpkins.

(*A* Ghost *goes to each side of stage and rolls out a pumpkin umbrella. A child is walking behind each.*)

Ghosts.
  We'll hide ourselves away,
  And when they come, we'll say: "O–O–OW–OW–U–U"
  They'll think it is an owl.
  And after that we'll growl; (*They growl.*)
  They'll think it is a dog.
  And after that a hog
  Because we'll grunt: (*They grunt.*)
  And if they come to hunt
  We'll give them a merry chase.

(*The* Ghosts *go behind the two umbrellas, so they cannot be seen by the audience.* Bre'r Rabbit *and* Susie *arrange the other* RABBITS *so that their legs are sticking out invitingly, while the rest of the* RABBIT *is hidden under the umbrella.*

The GOOD FAIRY *waves her wand—an electric light in it, if possible—and the full moon appears—with a light in it. The* OWL *calls and it is midnight.* GOOD FAIRY *disappears behind the mound.*

Two white boys come on stage, from the side, leading a white mule. A little colored boy is apparently riding on it.)

EZEKUAL. Dis yeah am de place all right.

AL. Yes, we're surely in the right place. Near a graveyard, a full moon, an owl to hoot, midnight. And we have a white mule. Ezekual, have you got your eyes crossed?

EZEKUAL. Yas sah.

OWL. (*Hoots.*) O–O–O–OW–OW–OW–U–U–U.

EZEKUAL. No sah, dis yere night air ain' good for me. My mammy done tole me, it'll pizen me and make me have the rematiz when I gits to be a ole man. Anyways I can't keep my eyes crost no longer, and lessen you has yo' eyes crost it ain't gwine do you no good at all to ketch a hind foot.

BOYS. Oh, come on, Zeke, be a sport!!

EZEKUAL. Boys, you see me looking at you. Well you look again and you ain't gwine see me at all. (ZEKE *makes a low bow to the* OWL.) Mr. Owl, effen any ghosts do come, you pay 'em my compliments an' tell 'em that if they wants to find me, to come to the third house from the cross-roads. It ain' no sense, at all, in jus' stayin' here an' waitin' for him. No, sah! Effen he wants me, he's jus' gotta come git me.

(ZEKE *runs off and* NICODEMUS *goes over to side of stage and sleeps.*)

AL. Well, we'll just have to go on without him. We can't stop now. Cross your eyes.

FRED. I can't cross my eyes. My mother won't let me. You cross yours. Oh! There's a rabbit! Two rabbits!

(*Fingers to lips, the boys tip-toe to the two* RABBITS. *Each boy stands back of a* RABBIT, *back to audience. He takes a lasso from around his neck or pocket and tries to get it around the foot of the* RABBIT.

The GHOSTS *slip around in back of the boys, back to the audience. They blow on the necks of the boys. The boys squirm. They then flick the boys lightly on the neck with their gloves. And again on the other side.*

The boys turn and face the GHOSTS *with a yell. The* GHOSTS *catch hold of the boys' hands, arms extended straight out from the shoulder. Boys pull their heads back, away from the* GHOSTS. GHOSTS *push their heads closer to boys, pushing them off-stage.*

Boys and GHOSTS *do any simple dance to ¾ time. Or:*
2 slides right, 2 slides left.
2 slides forward, 2 slides backward.
Turn around, etc., until boys have been danced off-stage at sides or back.

BRE'R RABBIT *and* SUSIE *take the little* RABBITS *to right side and have a pantomime conversation.* GHOSTS *frolic left side.* GOOD FAIRY *comes up on her mound in the rear.*

PUMPKINS *get up and walk forward and backward with their umbrellas, as though walking a tight rope. Then do "Dance of the Flowers," page 43 of "Dances, Drills and Story Plays" by Nina B. Lamkin, T. S. Dennison & Co. Or any other dance that they know.*

At the end of the dance the PUMPKINS *stand together, side front, partly facing the audience.)*

GOOD FAIRY. Well, little rabbits, are you satisfied at the night's work?

(LITTLE RABBITS *go over to the mound.*)

BRE'R RABBIT. Oh yes, Good Fairy, we thank you many times; and we will always remember your kindness to us.

GOOD FAIRY. Oh that's all right. And now, one last piece of advice, Bre'r Rabbit! Next Hallowe'en, keep your family at home. Then you will be in no danger of losing any of your four good feet. And now:

> The moon is hanging low, and the sky is turning blue.
> The owl is getting sleepy, and so are you;
> So we'll end this Hallowe'en as so many mortals do
> With a jugful of cider and a doughnut or two.

(*This may be used with the singing game "Jolly Is the Miller" found in "Twice 55 Games with Music"—The Red Book.*)

POEMS

ON A NIGHT OF SNOW

By Elizabeth J. Coatsworth

Cat, if you go outdoors you must walk in the snow.
   You will come back with little white shoes on your feet,
   Little white slippers of snow that have heels of sleet.
Stay by the fire, my Cat. Lie still, do not go.
See how the flames are leaping and hissing low,
   I will bring you a saucer of milk like a marguerite
   So white and so smooth, so spherical and so sweet—
Stay with me, Cat. Out-doors the wild winds blow.

Out-doors the wild winds blow, Mistress, and dark is the night.
Strange voices cry in the trees, intoning strange lore,
And more than cats move, lit by our eyes' green light,
On silent feet where the meadow grasses hang hoar—
Mistress, there are portents abroad of magic and might,
And things that are yet to be done. Open the door!

VILLANELLE

(A Protest Against the Habits of Ghosts)

By Dorothy Brown Thompson

Why shouldn't ghosts do something new,
   Instead of howling round at night?
There are so many things to do!

This hackneyed stuff they should eschew;
  (It seems they are not very bright.)
Why shouldn't ghosts do something new?

They might try making their debut
  At noon, with blasts of dynamite—
There are so many things to do!

Their garments should be red or blue,
  Not just monotonously white—
Why shouldn't ghosts do something new?

For steed, a yak—a kangaroo—
  A microbe—or a meteorite—
There are so many things to do!

Not wasting time with sad ado,
  But finding ever fresh delight:
Why shouldn't ghosts do something new?
There are so many things to do!

SMILING

By Dixie Willson

I met a Jack-o'-Lantern, Hallowe'en,
With the saddest face that I have ever seen!
For his mouth was turning down,
Both his eyes were made to frown,
And his forehead wrinkled crossly in between.
I thought it such a pity that his style
Had to keep him so unhappy all the while
For, as everybody knows,
Just the nicest thing that grows
Anywhere, on anybody, is a smile.

IMAGINATION

By John Davidson

There is a dish to hold the sea,
    A brazier to contain the sun,
A compass for the galaxy,
    A voice to wake the dead and done!

That minister of ministers,
    Imagination, gathers up
The undiscovered Universe,
    Like jewels in a jasper cup.

Its flame can mingle north and south;
    Its accent with the thunder strive;
The ruddy sentence of its mouth
    Can make the ancient dead alive.

The mart of power, the fount of will,
    The form and mould of every star,
The source and bound of good and ill,
    The key of all the things that are,

Imagination, new and strange
    In every age, can turn the year;
Can shift the poles and lightly change
    The mood of men, the world's career.

ON HALLOWE'EN

By Dorothy Brown Thompson

On Hallowe'en, what would you do—
If you were a witch, and the witch were you?

If I were a witch on Hallowe'en,
I wouldn't cook snakes in a big tureen,
And stir in frogs and a wall-eyed bat.
I'd nod my head to my old black cat.
Say, "Abracadabra" and "Presto, change!"
And then old Tabby would look so strange—
Like an ice-cream freezer with crook-tail crank;
I'd make some quickly, and then I'd thank
That nice old pussy and change her back;
Then we'd have a party, and—smack—smack—smack!

On Hallowe'en what would you do—
If you were a ghost, and the ghost were you?

If I were a ghost I wouldn't go
Just moaning round, like the tales you know,
At midnight, yowling behind some wall—
I wouldn't go out in the night at all.
With seven-league boots and invisible cloak,
I'd look for places to play some joke;
I'd go to a school where someone (like me)
Just couldn't remember the nine times three,
And whisper the answer, real soft—and say—
He'd get a one hundred per cent that day!

On Hallowe'en, if you're just you—
It's fun to plan all the things you'd do!

GAMES

AUTUMN AND HALLOWE'EN FUN
By Alice Crowell Hoffman

An Autumn-Leaf Game.—Let the children make a big heap of autumn leaves. Have the group line up on opposite sides of the leaf pile facing each other. There should be a like number of children on each side. When all is in readiness, the children join hands, forming a circle. They dance around the autumn leaves, singing to the tune of "Here We Go Round the Mulberry Bush,"

> Here we go round the autumn-leaf heap, autumn-leaf heap, autumn-leaf heap,
> Here we go round the autumn-leaf heap,
> All in the golden autumn.

As the last word is sung, each side tries to pull the other into the pile of autumn leaves. The side which first succeeds in doing this wins.

The Floating Jack-o'-Lantern.—A bright yellow balloon represents the jack-o'-lantern. Features may be painted on it, if desired. Stretch a cord across the room about three feet from the floor. Have half the children on one side, and half on the other. The floating jack-o'-lantern is tossed above the cord, and the children on each side, using their hands, try to bat it to the other side. When time is called, the side which does not have the floating jack-o'-lantern is the winner. The game may be repeated a number of times, since the children do not tire of it readily.

Scat, Black Cat.—The children sit in a circle with the exception of one, who is the Black Cat. The Black Cat gets down on all fours in the center of the circle and then goes up to anyone it pleases and says, "Miaow, miaow, miaow." The child before whom the Black Cat is miaowing must try to say three times, "Scat, Black Cat!" without laughing or smiling. If he can do this, the Black Cat goes up to another child and miaows. If a player fails to repeat the three words in the prescribed manner, he must exchange places with the Black Cat.

I Know a Goblin.—The leader explains that he knows a state in which there is a goblin; also that before he can count ten, the person to whom he points must try to name a city in that state. The players then form in two lines of equal number, facing each other. The leader stands between the two lines. He might begin the game by saying, "I know a goblin in Kentucky. Where does it live?" He points suddenly to a player and counts ten. If the player cannot name a city in Kentucky before ten is reached, he drops out of line. The leader then names another state and points to a member of the opposite group. The side having the most members remaining in line at the close of the game is the winner.

HALLOWE'EN GAMES

By Alice Crowell Hoffman

Hiding the Witch's Broomstick

One of the players leaves the room. While he is gone, another hides the broomstick, which may be represented by a rod or ruler. The player outside is called in and told to hunt for the witch's hidden broomstick. When he nears the object of his search, the other players clap their hands loudly; when he moves further away from it, they clap softly. As soon as he finds the witch's broomstick, he chooses another player to leave the room, and the game goes on as before.

Goblin over the Water

Someone is chosen to be the Goblin. All the others join hands, forming a circle around the Goblin. They dance around, saying:

> Goblin over the water,
> Goblin over the sea,
> Goblin caught a black cat
> But he can't catch me!

As soon as the players reach the last word of the rhyme, all stoop very low. This is the Goblin's chance to tag someone before he can stand erect. If the Goblin succeeds in tagging someone, the two exchange places. If the Goblin does not tag anyone in the first attempt, he must take another turn.

Don't Tread on the Black Cat's Tail

The black cat's tail is represented by a rather long, narrow strip of black cloth or paper, laid in the center of the room. The players stand in two lines of equal number, facing one another, and are equally distant from the black cat's tail. When all is in readiness, the players join hands, forming a circle, and skip merrily around the tail of the black cat. Someone suddenly calls, "Oh, don't tread on the black cat's tail!" This is the signal for a general struggle and pulling, each side trying to get the members of the other side against the tail of the black cat. Hands must be held tightly during the struggle. Any player who is pulled so that he touches the tail of the black cat must leave the group. Hands are clasped by the two adjoining players to fill the gap, and the game goes on. The side having the largest number of players when time is called is the winner.

Nut Circle

The players are divided into two groups of equal number. The captains of each side take their places and the members of their groups line up behind them, forming a straight line. Each player has a nut. In front of each captain a circle, about a foot in diameter, is drawn on the ground or outlined with autumn leaves. When the signal to begin is given, the captain of each line runs to the circle in front of him and throws in his nut. As soon as a captain gets back to his line, he touches the player next to him. This player then runs and drops a nut into the circle, returning to tag the next player as a signal for him to run and do likewise. Thus the game goes on, down both lines simultaneously. The side which first gets all the nuts into its circle is the winner.

A PARTY

A FIRST-GRADE HALLOWE'EN PARTY

By Helen Emily Snyder

One spring the kindergarten children planted in their garden pumpkin seeds that had been saved from their Hallowe'en pumpkins. On their return to school in the fall as first-graders, the children found a crop of seventeen pumpkins of assorted varieties and sizes.

The question of what to do with them arose. They were harvested and placed on a low shelf under a window, pending our decision. We could make pies of them. We could make jack-o'-lanterns. Finally came the desired response: We could give a Hallowe'en party. So we planned to give a party and invite the second grade, and one or two adults.

After discussing the party from various angles, we decided that the following items would be necessary, and placed the list on the blackboard.

invitations	doilies
decorations	favors
food	place cards
games	napkins
prizes for games	fortunes

In preparation for the event, we began by writing the invitations. They read as follows:

CELEBRATIONS FOR HALLOWE'EN

Please come
to
Our Hallowe'en Party
Wednesday, Oct. 31, 1935
10 to 11:30 A. M.
First-Grade Room

Much practice in writing the invitations was necessary before the results were satisfactory. Then the copies were decorated with appropriate seasonal emblems gleaned from the children's imaginations or past experiences. They were folded, addressed, and delivered ten days before the party.

We made the favors next—black cats about five inches long, cut from black construction paper. For these, I cut a cat's body with legs attached. Patterns for head and tail were cut separately. The children drew the cat faces. The heads and tails were fastened to the bodies with small paper fasteners, and strung with black thread so that they could be moved up and down like a jumping jack.

From black construction paper, 22 by 2 inches, we made headbands. Four-inch circles, cut from orange paper and decorated with pumpkin faces in black crayon, were pasted midway between the two ends of the headband. The ends were lapped and joined with two paper clips, making the band adjustable.

For prizes, we made three beanbags of approximately the same size. The first bag had a jack-o'-lantern face outlined with a running stitch in black embroidery cotton, on a 6-inch circle of orange felt. Another 6-inch circle of orange felt was cut for the back of the bag. The two pieces were then blanket-stitched together with black embroidery cotton, and filled with beans.

The second bag also had a jack-o'-lantern face outlined on orange felt with black embroidery cotton. In addition, this bag had a witch's pointed cap of black felt. The two pieces were blanket-stitched together with black embroidery cotton. The third bag, made of black felt, was a cat head with ears. We used orange embroidery cotton to outline the features, and blanket-stitched the two pieces together. Two extra jack-o'-lantern bags were made for use in a game.

The games we selected were Beanbags, Ninepins, and Pin the Nose on the Jack-o'-Lantern. For the game of Beanbags, one child painted on cardboard, 18 by 24 inches, a large orange pumpkin, with features outlined in black. The mouth was made round, and cut large enough to accommodate the beanbags. When the pumpkin had been cut out, it was mounted on a standard. Two beanbags were used, and a score of five was credited when a player tossed a bag into the mouth.

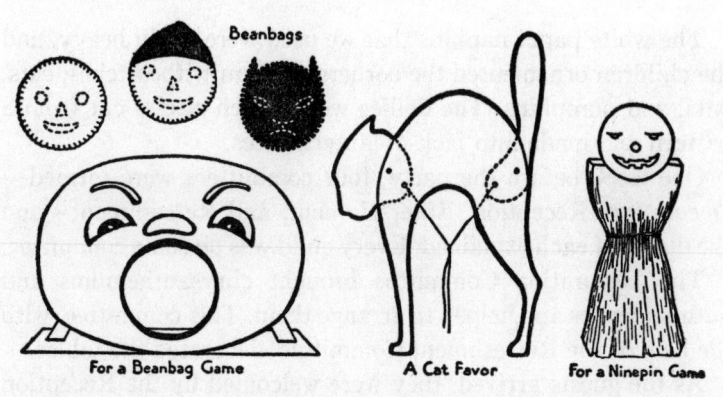

For a Beanbag Game   A Cat Favor   For a Ninepin Game

Ninepins were made from 12-inch paper sacks. The sack was opened, squeezed in at the middle, and tied with an orange string. A 4-inch pumpkin-head face was drawn on orange paper, cut out, and pasted on the sack's closed end, which represented the shoulders. These little men when placed in formation were bowled over with a tennis ball. A score of one was given for each felled man.

For Pin the Nose on the Jack-o'-Lantern a child painted a large noseless jack-o'-lantern face on wrapping paper 18 by 24 inches. Then the number of noses needed for the guests at the party were drawn, colored, cut, counted, and placed in a box with pins.

The place cards were made of white drawing paper 6 by 3 inches, folded lengthwise. They were decorated and the names were written on them.

The fortunes were written on paper 6 by 9 inches. They were decorated, folded, punched, and a long orange string was tied to each one, since they were to be placed in two hollowed-out pumpkins. Some of the fortunes are given below.

> You will go to a party.
> You will have some new clothes.
> You will see a picture.

The white paper napkins that we used were fairly heavy, and the children ornamented the corners of them with witches, cats, bats, and pumpkins. The doilies were 8-inch circles cut from a pattern and made into jack-o'-lantern faces.

One week before the party, four committees were formed—Decoration, Reception, Entertainment, and Refreshment—and the duties of each explained. Every child was on some committee.

The Decoration Committee brought chrysanthemums and autumn leaves and helped to arrange them. This committee, with the help of the Refreshment Committee, decorated the tables.

As the guests arrived, they were welcomed by the Reception Committee, which looked out for them generally during the party.

The games were explained, managed, and scored by the Entertainment Committee. The names of all present were written on the blackboard, and the Entertainment Committee marked the scores after the names. This committee also awarded the prizes.

Early on Hallowe'en morning the tables were set. Small tables were placed together to make two long ones. They looked very festive, with a doily, napkin, cat favor, headband, and candy basket at each place. From the center pumpkins, holding the fortunes, orange strings radiated to the doilies. Jack-o'-lanterns and autumn leaves added color.

The results were very gratifying. The children found an actual need for writing in the frequent lists that they made, the invitations, the icing recipe, and the fortunes. They found a use and a need for numbers when scoring games. They realized that a successful party needs to be planned, and that it is well to have two or three extra of everything in case of accident or extra guests. The social results were marked. The children learned the responsibility of the hostess, that the guest's pleasure comes first, that a hostess may participate in games but take no prize, and that the hostess must make all feel at home and happy.

ACTIVITIES

A PUMPKIN GAME FOR HALLOWE'EN
By Elizabeth Shark

All but the "pumpkin" form a circle holding hands. The "pumpkin" is in the center blindfolded. Those in the circle skip around, saying:
"Pumpkin, pumpkin,
Yellow-skin pumpkin,
Catch me if you can."
The "pumpkin" then tries to catch someone. The circle may move anywhere, but must not break clasps. The one caught is the next "pumpkin."

Variation: The "pumpkin" is not blindfolded, and the circle may break after saying the rhyme.

HALLOWE'EN MASKS
By Zeda A. Wahl

Inexpensive and usable Hallowe'en masks may be made from the large white paper sacks into which groceries are put. First, slip the sack over the head to determine the location of eyes, nose, and mouth. Mark these and remove the sack from the head. Cut out the features in proper shapes. Color lips, eyelashes, eyebrows, and hair on the sack. Either crayons or colored chalk may be used. Bats, cats, owls, and so on, may be cut from black paper and pasted on the top and back.

HALLOWE'EN MASKS MADE OF PAPER BAGS
By Mary B. Grubb

Many children enjoy making their own masks for Hallowe'en. Provide each child with a paper bag, large enough to slip over the head easily without tearing. It is well to have a few extra bags in case some of the finished masks are not satisfactory.

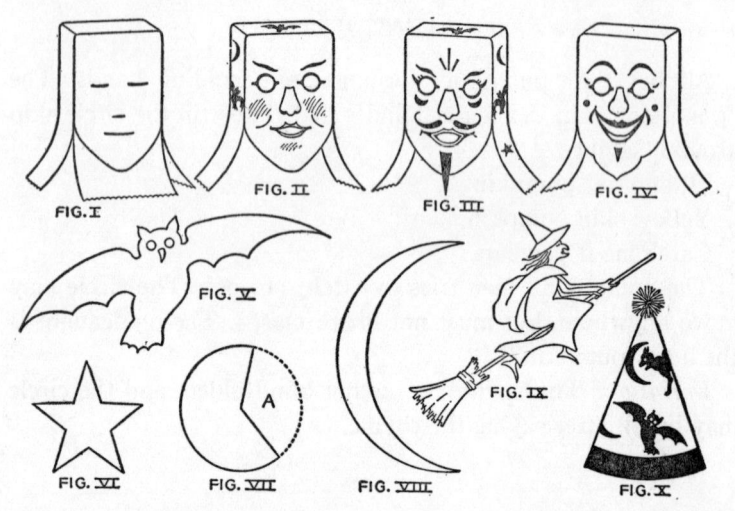

Other necessary materials are: scissors, paste, black and orange paper, and either crayons or water-color poster paints.

To show how the mask is made, have a child stand on a low chair in front of the class. Split a bag at the open corners, and slip it over the child's head. Locate the eyes, nose, and mouth by light lines made with blackboard crayon, such as those shown in Figure I.

Remove the bag, and draw a face, using the lines of Figure I as a basis. Cut openings for the features. Modify the shape of the eyes with black lines.

Try the mask on the child. If the features are satisfactorily placed, shape the bottom to fit the chin (Figure II), after removing the bag. Then the mask is ready to decorate. In coloring, make the lines heavy.

The children should develop their own ideas for decorating their masks. Give each one several pieces of paper the size of the front of his paper bag, to work on. Lead them to see that bold, rather than dainty, decoration is appropriate.

Figures III and IV suggest ways to finish the face. Fine strands of crêpe paper may be used to represent hair and whiskers. Some children like to draw a face on the back of the mask, to add to the fun.

Another way to decorate the mask is to paste on the sides, top, and back, figures cut from orange or black paper. Suitable designs are a black cat, bat (Figure V), star (Figure VI), moon (Figure VIII), jack-o'-lantern, and witch (Figure IX). Gummed seals similar to these designs can be used if preferred.

Pupils of third and fourth grades may wish to make original accessories, such as a cap (Figure X). It is made of heavy wrapping paper. Cut a large segment of a circle (Figure VII), and decorate it with drawing or cut-paper designs. Join the edges together with paste. Make the pompon of crêpe paper.

For a clown's mask use a small white paper flour sack, turned inside out.

As a safety measure, the children should be cautioned not to wear their masks on the way home. They do not fit securely, and may unexpectedly slip over the eyes.

Celebrations for Book Week

PLAYS

CHARACTERS' CABARET *

By Mirjane Strong

CHARACTERS

Lady Macbeth
Tarzan
Alice (From Wonderland)
Don Quixote
Huckleberry Finn
Becky Sharp
Mephistopheles
Scarlett O'Hara
Mr. Pickwick
Robinson Crusoe
Sherlock Holmes
Esmeralda
Mother Goose
First Witch
Second Witch
Third Witch
Romeo
Juliet
Hamlet
Macbeth

---

* All rights reserved: No performance of this play may be given without permission from, and payment of royalty of five dollars to, Mirjane Strong, 835 S. Sheridan Road, Highland Park, Illinois.

TIME: *The present.*

SCENE: *Cinderella's ballroom, which has been arranged like a night club with small tables and subdued lights. The dance floor is center back between two doorways, curtained with heavy portières. A small microphone stands in one corner of the floor. There are three tables on the stage and the seating must be accurate for the action. The table down left* * *seats* DON QUIXOTE, *up stage;* HUCK FINN, *down stage;* ALICE, *right; and* MOTHER GOOSE, *left. The table down right seats* SHERLOCK HOLMES, *up stage;* ROBINSON CRUSOE, *down stage;* ESMERALDA, *right; and* SCARLETT O'HARA, *left. The third table, which is right of center and nearer the dance floor, seats* LADY MACBETH, *up stage,* BECKY SHARP, *down stage;* MEPHISTOPHELES, *right; and* TARZAN, *left.*

As the curtain rises an orchestra is playing a current dance hit and the following guests are dancing: ALICE *with* DON QUIXOTE, *whose sword gets in everyone's way and whose elaborate apologies are even more trying:* ESMERALDA *with* ROBINSON CRUSOE; SCARLETT O'HARA *with* SHERLOCK HOLMES; *and* LADY MACBETH *with* TARZAN. MOTHER GOOSE *and* HUCK FINN *are sitting at their table.*

During the dancing BECKY SHARP *arrives with* MEPHISTOPHELES. *They are shown to their table by* MR. PICKWICK, *who is master of ceremonies.* BECKY *and* MEPHISTOPHELES *sit watching the dancers. They whisper and smile together, obviously discussing their companions.*

On the last strains of the music, LADY MACBETH *and* TARZAN, *who have been doing some fancy stepping together, execute a few steps of the "Lambeth Walk,"* LADY MACBETH *waggling her dagger in the air instead of her finger.* TARZAN *gives a ballroom version of his famous cry. The other characters applaud.*

---

* Stage's, not audience's, right and left.

ALICE. (*Dodging.*) Lady Macbeth will put someone's eye out with that dagger!

DON QUIXOTE. (*Gallantly offering his arm to* ALICE.) Fear not, fair lady, for the order of knighthood, which I profess, impels me to protect you all.

(*He seats her with a flourish. The other dancers go back to their tables, talking and laughing.*)

ALICE. (*Looking around.*) Have you seen Cinderella, tonight, Huckleberry?

HUCK FINN. (*Grinning.*) I reckon Cinderella's kinda tired—her havin' to be up every night till midnight. I reckon she's gone to bed with a good book.

(BECKY SHARP *and* MEPHISTOPHELES *have been exchanging greetings with* LADY MACBETH *and* TARZAN *and the occupants of the next table. Conspicuous on the front of* BECKY'S *gown is an elaborate diamond breast pin.*)

SCARLETT. (*Enviously.*) Becky Sharp! Where ever did you get that darling pin! (*She examines it.*)

BECKY. (*Her hand going to her breast.*) Oh, my brilliants?—Lord Steyne gave them to me. Wasn't that sweet of him? *Imagine* Lord Steyne remembering poor little me!

SCARLETT. I can.

(BECKY *meets her look with an innocent kitten stare.* MEPHISTOPHELES *leans over and whispers something to* SCARLETT, *who giggles.*)

SCARLETT. (*Giving him a little push.*) Oh, go 'way with you!

(BECKY *looks daggers at them both—then turning her chair around, gives all her attention to* TARZAN.)

BECKY. Tarzan, do tell me about your work. It must be wonderful with all those apes!

TARZAN. (*Flattered.*) Well—

MEPHISTOPHELES. Scarlett, give me rarest pleasure.
Dance with me this coming measure?

SCARLETT. (*Glancing at* ROBINSON CRUSOE, *who is talking*

with ESMERALDA.) Oh, I have to dance the next one with Robinson Crusoe!—But I'll try and save the one after for you.

(*She gives him her most charming smile.* MEPHISTOPHELES *moves a little closer. The lights in the main part of the ball room dim and a spot-light accents the dance floor, as* MR. PICKWICK *appears through the portières. Applause.*)

HUCK FINN. Hurrah for Pickwick!

(*This is greeted with "sh-h-h-he's."* MOTHER GOOSE *lays a kindly restraining hand on his arm.*)

PICKWICK. (*Benevolently.*) Ladies and gentlemen—my good friends. This is indeed a pleasure! I am especially happy to observe so many of you here this evening, for, as you know, the money derived from our little entertainment goes to the comfort of underprivileged and neglected characters. Most of us here have the advantage of being classics or—(*He bows to* SCARLETT *and* TARZAN.)—on the so-called "best seller" lists—(SCARLETT *blushes prettily.*)—but many are not so fortunate. Consequently it gives me exceptional pleasure to be able to welcome you all here tonight and to present our entertainment, which is in the competent hands of the Shakespeare group. (*Polite applause. . . . He moves the standing microphone to the centre of the floor.*)

SCARLETT. (*Suppressing a little yawn.*) I'm not so long on Shakespeare, myself. (*She glances quickly over her shoulder to be sure* LADY MACBETH *did not hear.*)

ROBINSON CRUSOE. (*Smiling.*) You would appreciate him had Providence—or your Author—stranded you upon a desert island.

SCARLETT. Saints preserve us—what a thought!

BECKY. (*Complacently.*) I'm so glad to be doing my little part to help out all those unfortunate characters!

MEPHISTOPHELES. Our Becky has a heart of gold,
             If we forget, we're always told.

BECKY. (*Tapping his cheek with her fan.*) Sweet Mephistopheles!

(*The last tap is almost a slap.* MEPHISTOPHELES *smiles enigmatically.*)

SCARLETT. Poor Elsie Dinsmore—she was on the shelf before I was born.

BECKY. (*Sweetly.*) Cheer up, dear, you may be there yourself soon.

SCARLETT. (*With equal sweetness.*) I know, honey, just where you'd be if you hadn't worked your way onto the required reading list.

(MR. PICKWICK *has been looking at his watch.*)

PICKWICK. (*Into the microphone.*) Good evening, ladies and gentlemen. This is Mr. Pickwick addressing you from Cinderella's ballroom where we are broadcasting the Characters' Cabaret. The Three Witch Sisters will sing "The Brewers' Blues."

(*He bows gallantly to the* WITCH SISTERS, *as they come tripping in, and leaves the floor.*)

(THE THREE WITCH SISTERS [*from Macbeth*] *have the conventional hag faces and weedy hair; but their bare arms are fair and their figures girlish and graceful in clinging evening gowns. They group themselves about the microphone and, accompanied by the orchestra, "swing" in harmony:—*)*

THREE WITCHES. "Double, double, toil and trouble,
    Fire burn and cauldron bubble,
    I said bubble—"

FIRST WITCH. (*Swaying into as much of a dance as the restrictions of the microphone permit.*)
  "Round about the cauldron go,
  In the poisoned entrails throw,
  Sweltered venom, sleeping got,
  Boil thou first in the charmed pot!"

ALL. "Double, double, toil and trouble,

---

* The Witches' Song can be "swung" to several popular tunes such as "Stop—It's Wonderful."

I said trouble—" (*Liberties can be taken with the "patter" depending on the ingenuity of the singers.*)

SECOND WITCH. (*Weaving her body.*)
"Fillet of a fenny snake
In the cauldron boil and bake,
For a charm of powerful trouble,
Like a hell-broth boil and bubble."

ALL. "Double, double, etc."

THIRD WITCH. "Cool it with a baboon's blood,
Then the charm is strong and good!"

ALL. "Double, double—"

(*If needed, more words can be borrowed from the original text—but the briefer the funnier.*)

(*Great applause greets this.* THE SISTERS *go off, and the lights come up in the ballroom.* MR. PICKWICK *moves the microphone to one side, the orchestra swings into a dance tune and most of the couples leave their tables for the dance floor.*)

ROBINSON CRUSOE. (*Escorting* SCARLETT.) I mentioned before that my professional life precludes this activity. I trust you will bear with me—

(SCARLETT *reassures him and they commence to dance.* LADY MACBETH *dances with* MEPHISTOPHELES—*they get on very well together*—; TARZAN *dances with* BECKY *and* DON QUIXOTE *persuades* MOTHER GOOSE *to take a turn.* MR. PICKWICK *comes over to* ALICE'S *table and pats her on the shoulder.*)

PICKWICK. How are you, my dear? Are you enjoying yourself?

ALICE. Yes, very much, thank you.

PICKWICK. Well, well—(*He sits down and mops his bald head and wipes his spectacles.*) There—now we'll show these people how to dance, shall we? (*Rising.*)

ALICE. I should like to—do you mind, Huckleberry?

HUCK FINN. No—go ahead! I'll go talk to Esmeraldy about

that there hunchback of what-cha-ma-call-it.

PICKWICK. Ah, the hunchback of Notre Dame. Well, Esmeralda's the one who can tell you. (*To* ALICE *as they begin to dance.*) Now, a minuet is what I prefer—

(HUCK FINN *joins* ESMERALDA *and* SHERLOCK HOLMES *at their table.* ESMERALDA *describes the hunchback with gestures as* HUCK *has trouble with her broken English. Then he asks her to dance and they join the others, excusing themselves to* HOLMES, *who assures them that he prefers to study the dancing. The dance ends shortly and the couples return to the tables.*)

TARZAN. (*To* ESMERALDA.) *Voulez-vous danser avec moi?*
ESMERALDA. (*Giving him a bright smile.*) *Mais oui!*
HUCK FINN. How do you talk that stuff?

(SCARLETT *beckons to* HUCK *as he passes and whispers something that amuses him very much.*)

DON QUIXOTE. (*As he seats* MOTHER GOOSE.) Madam, it is a privilege to dance with one so light and graceful as your sweet ladyship.

MOTHER GOOSE. (*Blushing and laughing.*) Lauk a mercy on us, this is none of I!

ALICE. I liked the Witch Sisters. What comes next?

PICKWICK. Ah, wait and see.—Thank you, my dear, for dancing with an old fellow.

(*The lights in the ballroom dim again and* MR. PICKWICK *takes the spot-light after a few uneasy glances at a microphone hanging below the proscenium arch. Applause and scraping of chairs.*)

PICKWICK. (*Beaming.*) And now, ladies and gentlemen—(*He pauses.*)—we have Romeo and Juliet, who will give us their famous waltz. (*Considerable applause, and he bows himself off as* ROMEO *and* JULIET *come on and gravely go into their waltz. They dance beautifully—either to the waltz from the opera "Romeo and Juliet" or to a modern waltz. They are encored several times and may repeat a few measures.*)

BECKY. (*When the ballroom lights come up.*) They do quite well, don't you think? One never knows what these amateur performances will be.

LADY MACBETH. (*Indignantly fingering her dagger.*) Amateur!
  Why, Shakespeare's men and women trod the boards,
  Ere Thackery was e'en a twinkle in his father's eye!

BECKY. (*Hastily, eyeing the dagger.*) Oh, I didn't mean it that way, I assure you!

(MR. PICKWICK *has been looking critically at the suspended microphone and gesturing to some unseen person who is trying to adjust it.*)

PICKWICK. (*Quietly.*) Up a little—no, not so much—just turn it a little—here—(*He comes over to the tables, right.*) Forgive me for disturbing you—we are having a little difficulty adjusting the microphone—(*He struggles with an extra chair.*) but with the assistance of this chair, I think I can just manage—(*He starts to ascend the chair.*)

HOLMES. My dear fellow, hadn't I better do that for you?

PICKWICK. (*Smiling and panting.*) Oh, dear dear no, I wouldn't consider it, Sir—(HUCK FINN *has joined the group.*) —I shall merely—(*He loses his balance and is saved by* BECKY, *who being back of him, steadies him.*) Thank you—so good of you, my dear—now I can reach—(*He gives the cord a twitch. The lights flicker and flicker again and then go out altogether. The characters respond with the usual gasps and giggles and after a moment the lights come on.*) Now, what caused that? However it is all right now—and so is the microphone.

(MEPHISTOPHELES *is gazing upward humming the* Jewel Song *from "Faust."* SCARLETT *smothers a giggle.* LADY MACBETH *is smiling.* HUCK FINN *goes back to his own table. Suddenly a shriek disturbs the cheerful atmosphere.*)

BECKY. My diamonds! They're gone! (*She clutches her bodice.*)

PICKWICK. What!

BECKY. My brilliants!—they're gone! The diamond breastpin Lord Steyne gave me!

PICKWICK. (*Bewildered.*) Why, it can't be—there must be some mistake.

BECKY. (*Bursting into furious tears.*) But I tell you it IS gone—see for yourself—! (*Everyone has risen. Suddenly the lights go out again.* BECKY *shrieks.*) STOP THIEF!

DON QUIXOTE. (*His voice ringing out.*) Fear not, fair lady— (*There are sounds of a scuffle and a heavy body falling. Some woman gives a little shriek. There are more sounds of combat and heavy breathing, punctuated by—*) Fly not, thou rascally knave—I have thee— Thou—shalt leave thy life—a forfeit for thy temerity! (*Steel clashes against steel.*) And thou, too, scoundrel—do thy worst!

(*The lights all come on revealing* DON QUIXOTE *dueling with the standing microphone and enveloped in one of the heavy portieres, which came down when he grappled with it.*)

HOLMES. There—it's all right. No need for alarm.

(*Everyone is standing up and* HOLMES, TARZAN *and* HUCK FINN *have rushed to separate* DON QUIXOTE *and the portiere.*)

DON QUIXOTE. (*Still lashing about blindly with his sword.*) Let me at the dastardly rabble!

(TARZAN *wrests the sword from him while* HOLMES *and* HUCK FINN *untangle the portiere.*)

HOLMES. Nobly done, my friend!

(DON QUIXOTE *is so encumbered with clumsy armour that it takes three to get him to his feet.*)

DON QUIXOTE. (*Throwing out his chest and surveying the scene.*) Are they all slain?

HOLMES. You routed them all—it was magnificent!

Don Quixote. (*Modestly.*) God has made me a fortunate knight.

Alice. (*Taking his arm.*) Are you sure you're all right?

Becky. (*Shrilly.*) This is all very amusing, but where are my brilliants?

Pickwick. (*Bewildered by all this.*) But I don't understand—

Becky. (*Her voice rising.*) My diamonds, my diamonds! —I tell you—

Holmes. (*Soothingly.*) Now, if you will all be calm—

Becky. (*Furiously.*) I will not be calm! Nor will I leave this place until my diamonds are returned! (*Sarcastically.*) Mr. Sherlock Holmes, the case is yours!

Holmes. (*Gravely.*) At your service, Miss Sharp. I think I can guarantee that your jewels will be recovered before the evening is over. (*His tongue in his cheek, he proceeds to conduct the conventional investigation with lens, rule, etc.*)

Pickwick. Yes, of course they will be. Perhaps the pin came unfastened and fell to the floor—(*He starts to lift the table cloth and look under—then blushes and steps back.*) Forgive my zeal, Madam. Perhaps you will look yourself.

Becky. (*Looking half-heartedly.*) Of course it isn't here! (*Aside.*) Idiot!

Scarlett. Don't think about it now—think about it tomorrow. Mr. Holmes may find it.

(Becky *looks at her suspiciously.* Holmes *examines the front of* Becky's *bodice with his lens.*)

Becky. (*Tartly.*) Is this necessary?

Holmes. (*Gravely.*) Madam, it is not for pleasure, I assure you.

(Mephistopheles *innocently whistles a few bars from the* Jewel Song *while* Holmes *studies one of* Huck's *bare feet.*)

Huck Finn. (*Grinning.*) Want my toe prints?

Holmes. An excellent suggestion.—Ah, I see that you come

from America—Missouri, I should say. That clay mixture under your large toe-nail is quite distinctive.

(MR. PICKWICK *has been looking nervously at his watch, glancing uneasily in the direction of the orchestra, signalling the players to wait, etc. He now addresses* HOLMES *in an undertone.*)

HOLMES. Certainly, my dear fellow, go right on with your entertainment.

PICKWICK. —on account of the broadcast, you understand. (*He hurries off. The ballroom lights dim once more and* MR. PICKWICK *reappears in the spot-light, mopping his brow.*) Ladies and gentlemen, may I present The Prince of Denmark and The Thane of Cawdor.

(*Applause from the guests.* MR. PICKWICK *disappears. The orchestra plays an introduction and* HAMLET *and* MACBETH *in their conventional costumes, with the addition of top hats, enter from opposite sides of the dance floor. They both wear black face [minstrel] make-up.*)

HAMLET. How now, Macbeth, what lady did I see,
         With these two eyes, last even', accompany thee?
MACBETH. Good Hamlet, I swear to thee upon my life,
         No lady that—forsooth 'twas just my wife!

(*He slaps his thigh and roars with laughter in which the guests join, glancing at* LADY MACBETH *who enjoys it too.* MACBETH *and* HAMLET *then go into a tap-dance routine, which is greeted with much applause. When the lights come on,* HOLMES *is discovered, his eyes closed, his elbows on the arms of his chair, finger-tips together, "reasoning."*)

BECKY. (*Sarcastically.*) Well, Mr. Holmes, where are my brilliants?

HOLMES. (*Not stirring.*) I shall produce them for you shortly.

(MEPHISTOPHELES *leans forward.*)

MEPHISTOPHELES. Is it possible you have solved
         The myst'ry?—Tell us who's involved!

HOLMES. (*Coming to life.*) First of all I wish to question Mr. Pickwick. (*Astonished murmurs of* "Pickwick?" BECKY *sighs resignedly.* HUCK FINN *and* SCARLETT *giggle openly, and even* LADY MACBETH *is grimly amused.*) Pickwick, my friend, will you take this seat here. (HOLMES *places a chair for* MR. PICKWICK, *back to the footlights.*)

PICKWICK. (*Doubtfully.*) Indeed, I hope I can be of some assistance to you—(*He lifts his coat tails and sits down only to rise immediately with a cry—*) My goodness! (*Fastened to the seat of* MR. PICKWICK'S *trousers is* BECKY SHARP'S *missing pin.*)

BECKY. My pin!

HOLMES. Exactly. Your pin.

(*The characters crane their necks to see.* HUCK *is doubled up with laughter.* SCARLETT *is wiping hysterical tears from her eyes.* MOTHER GOOSE *exclaims* "Lauk a mercy!" *and there is a babble of questions and exclamations in character.*)

PICKWICK. (*Dislodging the pin with some confusion.*) I assure you I had nothing to do with this! I was entirely unaware of its presence until this very moment. (*This causes a fresh outburst of laughter. He hands the pin to* HOLMES.)

HOLMES. My dear fellow, I am sure you were. Of course the pin *may* have become loose and fastened on to your—er—person while you were fixing the microphone and Miss Sharp was steadying you from behind—it MIGHT, I say.

SCARLETT. (*Too innocently.*) Of course—that's just how it happened. So obvious.

(MEPHISTOPHELES *gazes thoughtfully heavenward.*)

MEPHISTOPHELES. Facts are stranger far than fiction,
         'Twas accident—that's my conviction.

HOLMES. (*Ignoring these interruptions.*)—On the other hand, the pin could have been transferred during the brief period of darkness, which, you will recall, occurred quite inexplicably while Pickwick was adjusting the microphone. (MR. PICKWICK *mops his forehead and looks at his watch.*) This, in my opinion, is the correct solution.

HUCK FINN. (*Grinning up at* HOLMES.) But you wouldn't want to tell us right out who done it, would you? Not afore all these folks.

HOLMES. Certainly not.

HUCK FINN. (*Disappointed.*) Aw g'wan—bet yuh don't know—

HOLMES. (*Ignoring him.*) I shall merely commission Miss O'Hara and Mephistopheles to return the jewels to Miss Sharp.

(*He hands the pin to* SCARLETT, *who takes it with mock gravity. Then she makes a deep curtsy and* MEPHISTOPHELES *a courtly bow and together they solemnly hand the pin to* BECKY.)

BECKY. (*Jabbing the pin into her bodice.*) I might have known it would be you two!

(MR. PICKWICK *mops his forehead again. The orchestra starts playing a dreamy dance tune.* MR. PICKWICK *again consults his watch.*)

PICKWICK. Dear me—(*He hurries to the standing microphone, watch in hand, as the couples move out onto the dance floor*—TARZAN *with* ESMERALDA, SCARLETT *with* MEPHISTOPHELES, DON QUIXOTE *with* LADY MACBETH, *etc.*) This is Mr. Pickwick saying good night to you from Cinderella's ballroom and the Characters' Cabaret.

CURTAIN

NOTES ON PRODUCTION: This play must move swiftly, action and dialogue often taking place simultaneously.

A person taking part would do well to refresh his mind with the character he portrays, since there is little dialogue and the characterizations depend on mannerisms and personality.

THE MISSING BOOKEND *

By Elbridge S. Lyon

CHARACTERS

Myra
Mother

Penrod
Ben Hur
Tom Sawyer
Lorna Doone
Sherlock Holmes
Robinson Crusoe
Alice in Wonderland

Right Bookend
Left Bookend

Scene: *Living room in the evening.*

Myra *is sitting in large chair reading. There is a table on which is a row of six books with one empty space, between white plaster bookends. These books must be as conspicuous as possible.* Mother *enters.*

Mother. Come, Myra, it is getting late.
Myra. I want to finish this chapter.
Mother. (*Looking over shoulder.*) Why you have just started a chapter.
Myra. But, Mother, she is out alone on the edge of the moor and darkness is falling.
Mother. Who is?
Myra. Lorna Doone.

* For permission to produce, consult the author, Chatham, N.J.

Mother. You read Lorna Doone last year. You know exactly what is going to happen to her.

Myra. But she needs help.

Mother. In that case, I guess you need help, too. You mustn't get so worked up. You must sleep. She is only a character in a book, you know.

Myra. Please—just this one chapter—anyway, till the wind stops blowing on the dune.

Mother. My dear child, if you wait for the wind to stop blowing, then you will want to wait for something else. Come, off to bed. Put up the book. (*She takes book gently from reluctant* Myra *and places it between bookends on table.*)

Myra. I hear the wind on the moor.

Mother. You hear the wind right here. It is a stormy night.

(*Wind is heard.* Mother *and* Myra *go off, putting out lights. While stage is dark, table and chair are removed. Curtain at back opens, or screens are removed, exposing in pale light a large-scale row of books with bookends representing same set that had been on table. The books are pieces of beaver board 20 inches wide by six feet high, or may be all in one piece, painted accordingly. Titles are painted at top. Books are Tom Sawyer, Alice in Wonderland, Lorna Doone, Ben Hur, Robinson Crusoe, Sherlock Holmes, and Penrod. Under each title stands an actor dressed to represent the proper character. The two bookends are figures with white faces and sheet togas as if made of plaster. They are each seated on a two-step pedestal with profile to audience and back against books.*)

R. Bookend. Whom have we got now?

L. Bookend. Same old bunch, I guess.

R. Bookend. I'm getting awfully stiff. Mind if I stretch? This gang has been leaning on me all day.

L. Bookend. All right. Shove them over.

(Right Bookend *stands up holding books with one hand,*

pushes them over towards LEFT BOOKEND, *who braces to hold them. Book characters lean slightly, and turn faces slightly toward left.* RIGHT BOOKEND *turns front, stretches, yawns and steps down from pedestal.*)

R. BOOKEND. (*Looking over books.*) Yep, same old bunch. I can't see why they don't ever get any new books. Something up to the minute like Gone with the Wind. By the way, didn't the old lady say something about the wind blowing and it storming?

(*Wind has stopped.*)

LORNA DOONE. The child heard the wind—it was from my country.

R. BOOKEND. There isn't any wind. I can't hear any.

LORNA DOONE. It stopped when the child went to sleep.

R. BOOKEND. I'll bet the kid has bad dreams.

LORNA DOONE. No, she is already sleeping peacefully, thinking how she can help Huckaback.

R. BOOKEND. Who is that?

LORNA DOONE. One of my characters that you wouldn't know.

(BOOKEND *sits on lower part of pedestal with elbow on upper part, resting.*)

R. BOOKEND. I've tried to read all these books, but I can't go most of them.

L. BOOKEND. I've read Alice in Wonderland 82 times, and I enjoy her more every time.

ALICE. (*Bowing.*) Thank you.

R. BOOKEND. That is the silliest book of all; no sense in it.

ALICE. You never read me through.

R. BOOKEND. I should say not. You're stupid stuff.

ALICE. Thank you, kind sir, but I make people think!

R. BOOKEND. You! Make people think? That's a good one—with your Dormouse and your Mad Hatter and other silly things.

ALICE. Who else ever played chess on croquet grounds? That is thinking, isn't it?

R. Bookend. For little children, maybe.

L. Bookend. Every day you hope for a new book to be brought in, and you haven't really read any of these.

R. Bookend. I've read Ben Hur. He's the stuff. Killings and intrigues all through.

Ben Hur. You didn't get my message. You only looked for excitement.

R. Bookend. Did you have a message?

Ben Hur. I foretold— Oh, what's the use?

L. Bookend. I understood—about the Messiah.

Ben Hur. I know you did. I enjoy having you read me. Most folks are like this other bookend, just read for amusement and miss the point entirely. Still, if we weren't interesting, nobody would read us.

R. Bookend. Lorna Doone certainly isn't interesting.

L. Bookend. Look how Myra devoured her.

R. Bookend. And she'll have indigestion all night.

Lorna Doone. Not at all. She is very happy.

R. Bookend. How do you know?

Lorna Doone. When a person is reading a book, the book is reading the person.

L. Bookend. Then when a person is in the middle of a book, the book is in the middle of a person?

Lorna Doone. Exactly.

L. Bookend. That is some mystery.

Sherlock H. Mystery—mystery—who said mystery?

L. Bookend. No, never mind, Sherlock Holmes, this is too deep for you.

Sherlock H. There has never been a mystery I couldn't solve. All I need is a magnifying glass.

R. Crusoe. You never were shipwrecked on a desert island, were you?

Sherlock H. Not me. I never got wrecked anywhere.

R. Crusoe. Then you never knew a real mystery. I didn't

even have any magnifying glass, but I followed footprints in the sand, and whose do you think they turned out to be?

PENROD. Your man, Friday.

R. CRUSOE. Right. How did you know?

PENROD. Huh, I read you long before I was turned into a book.

TOM SAWYER. I spent a week once on a deserted island in the middle of a river; so I know how you felt.

R. CRUSOE. Did you find any bones of dead natives?

TOM SAWYER. I caught a robber in a cemetery.

PENROD. Maybe he "saw yer?"

TOM SAWYER. What did you say, Penrod?

R. BOOKEND. This is nonsense.

L. BOOKEND. I guess there are lots of things in the book world that folks don't realize.

ALICE. Did you know that the Jabberwock was once a college professor?

R. BOOKEND. Who cares?

TOM SAWYER. I do.

PENROD. I do.

TOM SAWYER. Did you know that Penrod and I are the same soul; only he is me again a couple of generations later?

R. BOOKEND. More nonsense.

LORNA DOONE. If you would read both books, you would realize how much alike they are.

R. BOOKEND. Well, all boys are like that.

PENROD. Try as I would, I never could get any kids to paint *my* fence.

L. BOOKEND. Wouldn't humans be surprised if they knew that books compared notes this way and talked to each other?

R. BOOKEND. And what rubbish they talk.

SHERLOCK H. If I could write a book, I'd call it "The Fly in the Ointment," and you would be the fly.

R. BOOKEND. Who, me? Why?

R. Crusoe. You are always a killjoy.

R. Bookend. Rubbish.

Lorna Doone. That's right. Here we are, all congenial but you.

R. Bookend. Well, I hold you up, don't I?

Penrod. You don't do your share.

L. Bookend. It's high time you got up into your place. These folks want to rest on the other foot, and I am getting tired, too.

R. Bookend. Since you seem to be the favorite around here, you might as well hold them up a little longer. They are too weak to stand up alone. Maybe that is where the idea of "Book-Week" comes from. Nobody ever cares about bookends, I notice.

L. Bookend. Honest, I'm slipping.

R. Bookend. Here, my fine friends, lean on this. (*Gets up and gets a huge jardiniere, real or painted on board, and places it on top of pedestal against books. Characters lean slightly towards it and turn faces front.*) There you are. As for me, I am going down to the library to get a book to read.

(*Goes off. Black curtain is closed covering books and characters. There is darkness. Table and chair are replaced as before, books on table with one bookend as before, and on other hand is vase resembling the jardiniere. Dawn is approaching. As it gets lighter,* Myra *in wrapper comes in, takes Lorna Doone from books, and settles excitedly into big chair and reads.* Mother *enters.*)

Mother. My dear child, why did you get up so early?

Myra. It isn't early, is it?

Mother. Well, yesterday I couldn't get you out of bed an hour later than this.

Myra. I couldn't sleep.

Mother. I suppose I was the same when I was a child. Look at these books—what ever became of this bookend? It was here last night, wasn't it?

MYRA. I think so.
MOTHER. Did you put this vase here?
MYRA. No, Mother.
MOTHER. Look at me. Did—you—break the bookend?
MYRA. No, really I didn't.
MOTHER. You were the only one in here.
MYRA. I don't know what became of it.
MOTHER. That certainly is funny. I wonder where it can be.
MYRA. Maybe it went down to the library to get another book.
MOTHER. Why, Myra, what ever made you think of such a silly thing?
MYRA. (*Laughing.*) I guess I must have dreamed it.

CURTAIN

A NOTE ON THE PRODUCTION OF "BOOK FROLIC"

How Eleven Departments in a High School Helped Make Book Week a Grand Success

BY ANNE MADISON BEEMAN

The celebration of Book Week in our high school [*] proved to be a great success.

It was the Librarian's opportunity to obtain the interest of many departments of the school and at the same time provide an interesting week for the students.

The week opened with the special book displays in the library which attracted great attention throughout the week. Then there was the Book Week Assembly at which was presented the play, "Book Frolic." It was through this play that the splendid co-operation of the eleven departments was obtained; and the heads of these departments were responsible for the success of

[*] University High School, West Los Angeles, Cal.

the play.

The displays in the library offered so much interest to the students that a description of some of them is given. On a large display table opposite the entrance door was a splendid collection of brand new books. Perhaps you do not know what such a collection meant to our 1,600 boys and girls. They had not had the joy of seeing new additions for three long years and when a table was loaded with attractive new ones, you may know it meant a thrill to every student who had read and reread so many of the old shabby ones on our shelves. It was a real joy to hear their Oh's! and Ah's! and "O, boy, new books!"

Another display was the new rebound books. All of our old shabby ones had been sent to the bindery during the summer to be all dressed up in new suits. Upon their return we took the bright new book jackets we had saved and pasted them on the front covers of the books. It was just like taking an old house and painting it so that it looked like new. The students flocked to this table as they thought they were also new additions and were so surprised when they found their old favorites in bright new shiny covers.

There was a display of all the Newbery prize stories. Here also was the Newbery prize medal book which tells all about the authors who won the prize medals. There were other displays on different subjects such as airships, poetry, biography and travel.

There was a delightful nook which lent itself most charmingly to our Oriental display. As a background we had some very colorful posters of Japanese scenes and Japanese figures. Here we placed some of our most entertaining and attractive books on Japan and China. To complete the picture we had some exquisite Japanese dolls.

"Hobbies" of a number of students occupied another corner of our library. There was a collection of China animal dolls. A collection of mounted butterflies came next. Some were from

South America. There were three water color paintings painted by a B9 student. These were splendidly done and attracted great attention. A book plate display was most interesting. And of course no Hobby exhibit is complete without the stamp collection.

Then there was the exhibit of the play, "Book Frolic." The Art class that fashions beautiful objects from clay heard of the play and wished to fashion some of the characters. They decided to make it a class project. The result of the project was that there was the entire setting of the stage, a miniature figure of every character in the play even to the "text books," and "Freddy the Toad."

Appropriate posters relating to Book Week made by the Art Department were displayed in various nooks and corners with the addition of plants, ferns and flowers. The library was surely dressed up in its best clothes. The displays alone were worth all the trouble and work it took to prepare them.

The play was presented by the Junior Drama Playshop under the direction of the dramatics teacher. The play was made a project for every department that assisted in its presentation. The students of the Junior Drama Playshop read the play in class. Every student was required to read every book mentioned in the play so as to become familiar with every character. Try outs were then made. Each student in the class was given an opportunity to portray the different characters and then the class selected the ones best fitted for the different parts. The work was then begun on the play itself. Students were made responsible for the success of the play. There was the Student-Director, an Assistant Director, Stage Manager, Scenery Director, Lights, Costume Mistresses, Make-up Committee, etc. Nothing was left undone to make the production a success. The teacher of Drama has the ability to make students live the parts they portray. Rehearsals were daily with the final dress rehearsal with lights, and everything complete.

The Costume department made notes of the kind of costumes and items needed. First of all a visit was made to the costume room and costumes which could be used for any character were assembled. Then some costumes were made over. Then new material was bought for costumes not in stock. The student actors had to go to the costume designer and be measured and fitted for the costume to be worn in the part. Seventy costumes had to be made for this play. Among the most outstanding costumes were "Freddy the Toad"; "Fun with Figures"; the four Text Books, Mathematics, Spanish, Chemistry and Geography.

The sets for the play were made by the Art Department. The Art Director read the play to his Stage Crew class. Notes were made of all necessary articles, and sets that needed to be designed and painted. After the list was completed these items were designed on paper, either full size or to the scale. With the co-operation of the Woodshop Department the sets were then substantially constructed. The painting of articles such as spears, a mountain scene, trees for a forest, a moon and stars, a castle with lights in the windows and many hundred and one details and articles not noticed by the audience followed. Arrangements of lights for a night or day scene, a sunset, or the purple mists of evening were made.

Plants and trees were selected from the Floriculture Department to give a realistic appearance to the outdoor scene.

The Music Department furnished the music for the play and trained the students for the opening dance of the Queen's attendants.

Other dances such as the Dances of the Twins; the Japanese, the Scotch and the Dutch twins, the dance of "Fun with Figures," the four Text Books and Pinocchio's doll dance were trained by the Physical Education Department.

The program was mimeographed by the Text Book Clerk.

The whole Book Week project was a great success due to the splendid correlation and co-operation of the different heads of the departments, teachers, students and librarian. Here is the play.

BOOK FROLIC *

By Anne Madison Beeman

CHARACTERS

(In the order of their appearance)

MOTHER
PETER
SUZANNE
QUEEN OF BOOKLAND
FREDDY THE TOAD
PAGES
WOODLAND SPRITES
PETER PAN
KING ARTHUR
SIR GAWAIN
SIR PELLEAS
ARITHMETIC
GEOGRAPHY
CHEMISTRY
SPANISH
FUN WITH FIGURES
LONG JOHN SILVER
PIRATES
ALICE IN WONDERLAND
CAT
TWO
FIVE

* For permission to produce, consult Mrs. Anne Madison Beeman, 11800 Texas Ave., West Los Angeles, Cal.

SEVEN
ROBIN HOOD
DUTCH TWINS
JAPANESE TWINS
AMERICAN TWINS
PINOCCHIO
REBECCA OF SUNNYBROOK FARM
TOM SAWYER
HUCKLEBERRY FINN

ACT I: *Living room in the home of* MR. *and* MRS. WILKINS. *Evening about ten o'clock.*

ACT II: *Woodland scene—The Country of Bookland. Later—same evening.*

ACT III: *Same scene as Act I. Later—same evening.*

ACT I

SCENE: *Living room in the home of* MR. *and* MRS. WILKINS. *Evening.*

(*Seated at the table opposite each other are* PETER *and his little sister,* SUZANNE. *Both are studying. Books are piled on the table.*)

MOTHER. (*Calling from upstairs.*) Peter! Peter!
PETER. Yes, Mother.
MOTHER. It is getting near bedtime for you and Suzanne.
PETER. But, Mother, I have this dreadful home work to do. Chemistry, geography, and Spanish. I'll be through pretty soon, though.
SUZANNE. And I have this arithmetic.
MOTHER. Well, do not be long now, children. I expect you to go to bed soon.

PETER. O.K. We will.

(*Silence for a minute, both intent on their books.*)

SUZANNE. I wish I never had to study this arithmetic. I would rather read books instead.

PETER. Well, I suppose we have to learn all the things in these stupid text-books.

SUZANNE. Oh, I suppose so. (*Sighs.*) Numbers, numbers, numbers, there is no fun in figures. (*Becomes more studious. Writing numbers on a large pad.*) 2×2 is 4; 4×2 is 8; 2×32 is what? Peter, what is it?

PETER. Is what? I wasn't listening. Now what is it you want to know?

SUZANNE. What is 2×32?

PETER. 64, you silly.

SUZANNE. Oh, dear. (*Continues with her work for a few seconds, her head begins to droop, lower and lower. She finally puts her head on her arms on the table and goes sound asleep.*)

(PETER *glances at his sister and smiles and goes on with his work for a few seconds. He finally begins nodding, slips down in his chair, puts his head on his arms on the table and goes to sleep.*)

(*Curtain drops very slowly.*)

Act II

SCENE: *Woodland scene. Castles in the distance. Blue sky, with stars and moon. Trees with twinkling lights which go on and off. A Throne with two tall chairs at center of back stage. Faint music is heard.*

(PETER *and* SUZANNE *creep in very slowly and cautiously.*)

PETER. I wonder what place this is.

SUZANNE. Oh, Peter, isn't it beautiful?

PETER. Be careful, I hear someone coming. Let's hide and wait to see who comes in. Suzanne, you get behind that tree, and I'll hide here.

(*Puts finger to his lips for her to be quiet. The music becomes louder. It is Mendelssohn's music from A Midsummer Night's Dream. Enter the* QUEEN OF BOOKLAND, *followed by her* PAGES *and* WOODLAND SPRITES, *dancing as they come in.* FREDDY THE TOAD *follows them and takes his seat on a stool. The* QUEEN *goes to her seat on the throne. She smiles as they dance. After the dance the* QUEEN *comes down and her escort gathers around her and they suddenly see* SUZANNE *and then* PETER.)

QUEEN. Well, see this boy and little girl. Who are you? Do you know where you are?

PETER. I am Peter Wilkins and this is my sister, Suzanne. Can you tell us where we are? And who are you?

QUEEN. You are in Bookland and I am Queen of Bookland.

SUZANNE. Who else lives here? And who are these little folks who danced? (*Waves her hand toward the dancers.*)

QUEEN. All the characters in books live here and these are all my pages. You could not have come to a happier place.

SUZANNE. Oh, Peter, what fun we will have if we stay here!

PETER. (*To the* QUEEN.) We will stay if you will show us just what you do and let us see some of the people who live here. Could we see Robin Hood and King Arthur and—

SUZANNE. (*Interrupts.*) And could we see Alice in Wonderland, the Twins and Pinocchio?

QUEEN. Yes, and many more. We will show you what you have never yet seen.

SUZANNE. (*Claps her hands.*) Oh, Goody, Goody.

QUEEN. Now here comes our little boy who will never grow up, Peter Pan.

PETER PAN. (*Leaps on the stage and makes a low bow before the* QUEEN, *taking off his cap as he bows.*) What service may I render you, dear Queen?

QUEEN. Peter Pan, this boy, Peter and his little sister, Suzanne, are to be our guests tonight and they want to see their favorite Book Friends. I suppose the Bookish friends they do not like will insist on being here, but we will take care of them. Now what I want you to do, Peter Pan, is to announce them all as they appear.

PETER PAN. Oh, what fun! (*He skips back and forth lightly across the stage.*) I am ready, dear Queen. Shall I blow my trumpet?

QUEEN. Yes.

(*She mounts her throne again and the escorts go to back stage on either side of her throne.* PETER *and* SUZANNE *go over by* FREDDY THE TOAD.)

PETER PAN. (*Blows his trumpet, looks into the wings of the stage.*) Ho! Ho! Here comes King Arthur and his Knights.

KING ARTHUR. (*Sword in hand appears, followed by his two* KNIGHTS. *Everyone bows low before* KING ARTHUR, *except* PETER *and* SUZANNE, *and then they see the others bowing and so they bow also.* KING ARTHUR *advances to the* QUEEN *and bows and kisses her hand.*) What cause, Fair Queen, am I to defend tonight?

QUEEN. (*Steps down from the throne and takes* PETER *and* SUZANNE *to* KING ARTHUR.) These two children, Peter and Suzanne, are our guests tonight and you may see that no harm comes to them.

KING ARTHUR. It shall be as you wish. (*Turning to the two* KNIGHTS.) Sir Gawain and Sir Pelleas, keep constant guard on these two dear children and see that no harm comes to them.

(*The two* KNIGHTS *bow low to* KING ARTHUR *and then to* PETER *and* SUZANNE, *and the children bow back to them.*)

SIR GAWAIN. As thou hast commanded, my lord, so shall it be. No harm shall come to either Peter or Suzanne.

(*The* KNIGHTS *take position behind* PETER *and* SUZANNE.)

PETER. (*To* KING ARTHUR.) You live here too?
KING ARTHUR. Yes, in yonder castle. (*Points to castle.*)
PETER. Oh, how wonderful!
QUEEN. King Arthur, come, take the seat of honor. (*Leads him to the throne.*)
KING ARTHUR. Allow me, dear Queen.

(*He assists her to her seat and takes place beside her.* PETER *and* SUZANNE *resume their places by* FREDDY THE TOAD, *and the two* KNIGHTS *take position behind them. A great commotion is heard off stage.*)

PETER PAN. (*Looks into wings of stage and shades his eyes to see more clearly.*) Dear me, I see some people coming who will not be welcomed. (*He rushes to the* QUEEN.) It is those boresome Text Books, Arithmetic, Chemistry, Spanish and Geography. I knew they would show up as they always do.

(*Four figures dressed in long black robes, large black hats.* ARITHMETIC *has a panel on the front of his gown with the multiplication table on it.* CHEMISTRY *has* H_2O *in large white letters on his gown.* SPANISH *has written in Spanish in large white letters—"First Book in Spanish."* GEOGRAPHY *has a map of the world on front of gown.* CHEMISTRY *and* SPANISH *rush at the boy and* GEOGRAPHY *and* ARITHMETIC *rush at the girl.*)

TEXT BOOKS. (*All together.*) What about our lessons we are trying to teach you? What are you doing here?

QUEEN. (*Intervenes, takes the* TEXT BOOKS *over to front of the stage.*) Gentlemen, Gentlemen, a little self-control! Do not disturb yourselves. Just what is it you want?

(KNIGHTS *come closer to* PETER *and* SUZANNE.)

CHEMISTRY. Now, if you must know, this boy has an exam tomorrow, and as usual he does not know his lessons, and he will have a failure sure enough.

PETER. Dear Queen, I am sick of Chemistry and all the other Text Books. Can't a fellow have some fun without it being spoiled by text books, text books, text books?

KING ARTHUR. (*To* QUEEN.) Shall I engage these men in battle?

QUEEN. No, it is not so serious as that. Peter and Suzanne shall not be bothered, though.

PETER. Oh, Queen, (*Bows before her.*) I have an idea. You make the Text Books themselves get our lessons. If they are so worried, let them do something about it.

QUEEN. That is a splendid idea, Peter.

KING ARTHUR. That's the spirit, Peter.

QUEEN. Gentlemen, I command you to do the lessons for the children tonight. Here is wise Freddy to help you.

FREDDY. (*He is hopping up and down and clapping his hands. Goes to* TEXT BOOKS *and puts his arms on the shoulders of two of them.*) With pleasure, gentlemen. Bring forth the table and chairs for these wise ones.

(*Table and chairs and books are brought by four gnomes. The* TEXT BOOKS *sit down and start looking over the books with puzzled faces.* FREDDY *goes from one to the other showing them here and there in the books. They shake heads.* PETER *and* SUZANNE *look on with smiles and nudge each other.*

Commotion is heard in the wings. A clown comes on the stage and turns a couple of cart wheels. He is dressed in white and red, has a painted clown face and has figures all over his costume. He slaps the TEXT BOOKS *on the back. The* TEXT BOOKS *all look indignant.*)

FUN WITH FIGURES, THE CLOWN. Ha! Ha! So you have to work for once in your bright lives. Come, come now, this is no place for seriousness. (*Takes* ARITHMETIC *to front of stage.*) Arith, if you only had a sense of humor everyone would be crazy about you. Now, look at me, I dish out fun wherever I go. Now let me dish out some to you. Listen to some of your serious problems that can all be made like a game. I, Fun with Figures, I come to help the poor downtrodden boys and girls to make their way bright. Now listen, Arith, and answer this. A School teacher, on looking over the home work of little Willie asked him how long he had taken to do it. Willie replied: "I did it yesterday between 4 and 5 o'clock P. M. When I began, the hands of the clock were together and when I finished they were opposite each other." "Quite clever," says the teacher, "but what I want to know is, how many minutes you spent in doing the work?" Now, Arith, if you don't know the answer look me up, "Fun with Figures," in the library. (*The* TEXT BOOKS *all look disgusted.*) Now, Chem, I can show you how you have eleven fingers. Count all the fingers on both of your hands, when you have reached the last finger (10) start to count backwards on one hand, and say, 10, 9, 8, 7, 6, (*Emphasizing the 6.*) and then holding up the other hand you say, "and 5 make 11." (*Everyone laughs.*) Now, Geography, the wise one, come here. Two children were born in Indianapolis, Indiana—right? (*Pauses.* GEOGRAPHY *nods.*) in the same year, same month, same day, and same moment, twins, right? (*Pauses.* GEOGRAPHY *nods yes.*) They both lived to be exactly fifty years of age and then both of them shuffled off this mortal coil at one and the same instant; and yet one of them lived 100 days longer than the other. Can you answer that? (GEOGRAPHY *looks puzzled.*) I knew you couldn't. Well, I'll tell you. From the time they were born until they gave up their respective ghosts, each one made a tour of the world once a year, one going by the westerly route and the other by the easterly. Since the former gained a day each year, and the other lost a day each year, in 50 years the difference amounted to 100 days.

(*All laugh.*)

PETER. Oh, Gee! Why can't we do problems like that in school? Do you know any more?

FUN WITH FIGURES. Here's one for you. I'll show you how three threes are ten.

PETER. You'll have to show me. Three threes are nine.

FUN WITH FIGURES. (*Takes three books. Places them on the*

table and then picking up each one in succession and putting it back 3 times, counting as he does so, and finishing with No. 10 instead of 9.) Pick up the first book and lay it back on the table and say 1; do this with the second book and say 2; and the third book and say 3, this done repeat the operation with the 4th book and say 4; then the 5th and say 5 but hold this in your hand. Then pick up the other two and hold them saying 6 and 7. Now lay down the three books, one at a time on the table and say, 8, 9, 10. If you want some more look me up in the library.

(*Everyone claps.*)

FUN WITH FIGURES. (*To the* TEXT BOOKS.) Now, boys, put your books away and we will have a little dance. Come, come, let's clear the place here. (GNOMES *take away tables and chairs. Everyone backs to sides and back of stage, except* FUN WITH FIGURES *and the* TEXT BOOKS. *He lines up the boys for the dance.*) Now, boys, loosen up your old joints and follow me. For goodness' sake don't look so glum.

(*Very slow music. He leads them in a dance. The* TEXT BOOKS *dance it very awkwardly and stiffly.* FUN WITH FIGURES *does cart-wheels and fancy steps. At end of dance they dance off stage.*)

PETER PAN. (*Blows his trumpet and seeing a band of people coming, he rushes to the* QUEEN.) It's the pirates, the pirates of Treasure Island.

(*All are excited. The* KNIGHTS *come forward to guard everyone.*)

PETER. (*Rushes to* PETER PAN.) Oh, do you mean it is Long John Silver, the Pirate? Oh, I want to see him.

PETER PAN. Yes, and all his pirate band.

LONG JOHN SILVER. (*Hobbles across the stage with his band following. He looks around until he sees the* QUEEN *and* KING ARTHUR. *He goes over in front of the throne and, taking off his hat, makes a low bow, and beckons his men to do the same. All bow.*) Good evening, Queen and King Arthur, bless my soul.

QUEEN. Good evening, Long John Silver.

LONG JOHN SILVER. (*Glancing at* PETER.) And whom have we here? Who may this fine lad be? (*Moves over to* PETER, *as do the* KNIGHTS.)

PETER. I am Peter and I have read all about you, Long John Silver, but I never thought I would ever see you and I'm not a bit afraid of you either.

LONG JOHN SILVER. Say, you're a fine lad you are, and you're smart as paint. I seed you with them Text Books, how you made them do your lessons, I was watching you. You're a fine lad, sure enough, and as smart as paint. How would you like to be my cabin boy?

PETER. Oh, Gee, that would be great!

PETER PAN. Say, Peter, they might sing if you ask him. (*Pointing to* LONG JOHN SILVER.)

PETER. O, would they? Have them sing that song about the dead man's chest. Will they?

LONG JOHN SILVER. Sure we will, my fine lad. (*To his pirate band.*) Dooty is dooty, messmates, come with the song for the boy.

(*The* PIRATES *sing; after which they go off stage except* LONG JOHN SILVER *who goes over and sits on a stool.*)

PETER PAN. (*Blows his trumpet.*) Here comes Alice in Wonderland and the Cat and Robin Hood.

(ALICE *with the* CAT *and* CARDS 2, 5, *and* 7, *and* ROBIN HOOD *with his bow and arrow, come in and bow before the* QUEEN.)

QUEEN. Good evening, Alice. Good evening, Robin Hood.

ALICE. I managed to get away from the King and Queen and here we are, cards 2, 5, and 7 and the Cat.

QUEEN. I am so glad you came. We have two guests tonight who are seeing all their Book Friends. Alice, show the cat to Suzanne, and Robin Hood, show your bow and arrow to Peter. Perhaps Peter would like to shoot it.

(PETER *shows great interest in the bow and arrow.*)

ALICE. (*To* SUZANNE.) Would you like to have me make you short so you could crawl into Wonderland?

SUZANNE. (*To* QUEEN.) Could Alice do that to me?

QUEEN. She can only do that at my command; but we have many other things to show you.

PETER PAN. (*Blows his trumpet.*) Oh, see, here come all of the Twins. Here they are, the Dutch, the Japanese, and the American twins.

(*The* TWINS *all shyly appear and make their bow to the* QUEEN.)

PETER PAN. (*Rushes to the* QUEEN.) Perhaps the Twins would be happy to give their dances for Peter and Suzanne.

SUZANNE. (*To the* QUEEN.) O, do please ask them to dance.

(*Everyone on the stage begins to clap.*)

QUEEN. (*Rises and puts up her hand for silence.*) You will dance for us all. The Dutch Twins will give their dance first, then the Japanese Twins, and then the American Twins will give the tap dance which they have so recently learned.

(*All clap. Stage is cleared in front. At the end of each dance all on the stage applaud; and as each pair of* TWINS *finish their dance they dance off stage. After these dances are over,* ROBIN HOOD *is seen showing* PETER *how to shoot, and they are shooting into the wings.*)

PETER PAN. (*Blows his trumpet.*) Here comes Pinocchio, Rebecca of Sunnybrook Farm, Tom Sawyer and Huckleberry Finn.

(PINOCCHIO *and* REBECCA *walk in hand in hand and bow to the* QUEEN. TOM *walks in lazily eating an apple, with* HUCKLEBERRY *following.*)

PETER. (*As soon as he hears the name* TOM SAWYER *he loses all interest in the bow and arrow, and walks towards* TOM.) Hello, Tom.

Tom Sawyer. Hello, yourself.

Suzanne. (*To* Pinocchio.) Were you really a block of wood once?

Pinocchio. Sure I was; but look at me now. I can dance too.

Suzanne. Oh, Queen, please have Pinocchio dance for us.

Queen. Very well, Pinocchio, do your doll dance.

(Pinocchio *does the doll dance. All applaud at the end.*)

Queen. It is late now and we must go before dawn. We will have one more dance and then we must all say goodbye.

Peter. (*To the* Queen.) I wish I could take Tom home with me.

Tom. I will go if you will let Huck go with me.

Peter. O, that will be great.

(Tom *throws his arm over* Peter's *shoulder. Music of Midsummer Night's Dream again.* Queen's Pages *give the same dance as they did in the opening dance. As they are dancing one by one, the characters leave. The lights become dimmer and dimmer. The dancers dance off stage.* Peter, Tom *and* Huckleberry *slowly walk off with* Suzanne *and the two* Knights *following.*)

SLOW CURTAIN

Act III

Scene: *Same as Act I. Living Room of* Mr. *and* Mrs. Wilkins. Peter *and* Suzanne *asleep at the table in the same position as before.*

Mother. (*Calling from above.*) Peter, Peter, Suzanne!

(*No answer.*)

Mother. (*Voice sounds nearer as though she came down a few steps.*) Peter, Peter!

PETER. (*Wakes up and sleepily answers.*) Yes, Mother.
(PETER *shakes* SUZANNE.) Wake up, Suzanne.
MOTHER. Come to bed this minute.
PETER. Yes, Mother, we are coming.
(*They walk slowly out as the curtain drops.*)

POEMS

MY BOOKS

By Julia Johnson Davis

When falls the winter snow
I little care, nor yet what cold winds blow,
For here beside the fire
Are many friends of whom I never tire.
Jane Austen sits with me,
And oh, what company!
Or else the Brontës make the fireside glow
With their strange spirit. Dickens comes, and then—
Most lovable of men—
Dear Browning. Yet I've named not even ten
Of those who come and go.

When the December of
My life shall come, and those that now I love
The best, perhaps are gone,
I shall not be quite friendless and alone.
These same dear ones will be
Spring, youth and love to me.
I shall be young with them and happy too.
And who can tell? In that great After-place,
I, by diviner grace,
May touch their hands and look upon each face
With happiness anew.

IN A COPY OF BROWNING

By Bliss Carman

Browning, old fellow,
Your leaves grow yellow,
Beginning to mellow
As seasons pass.
Your cover is wrinkled,
And stained and sprinkled,
And warped and crinkled
From sleep on the grass.

Is it a wine stain,
Or only a pine stain,
That makes such a fine **stain**
On your dull blue,—
Got as we numbered
The clouds that lumbered
Southward and slumbered
When day was through?

What is the dear mark
There like an earmark,
Only a tear mark
A woman let fall?—
As bending over
She bade me discover,
"Who *plays* the lover,
He loses all!"

With you for teacher
We learned love's feature
In every creature

That roves or grieves;
When winds were brawling,
Or bird-folk calling,
Or leaf-folk falling,
About our eaves.

No law must straiten
The ways they wait in,
Whose spirits greaten
And hearts aspire.
The world may dwindle,
And summer brindle,
So love but kindle
The soul to fire.

Here many a red line,
Or pencilled headline,
Shows love could wed line
To golden sense;
And something better
Than wisdom's fetter
Has made your letter
Dense to the dense.

No April robin,
Nor clacking bobbin,
Can make of Dobbin
A Pegasus;
But Nature's pleading
To man's unheeding,
Your subtile reading
Made clear to us.

You made us farers
And equal sharers

With homespun wearers
In home-made joys;
You made us princes
No plea convinces
That spirit winces
At dust and noise.

When Fate was nagging,
And days were dragging,
And fancy lagging,
You gave it scope,—
When eaves were drippy,
And pavements slippy,—
From Lippo Lippi
To Evelyn Hope.

When winter's arrow
Pierced to the marrow,
And thought was narrow,
You gave it room;
We guessed the warder
On Roland's border,
And helped to order
The Bishop's Tomb.

When winds were harshish,
And ways were marshish,
We found with Karshish
Escape at need;
Were bold with Waring
In far seafaring,
And strong in sharing
Ben Ezra's creed.

We felt the menace
Of lovers pen us,
Afloat in Venice
Devising fibs;
And little mattered
The rain that pattered,
While Blougram chattered
To Gigadibs.

And we too waited
With heart elated
And breathing bated,
For Pippa's song;
Saw Satan hover,
With wings to cover
Porphyria's lover,
Pompilia's wrong.

Long thoughts were started,
When youth departed
From the half-hearted
Riccardi's bride;
For, saith your fable,
Great Love is able
To slip the cable
And take the tide.

Or truth compels us
With Paracelsus,
Till nothing else is
Of worth at all.
Del Sarto's vision
Is our own mission,

And art's ambition
Is God's own call.

Through all the seasons,
You gave us reasons
For splendid treasons
To doubt and fear;
Bade no foot falter,
Though weaklings palter,
And friendships alter
From year to year.

Since first I sought you,
Found you and bought you,
Hugged you and brought you
Home from Cornhill,
While some upbraid you,
And some parade you,
Nine years have made you
My master still.

OLD BOOKS

By Clinton Scollard

I have no craze for curios—
   A craving many folk affect,
Grim idols ranged in grinning rows
   And bottles, twisted-necked.

But an old book, this meets my need,
   Quarto or folio, as you please,
An ancient Marlowe, foxed and flea-ed,
   A first HESPERIDES.

Although the little worm and blind
    Has pierced the binding or the page,
And though the leaves be sered and lined
    With the dull rust of age,

Yet I am overmastered much
    By feelings I may not control,
As if there throbbed beneath my touch
    The poet's very soul.

POETRY

By Leonard Charles van Noppen

Poetry is the measure of the soul;
For, of that sea, she hath the power to sound
Its deepest deep, yea, to that calm profound
Below the tides of feeling. By one pole
She finds the opposite, and sings the whole,
Seeing the part, divining the full round
Beyond the crescent. Reason is the ground
Whence she springs, jubilant, to God, her goal.

Her wings are beauty, wonder is her song;
Yet sad her eyes, for she has wept too long,
And why she knows. But sorrow may not stay
Her soaring music, who, in her rapt flight,
Thrilling with vision, views, enthroned on light,
That sun whose wide circumference is day!

COUNTRY OF BOOKS

Anonymous

This workaday world is so trying at times,
    Folks chatter and squabble like rooks!

So the wise flee away to the best of all climes
Which you enter through History, Memoirs, or Rhymes,
   That most wonderful Country of Books.

And griefs are forgotten. You go on a tour
   More wondrous than any of "Cook's";
It costs you but little—your welcome is sure—
Your spirits revive in the atmosphere pure
   Of the wonderful Country of Books.

Your friends rally round you. You shake by the hand
   Philosophers, soldiers, and spooks!
Adventurers, heroes, and all the bright band
Of poets and sages are yours to command
   In that wonderful Country of Books.

New heights are explored; and new banners unfurled;
   New joys found in all sorts of nooks—
From the work-weary brain misgivings are hurled—
You come back refreshed to this workaday world
   From that wonderful Country of Books.

"STONE WALLS—"

By Robert Haven Schauffler

Shackled within the cell
   Of his immuring mind,
The poet burns to tell
   His message to mankind.

Alas that you and I,
   Captives in equal thrall,
Catch but a muffled cry
   And faint taps on a wall!

ADVICE TO WOULD-BE POETS

By Mary Sinton Leitch

Would you be a poet,
  Be silent till you drink
Deep of a rainbow
  At a river's brink!

You shall tread deftly
  Lest beauty be bereaved
By bruising of a flower.
  Your spirit shall be grieved

When a bough is broken,
  Else from your lips will come
No elegy, no idyll,
  Or Prothalamium.

When you hear the world's laughter
  And feel the world's grief
In the wash of a wave,
  In the stir of a leaf;

When there shall fall upon you
  The shadow of a wing,
Though never a bird is in the sky,
  Then sing!

ENVOY

By Francis Thompson

Go, songs, for ended is our brief, sweet play;
  Go, children of swift joy and tardy sorrow:

And some are sung, and that was yesterday,
   And some unsung, and that may be tomorrow.

Go forth; and if it be o'er stony way,
   Old joy can lend what newer grief must borrow:
And it was sweet, and that was yesterday,
   And sweet is sweet, though purchasèd with sorrow.

Go, songs, and come not back from your far way:
   And if men ask you why ye smile and sorrow,
Tell them ye grieve, for your hearts know Today,
   Tell them ye smile, for your eyes know Tomorrow.

COUNSEL

By George Sterling

For poetry, one should be fond of living,
   And not too free from care and humbler tasks,—
With curious mind, and heart that's used to giving
   More than it ever asks.

For poetry, one must be apt at playing,
   And not at all afraid of make-believe,—
Eager to join Imagination straying,
   Even if she deceive.

For poetry, one needs have much in vision
   That unseen aura common to all things,—
Must hold the crying doubt in half-derision,
   And greatly trust to wings.

For poetry, one mustn't fear a blunder,
   But laugh at facts and let the soul run wild,

Roaming that land of dream and truth and wonder
  Where meet the sage and child.

For poetry, today must be tomorrow,
  And Beauty ever loyal to our trust,
Waking her music at the heart of sorrow
  And rainbows in the dust.

A PRIMARY STORY

THE LITTLE BOOK PEOPLE

By Goldie Grant Thiel

The old grandfather clock on the stair landing was striking eight. Jane tried to go to sleep, but she kept thinking of the fairies that her new story-book told about. Suddenly she heard a tiny voice say: "I'm glad I came to live with Jane!"

"You'll be sorry, New Book!" a gruff little voice answered. "She isn't a bit nice to live with!"

"You must be mistaken!" said the first voice. "She looks very nice."

"Yes, she does," the gruff little voice said, "but she certainly abuses us!"

"Indeed she does!" chimed in several voices.

The voices came from the floor beside Jane's bed, and she wondered who could be talking. Very, very quietly she peered over the edge of the bed.

There on the floor were several of her books—only they didn't look like books now. They looked like queer little people, with book bodies, tiny legs and arms, and serious little faces. They were standing in a circle.

"They are little Book People," thought Jane. They kept right on talking.

"See what she did to me!" Jack and the Beanstalk Book stood up, flipped itself open, and pointed to the corners of its pages. "Every time Jane stopped reading me, she turned down the corner of one of my pages, and the corners broke off."

"If you think that you've been badly treated," said Mother Goose Book, "look at me. One day when I was brand-new Jane opened me, laid me face down on the floor, and ran out to play. Someone stepped on me and broke my back."

"I've *two* breaks in my back!" wailed Blue Fairy Book. "Jane opened me the first time without properly breaking my binding, and of course my back broke. Then, one day she put a pencil between my pages to mark her place, and left me in a chair. Someone sat on me, and my back broke again."

"My back is all right," spoke up Little Red Riding Hood Book, "but my dress is badly soiled."

"Look at me!" said Robinson Crusoe Book. "Jane left me outdoors one night and it rained. I'll have to go about in rags the rest of my life, just because Jane didn't put me in my house."

Jane could stand it no longer. She leaned over the edge of the bed. "I'm sorry!" she said. "If you'll only tell me what to do, I'll promise never to hurt you again. Where is your house?"

"It's the bookcase!" explained Robinson Crusoe Book.

"There are several things that you can do to take care of us," said Blue Fairy Book. "Keep us in the bookcase when you are not using us. Wash your hands carefully before handling us. Use a bookmark."

"You should never, never open a new book without properly breaking the binding!" said New Book. "Take me in your hands and hold me so that my back rests on the table. Now let my covers drop down until they rest on the table, and then run your finger along the crease between my front cover and my pages, pressing gently all the time. Do the same with my back cover. Now take a few pages from the front of the book, then a few from the back, until you have gone all through the book."

Jane began running her finger along the creases. Suddenly someone said: "Wake up, Jane. Wake up!" Jane's eyes opened wide. It was morning.

A PRIMARY STORY

"I must have been dreaming," thought Jane.

She dressed quickly. When she was ready to go downstairs, she picked up all of her books and put them in the bookcase. Then she properly broke the binding of her new book. Last of all she cut the picture of a flower from a seed catalogue and pasted it on a strip of paper for a bookmark.

Questions

Where should books be kept when not in use?
What will help keep your books clean?
Should you turn down the corner of a page to mark your place?
What is meant by "breaking" the binding of a new book?
How did Jane make a bookmark?

THOUGHTS ON READING

THE THREE JOYS OF READING
Anonymous

Men do brave deeds on the sea, in far-off lands, or in war, and these deeds are the subject of song and story. Youths who are looking forward to heroic careers, and men and women to whom life has brought few thrilling experiences, like to hear these tales. A well-told story opens the door to a new pleasure in living. An animal knows only the present. He is hungry, or tired, or his life is in danger, or he is well fed and sleepy. But boys and girls, and men and women, too, not only have their daily experience to draw upon, but through books and magazines and papers they can enter into the experience of others, so that they may live many lives in one.

Aladdin had a wonderful lamp. By rubbing it he could be anywhere he chose or could possess anything he desired. Such a lamp the reader of good books possesses. You come in from work or play, curl yourself up in a big chair before the fire, open your book, and in a twinkling you are whisked away to a new world. Your body is there, curled up before the fire, but enchantment has come upon you. In imagination you are with Sindbad the sailor, or with Robinson Crusoe, or with King Arthur, or you are in the Indian jungle, or on a ship sailing the South Seas, or you are hunting for Treasure Island. And you have it in your power to take these wonderful trips instantly; no railway tickets are required, no long delays. You may go on a journey to the other side of the world or into the South Polar ice or out on a western ranch. What is more wonderful, you may go back a century, or ten centuries; through this Aladdin's lamp of reading you are master not only of space, but also of time. Thus the first joy of reading is the privilege of taking part in the experiences of men of every time and every portion of the world. You multiply your life, and the product is richness and joy.

The second joy of reading is even greater. Not only the world of adventure is open to you by means of books, but also a life enriched by the wisdom that has been gathered from a thousand poets and historians as bees gather honey from a thousand flowers. There is a story of a great Italian of the sixteenth century who found himself in the prime of life without a position, without money, and even compelled to become an exile because of a revolution. He retired to a farm remote from all the scenes in which his previous life had been passed. All day he worked hard, for only by hard work could he live. But in the evenings, when work was done, when horses and oxen and the laborers who had toiled with them all the day had gone to sleep, this man put on the splendid court dress he had worn in the days of his prosperity, days when he had associated with princes and the great ones of the earth, and so garbed he went into his library and shut the door. And then, he tells us, for four hours he lived amid the scenes that his books called up before him. He found in books an Aladdin's lamp that transported him to past times, that revealed the secrets of Nature, that showed him what men had accomplished. Through history, he re-created the past. He could call on the wisest of men for counsel, and he forgot during these hours his weariness and pain.

Many men, like this great Italian, have found happiness and strength in books. There was once a boy in a frontier cabin who was eager to know all that could be learned about life. His days were long and hard, but he was dreaming of things to

in the matter of public library service. They must be given opportunities for continuous self-education and self-development if they are to stabilize and not endanger the more leisurely democracy of tomorrow.

The financial situation is admittedly a problem, but there seem to be ways of solving it. County or regional libraries may be needed rather than local, to provide maximum service at minimum cost. State aid for libraries may be necessary to supplement local financing. Perhaps only an aroused public opinion is the answer. In more than a score of communities during the last four years where citizens have recognized the need for more adequate library support, the appropriations have been materially increased in spite of financial stringency. A citizens' council in one city where the library had been drastically cut increased the library's appropriation for the next fiscal year by 25 percent. In still a third city, $75,000 cut from an already reduced budget for 1933–34 was restored by popular demand.

BOOKS

Give a man this taste [for good books], and the means of gratifying it, and you can hardly fail of making a happy man. You place him in contact with the best society in every period of history—with the wisest, the wittiest, the tenderest, the bravest, and the purest characters who have adorned humanity. You make him a denizen of all nations, a contemporary of all ages.
—Sir John Herschel

In Books lies the soul of the whole Past Time: the articulate audible voice of the Past, when the body and the material substance of it has altogether vanished like a dream. . . . All that Mankind has done, thought, gained, or been; it is lying as in magic preservation in the pages of Books.
—Carlyle

POEMS IN PANTOMIME

POEMS IN PANTOMIME
By Kathleen Carmichael Dietz
(An Exercise for Grade 3 or 4)

For some time Minnequa School had been deep in a poetry project worked out between the library and the art room. Each child found a poem in the library and learned it. Then in the art room he drew an original illustration for it. The enthusiasm over this project furnished an inspiration for our Parent-Teacher Association program when it was the third-grade children's turn to entertain.

Twelve poems were given in pantomime. These were divided into two groups in order to facilitate stage setting. There were five indoor scenes and seven outdoor. Each poem was spoken by a different pupil, who stood at one side of the stage facing the audience, apparently unconscious of the dramatization.

The stage had a dark blue back drop. For the first group, the stage was set with a fireplace, a small cupboard having glass doors, a miniature dining table and chairs, a rocking chair, and some toys.

The first poem was "Tea Time," by Grace Noll Crowell. The curtain opened on a mother who sat rocking and sewing, and several children who were playing before the fireplace. This poem was very easy to act—folding work away, tying on an apron, setting the table with real dishes, bringing in quivering jelly, and finally the family's gathering around for tea. (Red art paper with the base glued to a dish was used for the jelly.)

"The Cupboard," by Walter de la Mare, was given next. There were a jar of lollipops and a plate of cookies in the cupboard. The little girl who received them actually sat on "Grandma's slippery knee."

"Animal Crackers," by Christopher Morley, gave one boy a chance to show his nice table manners as he sat eating animal crackers and drinking cocoa.

(Real lollipops, cookies, animal crackers, and cocoa are effective to use, if one is certain that there will be no actually hungry children in the audience.)

"Boots," by Leroy Jackson, was recited by a curly-headed little boy with mischief in his eyes. How he strode across the stage when he "walked from here to China"!

"The Barber's," another poem by Walter de la Mare, was especially pleasing to the audience, since the barber had a pair of shears which he manipulated skillfully enough to produce a very audible "snip-snap and snick-a-snack." The customer was consulted as to her preference for "bear's grease or bay rum." She paid him from her purse and "shin-shan-shinnied" out with a joyous little skip.

For the outdoor poems the stage was cleared, and then reset. We used growing plants, a low box "planted" with large pansies painted on cardboard, and stars of gold paper on the back drop.

A chimney was necessary for the first poem of this group, "Fairies and Chimneys," by Rose Fyleman. For the chimney a heavy wooden box, whose sides were covered with red brick crêpe paper, was utilized. Four fairies sat in the chimney, arms across one another's shoulders, taking care that they did not crush the wings of silver, rose, and blue. They swayed back and forth while they were "singing all together and warming up their toes." The flowers were not used in this setting, but the gold stars were.

"Frilly Tilly," by Leroy Jackson, was recited by a little girl

POEMS IN PANTOMIME 367

with curls, wearing a "fluffy, ruffly dress."

"Rain in the Night," by Amelia Josephine Burr, was the inspiration for an experiment in presenting Boots, a very lively black and white kitten. A bait of salmon enticed him to remain on the stage to lick the fish off his paws—"washing his little dirty feet."

"Have You Watched the Fairies?" by Rose Fyleman, was acted by fairies who "dried their wings," and "danced to little fairy tunes." Because the fairies must "dash off behind the stars," the gold stars were used on the back drop.

In "Baby Seed Song," by Edith Nesbit, the curtain opened on two little boys in brown suits of paper cambric. They were kneeling in tight little balls, heads down, salaam fashion. As the poem was given, they slowly "grew" until, at last, they were up, and one was holding a sunflower and the other a poppy.

"The Elf and the Dormouse," by Oliver Herford, called for a large toadstool, which was made of mounting board and colored with crayon. The elf wore a tight-fitting costume of bright red, and the dormouse a black one which had a cardboard tail about a yard long.

"The Moon's the North Wind's Cooky," by Vachel Lindsay, was our last number. While a small boy in the foreground "ate" an immense yellow cardboard cooky, a second boy at back of stage, in baker's cap and apron, sifted flour and "kneaded a crisp, new moon."

Children's love of costumes, of dramatizing, and of poetry all combined to make the presentation of poems in pantomime a happy occasion.

The poems used may be found in the following volumes. They are listed in the order presented.

"Tea Time," in *Miss Humpety Comes to Tea,* by Grace Noll Crowell (Dallas, Texas: The Southwest Press).

"The Cupboard," in *Peacock Pie,* by Walter de la Mare (New York: Henry Holt & Co., 1930).

"Animal Crackers," in *Silver Pennies,* compiled by Blanche Jennings Thompson (New York: The Macmillan Co., 1928).
"Boots," in *Peter Patter Book,* by Leroy Jackson (Chicago: Rand McNally & Co.).
"The Barber's," in *Peacock Pie.*
"Fairies and Chimneys," in *Fairies and Chimneys,* by Rose Fyleman (New York: Doubleday, Doran & Co., 1920).
"Frilly Tilly," in *Rimskittle's Book,* by Leroy Jackson (Chicago: Rand McNally & Co.).
"Rain in the Night" and "Have You Watched the Fairies?" in *Silver Pennies.*
"Baby Seed Song," and "The Elf and the Dormouse," in *Required Poems for Reading and Memorizing,* First and Second Grades (Dansville, N.Y.: F. A. Owen Publishing Co.).
"The Moon's the North Wind's Cooky," in *Silver Pennies.*

A GAME

MAGIC RING—A GAME OF POETRY APPRECIATION

By Edna Flexer Stuart

"Let's play Magic Ring!" several girls' voices exclaimed.

"Don't you want to have stunts tonight, instead?" their adult leader questioned.

"No, Magic Ring!" chorused a hundred girls sitting about a bonfire on the beach at their camp.

"Very well," the leader replied. "How shall we start?"

"'Souls,' first." Without further ado, like a chant came the girls' favorite:

> My Soul goes clad in gorgeous things,
> Scarlet and gold and blue,
> And at her shoulder sudden wings
> Like long flames flicker through.*

Across the water, the crimson streaks of a particularly glorious sunset lingered on as though to illustrate the choice. Raptly, the girls watched while the colors faded and the stars came out, as, for an hour, they recited together poems that they loved. Most choices were expressions of ideals, of ways of life.

The beauty of the surroundings, the light on the girls' faces as they sat about the fire, made a profound impression on a schoolteacher visitor that evening.

"This has been a revelation to me," exclaimed the teacher,

* From "Souls," in *Myself and I*, by Fannie Stearns Davis. Used by permission of The Macmillan Co.

"and I should like to ask you a few questions. How do you get the girls to learn so many poems? How did you make them like to spend an evening reciting them?"

"Try to keep them from it!" twinkled the camp director. "We have a counsellor here this summer who attempted to substitute the stunts usually found in all camps at our evening fires. But the girls insisted on playing Magic Ring, as they call it, and the counsellor finally gave in. She is keeping a notebook of poetry herself now. She says that it is the first time in her life she ever cared for it. Throughout her school days, poetry was just dissection; now she has discovered it to be crystallized truth beautifully, rhythmically stated."

"Crystallized truths! Tonight it surely seemed so. This evening it was almost a rhythmic philosophy. I can imagine the girls recalling certain lines to solve their problems a bit later in life.

"But how did it all start? These girls appear to be human—good athletes, fun-loving. Did they take naturally to poetry?"

"It began this way. One evening a number of us were sitting in a ring around a fire like this one and we started to say lovely poems. One after another, we each gave our favorites. Before we knew it, the evening had gone. 'It has slipped by like magic,' said one girl. 'It has been the loveliest evening we've had,' confided another. 'Let's play it again,' said still another.

"'I know,' came a sudden inspiration, 'we might call the game Magic Ring and sit in a circle as we did tonight. Then the evening will slip by again with beauty and magic,' and so, Magic Ring started. The girls bring their favorite poems and these are posted where all who care may copy and learn them and so, year by year, we have collected a remarkable anthology of poems girls love. They have better taste than we adults accredit them, I am sure you will agree."

"I should like to try this in my school," burst forth the teacher.

She did try and it did work. For five minutes in the morning, her seventh grade was privileged to play Magic Ring. Poems were brought in voluntarily. Those they all liked were posted and the children who desired to do so learned them. No study or discussion of them was made. But at the end of the term it was discovered that the pupils had memorized many poems. In addition, they had gained a real taste for poetry.

TESTS AND SUGGESTIONS

A TEST FOR BOOK WEEK
By Juanita Cunningham

I. *Opposite the number of each book, write the letter for the author of the book.*
  1. *The King of the Golden River*
  2. *Heidi*
  3. *Little Women*
  4. *Hiawatha*
  5. *The Jungle Book*
  6. *The Call of the Wild*
  7. *Rip Van Winkle*
  8. *Treasure Island*
  9. *Snowbound*
  10. *The Great Stone Face*
  11. *Christmas Carol*
  12. *The Other Wise Man*
  13. *The Vision of Sir Launfal*
  14. *Rebecca of Sunnybrook Farm*
  a. Kate Douglas Wiggin
  b. John Greenleaf Whittier
  c. James Russell Lowell
  d. Johanna Spyri
  e. John Ruskin
  f. Jack London
  g. Henry W. Longfellow
  h. Louisa M. Alcott

i. Robert Louis Stevenson
j. Washington Irving
k. Nathaniel Hawthorne
l. Henry van Dyke
m. Rudyard Kipling
n. Charles Dickens

II. *Write Yes or No after each of the following questions.*
1. Is *Hiawatha* written in prose form?
2. Did Heidi live in America?
3. Was Black Beauty a dog?
4. Did Evangeline finally find Gabriel?
5. Were the Mohicans early pioneers?
6. Was John Silver a sailor?
7. Did Hans Brinker win the silver skates?
8. Was Sleepy Hollow in the state of Virginia?
9. Was Tiny Tim an orphan?
10. Was Rip Van Winkle an industrious man?

III. *Opposite the number of each of the following book characters, write the name of the book in which it appears.*
1. Little John
2. Ichabod Crane
3. Gluck
4. John Silver
5. Rowena
6. Friday
7. Philip Nolan
8. Meg
9. Peter (a goatherd)

IV. *Each of the following books can be classified as Biography, History, Travel, or Adventure. Opposite the number of each that is Biography, write* B; *History,* H; *Travel,* T; *and Adventure,* A.
1. *American Hero Stories,* by Eva March Tappan
2. *The Story of My Life,* by Helen Keller
3. *Adrift on an Ice Pan,* by Sir Wilfred T. Grenfell
4. *Inventions and Discoveries of Ancient Times,* by Wil-

liam L. Nida

5. *Westward Ho!* by Charles Kingsley
6. *Florence Nightingale, the Angel of the Crimea,* by L. E. Richards
7. *A Boy's Life of Theodore Roosevelt,* by Hermann Hagedorn
8. *Treasure Island,* by Robert Louis Stevenson
9. *Hero Stories for Children,* by E. A. Collins and L. Hale
10. *Across the Plains,* by Robert Louis Stevenson
11. *Robinson Crusoe,* by Daniel Defoe

V. *Place the letter A opposite the number of each of the American writers; E opposite the number of each of the English writers; and S opposite the number of each of the Swiss writers.*

1. Henry W. Longfellow
2. Johanna Spyri
3. James Russell Lowell
4. Louisa M. Alcott
5. Daniel Defoe
6. Henry van Dyke
7. John Greenleaf Whittier
8. Johann Rudolf Wyss
9. Rudyard Kipling
10. Alfred Tennyson
11. Washington Irving
12. Edgar Allan Poe

VI. *Underline the word or group of words within each parenthesis which best completes the sentence.*

1. When reading silently we should read (rapidly, slowly).
2. We should read (fewer, more) than one hundred fifty words a minute.
3. The climax of a story is usually near the (beginning, end, middle) of the story.
4. We can appreciate the books we read more if we (know, do not know) about the authors who wrote them.
5. When we find words in our reading with which we are not familiar we should (skip them, learn their meanings and correct pronunciations).
6. Reading is a (valuable, wasteful) way to spend leisure.

7. Books should be (carelessly, carefully) handled.
8. Never read a (good, interesting, worthless) book.
9. Develop a desire to read (fiction, history, different classes of books).

Key to Tests

I. 1. e   5. m   9. b   13. c
    2. d   6. f   10. k   14. a
    3. h   7. j   11. n
    4. g   8. i   12. l

II. 1. No   4. Yes   7. Yes   10. No
     2. No   5. No   8. No
     3. No   6. Yes   9. No

III. 1. *The Merry Adventures of Robin Hood*
     2. *The Legend of Sleepy Hollow*
     3. *The King of the Golden River*
     4. *Treasure Island*
     5. *Ivanhoe*
     6. *Robinson Crusoe*
     7. *The Man without a Country*
     8. *Little Women*
     9. *Heidi*

IV. 1. H   4. H   7. B   10. T
     2. B   5. A   8. A   11. A
     3. T   6. B   9. H

V. 1. A   4. A   7. A   10. E
    2. S   5. E   8. S   11. A
    3. A   6. A   9. E   12. A

VI. 1. rapidly
     2. more
     3. end

4. know
5. learn their meanings and correct pronunciations
6. valuable
7. carefully
8. worthless
9. different classes of books

SUGGESTIONS FOR BOOK WEEK

By Fanora Voight

The possibilities in Book Week are infinite, offering opportunity for growth throughout the entire year. The home, the school, the church, the library—each has its field, ripe for development, if those in charge will but use initiative in promoting the purpose of this Week. Below are listed various suggestions. A contest between grades or rooms may be developed, and the winners entertained at a party, to which each pupil comes dressed as a book character, and at which book contests and games are played. A radio program may be used as a part of the entertainment.

Book Week Activities

1. Have plays, pageants, and puppet shows, featuring characters from books.
2. Have exhibits, featuring:
    a) Clay models of favorite characters from books.
    b) Scenes from books, drawn or modeled in a box.
    c) Paper dolls of characters taken from literature.
    d) Community posters about good books.
    e) Illustrations from a good story.
3. Have an exhibit of books brought from home. Invite the parents.
4. Interest children in earning money for books and re-

porting how they did it.

5. Locate on a world map the regions used as the settings for well-known books. (For instance, on Juan Fernandez Island write *Robinson Crusoe*.)

6. Have a book parade and select the costume most illustrative of a book or a character in a book.

7. Assign essays on "My Favorite Book."

8. Have a list made of favorite books for girls and boys.

9. Make book ends, bookmarks, book covers.

10. Make a list of suggestions about the care of books.

Book Week Tests

I. *Write the names of the characters suggested by the following:*

1. Three Golden Apples.
2. From king to jester.
3. Bulrushes.
4. The Catskill Mountains.
5. Acadia.
6. A bunch of keys.
7. The Forty Thieves.
8. The founders of Rome.
9. Sherwood Forest.
10. A puppet.
11. A magic traveling cloak:
12. A dog nurse.
13. Sleepy Hollow.
14. A coat of many colors.

II. *Check the words which best complete the following sentences:*

1. Robinson Crusoe made his clothes of:
    a) wool.
    b) skins.
    c) cotton.
2. Silas Marner was:
    a) a ne'er-do-well.
    b) a spendthrift.
    c) a miser.
3. Cinderella lost:
    a) her diamond necklace.

  b) her bright red shawl.
  c) her glass slipper.
 4. Robin Hood used:
  a) a shotgun.
  b) a bow and arrow.
  c) a sword.
 5. Hiawatha lived in:
  a) a castle.
  b) an igloo.
  c) a wigwam.
 6. Tom Sawyer:
  a) whitewashed the fence.
  b) shot an arrow.
  c) flew an airplane.
 7. Heidi had:
  a) a goat.
  b) a German police dog.
  c) a Maltese kitten.
 8. Daniel Boone wore:
  a) a tailored suit.
  b) silk pajamas.
  c) a suit of skins.
 9. Hitty was the name of:
  a) a doll.
  b) a Newfoundland dog.
  c) the sweetheart of Ivanhoe.
10. Ivanhoe was in love with:
  a) Pollyanna
  b) Rowena.
  c) Maid Marian.
11. Robert the Bruce watched:
  a) a bullfight.
  b) a spider.
  c) an automobile race.

12. *The Sketch Book* is:
   a) a fairy tale.
   b) a collection of short stories.
   c) a poem.

III. *Name the author of each of the following books:*
   1. *The Jungle Book.*
   2. *Huckleberry Finn.*
   3. *Daddy Long Legs.*
   4. *The Wonder Book.*
   5. *Penrod.*
   6. *The Old Curiosity Shop.*
   7. *Treasure Island.*
   8. *The Call of the Wild.*
   9. *Smoky.*
   10. *Coronado's Children.*
   11. *The Deerslayer.*
   12. *Westward Ho!*
   13. *Little Women.*

Key to Tests

I.
1. Atalanta.
2. King Robert of Sicily.
3. Moses.
4. Rip van Winkle.
5. Evangeline.
6. Bluebeard.
7. Ali Baba.
8. Romulus and Remus.
9. Robin Hood.
10. Pinocchio.
11. The little lame prince.
12. Wendy, Peter Pan.
13. Ichabod Crane.
14. Joseph.

II.
1. (*b*) skins.
2. (*c*) a miser.
3. (*c*) her glass slipper.
4. (*b*) a bow and arrow.
5. (*c*) a wigwam.
6. (*a*) whitewashed the fence.
7. (*a*) a goat.
8. (*c*) a suit of skins.
9. (*a*) a doll.
10. (*b*) Rowena.

11. (*b*) a spider.
12. (*b*) a collection of short stories.

III.
1. Rudyard Kipling.
2. Mark Twain.
3. Jean Webster.
4. Nathaniel Hawthorne.
5. Booth Tarkington.
6. Charles Dickens.
7. Robert Louis Stevenson.
8. Jack London.
9. Will James.
10. J. F. Dobie.
11. James Fenimore Cooper.
12. Charles Kingsley.
13. Louisa M. Alcott.

ACTIVITIES

A POETRY BOOKLET

By Gladyce Englerth

Since children often have a dislike for poetry, I arouse their interest by the following method, which I find very helpful.

Each pupil brings a picture to illustrate some part of each poem studied. He mounts the picture and writes the appropriate part of the poem below. At the end of the term the pupils make booklets of their mounted poems.

This device, besides creating a greater interest in poetry, helps to improve the children's writing. The pictures also furnish many lessons for art discussion.

A BOOK PAGEANT

By Katharine Nickel

There seemed to be a need in our school to create a desire to read good books and poems. Consequently my fifth- and sixth-grade pupils worked out a book pageant for an assembly program.

When the curtain was drawn back, a girl was seen lying on a couch, reading a book. Soon she fell asleep. Then a pupil entered, dressed in the costume of the main character of the story represented, gave an interesting introduction to the story, and disappeared blithely through an opposite door. This was repeated until each pupil had given a brief introduction, *résumé*, or incident. Some of the many characters represented were Gulliver, the Barefoot Boy, and Peter Pan.

This exercise gave the pupils practice in writing suitable paragraphs to introduce their books, in giving them orally, in appearing before an audience, and in using their own creative powers in preparing suitable costumes. The pageant was enjoyed, and many pupils who saw it expressed an enthusiastic desire to read the stories represented.

A BOOK-WEEK DRAMATIZATION

By Mae Foster Jay

One sixth grade worked out in class an original play using book characters. These characters, in costume, presented themselves to the audience as being free for a short time from the books in which they belonged. They were on their way to a party at the palace of the Princess Ozma. In the palace was a broadcasting station, where each character gave through the microphone a *résumé* of the book in which he appears.

While refreshments were being served at the palace, a voice off stage was heard exclaiming, "Mother! Whatever can have happened to my book? Tom Sawyer is not in it! Where can he be?"

"We've stayed too long!" the book people cried, and hastened away to get back into their books.

TEACHING POEMS

By Jennie E. Roper

My pupils were not interested in the study of poems. They sometimes failed to understand and enjoy them, and were unable to visualize the pictures presented by a poem. The following plan, which may be used for many poems, has been both helpful and interesting to my third grade.

In studying "The Brook," by Tennyson, I asked my pupils whether they would not like to make a booklet about it. They decided that this would be interesting. Eight pieces of white notebook paper were used for the booklet, with colored drawing paper for the cover. Several cover designs were suggested, and each pupil was asked to use two contrasting colors in working out his own design.

After the booklets were completed, pictures describing the different lines of the stanzas were found and cut out. These were pasted on the white pages, and the appropriate lines were written beneath the pictures.

When the entire poem had been illustrated in this manner, the children had a very good mental picture of it, and had memorized it.

A BOOK RECITAL
By Helen Reed

Rural teachers often find it difficult to interest some children in reading. I began early in the year to talk about a book recital. We discussed different authors and stories, and secured a number of books from our state traveling library. Soon even the beginners were asking for books to read. About the middle of the year each child was to choose his favorite book to review for the recital, to which parents were invited. This was the most educational entertainment that our school ever gave, and the children are wondering whether we have time to prepare for another before school closes.

TEACHING POETRY

By Sara Mae Spearing

In teaching poetry I find that questions, suggestions, and pictures help create in the classroom a desire to hear poems read aloud. The children listen just for the beauty of the words, the rhythm, and the story. Usually after I have read a poem, the children ask to have it read again. After the poems read for appreciation only, I read a poem that the class might like to learn. As an experiment, I read poems written by children, such as poems by Nathalia Crane and Hilda Conkling. I found that the pupils enjoyed them, and suggested that they might write a poem. The results have been most pleasing. The art department co-operated with us by making books in which to keep our poems. We add to these books as the children create the poems. Only the best are kept. This has indeed been a splendid project in creative work.

MEMORIZING POETRY

By Margaretta McCoy

The following method has been helpful for interesting upper-grade pupils in reading and memorizing poetry. The class is divided into several groups, each containing pupils from the upper, middle, and lower third of the class. After a poem has been read and discussed, we set a day for a group activity. Each pupil may memorize as much of the poem as he wishes. Each stanza memorized and given orally without a mistake counts one point for the group. Therefore the pupils understand that it is better to learn one stanza well than to half-memorize the entire poem.

Since the group instinct is very strong in upper-grade pupils, each shares to the extent of his ability in this activity.

ILLUSTRATING POETRY

By Laura A. Holderness

Children like to illustrate, and narrative poems lend themselves very nicely to this kind of work. Recently we tried the plan of teaching many narrative poems to develop an appreciation of poetry in the sixth grade. After a poem had been taught, we asked each child to choose the subject he liked best in the poem for his illustration.

"The Pied Piper" was the poem that the class as a whole seemed to enjoy most. The poem was taught as an appreciation lesson in poetry. During the summary the class was asked to make a list of the pictures in the poem. One child wrote on the blackboard the suggestions given by the pupils. We then had an informal class discussion, under the guidance of the teacher, to decide which pictures were best to illustrate. When we had eliminated the least desirable, we went over the revised list to see whether these pictures really would tell the story.

There were very few changes made. In nearly every case we noticed that the child chose the illustration he himself had mentioned. The class period ended with the suggestion from the teacher that each child come the next day with his picture clearly developed in his mind as to the relation of objects and colors desired. It was further suggested that the children make a diligent search for pictures of rats, mountains, and any objects or characters which would serve as guides in making cut-outs for the poem. These would be placed on the blackboard ledge.

When the class assembled the next day the children found dark brown mounting paper, 9 by 12 inches, a pair of scissors, and a bit of paste on each desk. Each child chose from the teacher's desk an 8-inch square of colored paper for the background of his picture, and also squares of paper from which to make his objects. Then the cutting began. The teacher watched, making suggestions only when she found it necessary. At times the children would quietly step to the blackboard to look at the objects they were cutting.

When the cutting was done, each child carefully placed his cut-outs the way he thought they should be mounted. If the teacher gave her consent, he pasted them on the mounting paper. At the end of the period the story of "The Pied Piper" in pictures was completed for display.

A BOOK WEEK ACTIVITY

For Primary Grades

By Eleanor Haack

I. Motivation.
   As the date for Book Week was near, the children became interested in planning a program for it.
II. Children's objective.
   To learn interesting facts about books to be presented at an assembly program.
III. Teacher's objectives.
   A. To have children see the need of books.
   B. To develop an appreciation of, and a love for, good reading.
   C. To develop good reading habits.
   D. To acquaint children with good books.
   E. To broaden children's interests and choices in reading.
   F. To use the table of contents to find pages quickly.
   G. To appreciate the use of books for pleasure.

ACTIVITIES

- H. To learn about the physical features of a book.
- I. To encourage proper handling of books.
- J. To establish right habits of conduct in a library.
- K. To build up an appreciation for libraries and their services to a community.

IV. Procedure.
- A. We gathered all the information that we could find concerning the history of Book Week.
- B. We talked about the physical features of books. (Book jackets, size of books, cover, binding, print, and paper.)
- C. We also discussed the contents of books. (End papers, flyleaf, title page, date of publication, publisher, author, illustrator, dedication, frontispiece, table of contents, illustrations, etc.)

V. Activities.
- A. We visited the city library in a group. We were introduced to the children's librarian. We looked at books in the children's section.
- B. We set up a library in our schoolroom.
    1. Made the bookcases from orange crates.
    2. Made chairs from orange crates.
    3. Repainted old chairs and tables.
    4. Made a large poster: Be Courteous in the Library.
    5. Made smaller posters to illustrate scenes from favorite books.
    6. Made exhibits of papier-mâché figures to represent book characters.
- C. We wrote story reviews. We also wrote original stories, which in some cases were dedicated and illustrated.
- D. We used the library in connection with various kinds of work. The children learned that books other than nature readers had nature stories.
- E. Bookmarks were made in our handwork periods. Some

pretty ones were made with embroidery floss and colored beads. These were finished in time to be used as Christmas gifts.

VI. Outcomes.
- A. The children began to show a deeper and more desirable feeling for books. This led to a discussion of the good treatment of books. We composed a story about a boy who dreamed that he was a mistreated book. This story was dramatized.
- B. As the children's interest in books broadened, they became acquainted with many characters in books which were on their reading level.
    1. Some children made dolls to represent these characters. Through this there developed an interest in mitten puppets. Each child chose a book character which he was interested in making.
    2. A puppet stage was made for us. We had much fun dressing our puppets and making stage scenery. With our puppets we played several stories for our Book Week program. A number of children, otherwise shy and conservative, were happy to participate in this part of the program.
- C. We discovered that the day on which we planned to give our program was Robert Louis Stevenson's birthday. This stimulated a great interest in Stevenson's poems. We dramatized "Pirate Story," and read several other poems which we had learned.
- D. We invited the new librarian of our public library to see our program. We were glad that she could be there. At the close of the program she was introduced by one of the girls.
- E. The day following our presentation we were invited to give our program at the public library on Saturday during the children's story hour.

F. The children enjoyed this project, and I am sure that an early interest in books was created.

BIBLIOGRAPHY

Meader, Deborah: "Hand Puppets with Papier-Mâché Heads," in THE INSTRUCTOR, February 1938 (Owen).

Stevenson, Robert Louis: "Pirate Story," in *A Child's Garden of Verses* (various publishers).

Warner, Frances Lester: *Ragamuffin Marionettes* (Houghton Mifflin).